Decadence

Decadence
Radical Nostalgia, Narcissism, and Decline in the Seventies

by JIM HOUGAN

WILLIAM MORROW AND COMPANY, INC.
NEW YORK   1975

Copyright © 1975 by James Hougan

All rights reserved. No part of this book may be reproduced or utilized in any form or by any means, electronic or mechanical, including photocopying, recording or by any information storage and retrieval system, without permission in writing from the Publisher. Inquiries should be addressed to William Morrow and Company, Inc., 105 Madison Ave., New York, N.Y. 10016.

Printed in the United States of America.

1 2 3 4 5   79 78 77 76 75

Library of Congress Cataloging in Publication Data

Hougan, James.
   Decadence: radical nostalgia, narcissism, and decline in the seventies.

   Includes bibliographical references.
   1. United States—Social conditions—1960- I. Title.
HN59.H68   309.1'73'092   75-12993
ISBN 0-688-02950-7

Book design by Helen Roberts

For Carolyn & Daisy

The newcomer examines [a civilization] without calculation and is in a better position [than a native] to grasp its failures. If it is declining, he will agree, if need be, to decline too, to remark upon it and upon himself the effects of *fatum*. As for remedies, he neither possesses nor proposes them. Since he knows you cannot *treat* destiny, he does not set himself up as a healer in any case. His sole ambition: to keep abreast of the Incurable.

E. M. Cioran

Let a smile be your umbrella.

Popular Refrain

Preface

It's amazingly simple. Things fall apart. There's nothing you can do. Let a smile be your umbrella.

It seems inevitable that a writer who describes the impending, *unavoidable* collapse of his culture will raise the upper lips and nostrils of some liberal critics and readers. Felonious nouns—"doomsayer" and "pessimist"—will be applied to him, and his book will enter the world in the brands and bandages of negative verbiage. But such judgments assume too much.

In particular, those who accuse the "doomsayers" of pessimism assume that all men and women share their affection for, and have an equal stake in, the moribund society. That's a mad assumption, and it would be best to correct it in advance.

It is the thesis of *Decadence* that, for some few hundred years, we've been living within an evolving *regime of culture,* an industrial Order whose internal pressures have—despite its expanding sphere of influence—increased to nearly stellar intensities. In the United States, we live within a machine-of-nation, a cultural Gizmo whose functioning is absolutely dependent upon an ever-increasing number of strategic resources, both "natural" and not. As Harvard's resident Brainiac, B. F. Skinner, realizes, we can no longer afford the "variables" of freedom-'n-dignity. Nor any other variables, for that matter: if each part of the whole does not function perfectly and predictably, the system will not function at all.

All this is a way of saying that we've reached the end of the Industrial Age. Those who view Progress as a fate worth capitalizing—an inevitability or biological *right*—expect the "post-industrial age" to emerge as a meld of the Renaissance and the New Deal. There is nothing rational about this faith in Progress, however, and those who look forward to a "greening" of America will (along with everyone else) live to see the culture pruned. There's nothing that anyone can do about this, either collectively or solo. The same centrifugal forces that drive so many of us to the edges of the culture—to wand-waving gurus, glitter-rock, and gold—reduce all social movements to a wasting narcissism. Indeed, we're beyond the help of movements. Marx is, as always, dead, and "the masses" are only the Wad.

That History recycles cultures more often than revolutions do is obvious, ironic and (in the present case) *okay*. Those who would tinker with the culture, adjusting its socioeconomic knobs, labor under the delusion that a society which is industrial can also be humane and responsive. In fact, reform is meaningless when it's not impossible. The rationalization of labor and the state, begun in the seventeenth century by well-intentioned men whose names are now highways, has delivered us into a misery-dependent world. For the most part, we live in boxes owned by banks, labor senselessly, eat synthetically, ball methodically, compulsively, or desperately, and read for entertainment. For the rest . . . well, the rest do without. Suffering, as much as oil, is the juice of industrialization.

So *Decadence* is not a pessimistic book. To diagnose the society as Incurable, its malaise terminal, is something of a relief. That we can prescribe no regimen—except to act as witnesses and to indulge in those existential entertainments which are still available—may be futilitarian, but that in itself is no crime. Nero correctly understood that beauty, music and irony can co-exist with disintegration, that the inevitable can be accompanied on the violin.

We have, then, arrived in a rush at history's watershed only to find that the dam is about to burst. That rupture will be catastrophic but—have you ever seen a dam burst? All sorts of things are freed.

Advertisements

PART I. *THE INCURABLE*

**I Rennie Davis and
   the Drummer of Niklashausen   17**
   1. The Apocalyptic View   18
   2. Ellul, Fuller, Skinner, Stent, Bell, Cayce, the Mormons, and That Whole Crowd   23
   3. Science and Salvation   26
   4. Millenarian Preconditions: Signes of the Times   32
   5. The Unraveling of America: Charles Manson and Jan Bockelson   37
   6. Technical Fragility: Scenario from the *Fiery Flying Roll*   44

II Breakthrough in the Gray Room   50
   1. Preliminary Definitions: Technique and the Technical Phenomenon   50
   2. Alvin Toffler: Pimping for Progress   52
   3. William Burroughs: Reflections on the Heavy Metal Kid   57
   4. The Technical Chreod: Rationalizing the Ovaries   61
   5. From *I Ching* to *The Whole Earth Catalog*   66

III Freedom as Epilepsy 71
1. The Black Hole of Technique: The Inventor as Midwife 71
2. You Are What You Drive: *Brewster McCloud* and Aztec Sacrifice 74
3. Alphaville versus Betaville 78
4. The "Standard of Living" versus the "Quality of Life" 82
5. Charles Whitman, Lordstown, and the Disease of Reason 86

IV Gizmo and Siege 95
1. The "EM's" Quarters; the Technical Police 95
2. Problems of Technology Assessment 100
3. The Mystique of Reason (A Report on an Encounter between Dr. Frankenstein and Mr. Nader) 105
4. Nostalgia and Persecution 108
5. "Fag-Waves of Mexican Dope and Chicom Ideology" 112
6. The Future: Why It Hasn't Any 116

PART II. *AND THE DECADENT*

V The Unmaking of a Katakulchur 127
1. *The Whole Earth Catalog* 127
2. Myth of Counterculture 128
3. Beats and Freaks: From Job to Atlas to Noah 132
4. Tabular Transitions; Millenarian Discontents 138
5. Ebbing of "The Plague"; New Left Co-optation 145
6. Collective Narcissism: The Media Warp 151
7. The Sears, Roebuck of Postindustrial Cataclysm 155

VI Expatriate Rust   158
1. An Aside   158
2. Psychic Reflex   162
3. Inertial Observers   169
4. Ibiza and Racine   171
5. Oscillation: The Habit of Stupidity   174

VII America Flambé   182
1. Toynbee and the Metacrisis   182
2. Frankenstein: Seizing the Means of Reproduction   186
3. Alpha and Omega Cultures   190
4. Radical Nostalgia   193
5. Decadence   196

VIII Decadence: A Defense   202
1. Existential Stardom   202
2. An Ideology of Style?   205
3. Playboys, Poets, and Cranks   207
4. The Avenue   212
5. Tea at the Palaz of Hoon (Bye-bye, Canada Dry)   223

Acknowledgments   **237**

Recommendations   **239**

Footnotes   **249**

THE INCURABLE

I. Rennie Davis and the Drummer of Niklashausen

> To God in heaven we complain
> Kyrie Eleison
> That the priests cannot be slain
> Kyrie Eleison . . .
>
> *Old prayer*

Success and history both smell sweet. It's the odor of corruption, of something moldering within, a deadness or decay.

Climbing through the ruined fairy fort of the counterculture, stumbling over trunkfuls of unkept promises and empty threats, the desiccated bones of the American Left, I'm nearly overwhelmed by clouds of camphor and historical rot. It's all so dim and still, as if the very nerve ends of the culture had succumbed to a brownout of the most visceral kind. Outside —the gates and gears of industry, the noise, the numbness, the ubiquitous petering out of all and everything. Entropy or "chocolate in the veins". . . whatever you want to call it.

And yet, there is something seismic here, as if fermentation is taking place in a dangerously enclosed space. Poking deeper, we find the proliferation of what can only be called "the literature of catastrophe"; the multiplication of messianic sects, both passive and revolutionary; the increasing intersections of science and eschatology; the continuing retreat from the cities to the deep countryside; the ongoing fragmentation of all social movements, and the awakening of a squalid ethnicity based upon canards of gender, race, "heritage," social analysis, and sexual inclination. We divide and subdivide, moving ever deeper into the isolation of our private Gobis.

These symptoms are in no way unique to the present age, but reappear like the stitches in a seam that runs through history. In many ways, the present seems to be a reenactment of the medieval age. Conceptual arithmetic suggests that this decade or the next will end in a spasm of millenarian upheaval unmatched in its intensity since the proper authorities put a torch to John of Leyden in 1536. What follows is a map to the coming upheaval.

1. The Apocalyptic View

Whether cultural agnostics or true believers, members of post-World War II generations have so far tended to hold one conviction in common: mankind is at a critical stage whose resolution will soon result in the total transformation of all and everything. We do not expect to recognize the future. Beyond this, there's little agreement. The impending transformation is variously seen as Judgment or the Juggernaut, salvation or catastrophe. The catalyst responsible for the expected change is—take your pick—a guru-messiah delivering bliss; economic development proceeding exponentially to ecological disaster; political revolution generating utopia or hell; cybernetic malfunction igniting nuclear holocaust; politically motivated behavior-modification policies establishing the perfect robot society; and so on down an ever-lengthening list. Crisis, catastrophe, and transcendence are possibilities that are both chronic and acute, subjects discussed as often in the think tanks of Southern California as they are in the ashrams of Ibiza.

Those who see the coming metamorphosis as the product of some external agent (e.g., Christ or the nuclear Grand Guignol) are complemented by those who insist that the change will derive from mental high jumps made possible by new techniques in psychoanalysis (e.g., primal therapy), behaviorism (e.g., biofeedback), ESP, or drug experimentation. Indeed, there is a neat balance between those who see humanity transformed by a changed world and those who see the world transformed by a changed humanity. But, whichever is the case, it adds up to the same thing: utter metamorphosis.

Those who assert this view most frequently, forcefully, and publicly tend to be advocates of one thing or another. But the expectation of radical change is held by a vast number of "ordinary" people whose feelings are more often articulated in bars and on buses than they are in print. Unlike the proselytizers, who forage for converts among the young and the intellectuals, the majority of people are confident of no particular solution. They put their faith in God or Science, the President, grace, or R and D. They confront the future almost stoically, confident that *somehow* they will endure whatever comes. ("Well, if it comes right down to it: I've got my rifle—there'll always be enough to eat.")

There are different ways of dealing with the anxieties raised by the future. Those who have sufficient courage or single-mindedness will radically alter their present conditions and occupations to conform more closely with their anticipation of tomorrow: they'll emigrate to Brazil, start a commune, run for office, hoard money and consumer goods, or meditate around the clock. But, as Susan Sontag made explicit in her essay "The Imagination of Disaster," most people will simply neutralize their anxieties by surrendering to fantasy.[1] And if fantasy is in inadequate supply, there is a surfeit of hand-me-down catharsis available on television. It may also be the case that we sublimate our anxieties through consumption: there's an element of hoarding in the acquisition of a second car, a second home, a third television—as if each acquired object is an obstacle in the path of an onrushing disaster. Buying goods may be a deluded attempt to buy time.

If there is a single cause of our collective anxiety, it is technique. The technological imperative—that technique automatically maximizes the efficiency of means—suggests that nothing is permanent, and that what is technically possible is technically inevitable. If a more efficient means of doing something *can* be achieved, it *will* be achieved, regardless of any "secondary consequences" to individuals or mankind. A seemingly a priori skepticism about the infallibility of technique informs the young with gloom, and forces their optimism through the narrow sieve of one *deus ex machina* or another (guru, wonder drug, or revolution). This same skepticism informs others with a militant conservatism: the world, it seems, is too fragile to be entrusted to tinkerers and reformers —if we can't go back, it's best to stay where we are. (I'm reminded of a scene in Frederick Exley's memoir, *A Fan's Notes,* in which a barfly stares unblinking at a televised football game, muttering over and over, "Slow it down! Just, slow. it. down.") And some others, of course, will find redemption in their pessimism, surrendering to the inevitability of decay.

Common sense has long insisted that if errors *can* be made, they *will* be made. What makes this belief qualitatively different to hold in the twentieth century than before is that errors become more expensive as the methods we use become more powerful and all-effective. Technical error by the Strategic Air Command, for instance, can be total and *incorrectable* by virtue of that entity's function. One false move and we've had it.

Similarly, simple observation of technological development(s) suggests that (in the past thirty years) almost everything has "gotten better"—except the quality of life, which has gotten worse.

We can debate the accuracy of these beliefs, but what is unarguable is that they are widely held, particularly by the young, whose stake in the future is profound. Countercultural activity in the 1960s was the first sign that our collective anxieties had reached a depth sufficient to generate what amounted to a popular, if premature, millenarian revolt. Indeed, the only way in which reference to a "counterculture" makes much sense is if, by that term, we mean a loose conglomeration of widely divergent millenarian outgroups.

"Counterculture" was a convenient but misleading term. It suggested a monolith built upon an indiscriminate unity which the young never felt. If anything, those who came of age during the 1960s were one of the most divided generations the planet has ever seen. The macrobiotic, acidhead, Jesus freak, communard, and Weatherman were poles apart in analysis and style, and were mutually contemptuous. While they shared a set of basic rejections, their enthusiasms were inherently divisive. Only in a single sense could they be thought of as in any way homogeneous: that's the sense in which each faction felt itself to be an elite with a communal mission whose goal was to enlighten or improve the world through its immediate and radical transformation. In every other way, the "counterculture" was a myth of liberal intellectuals (like me), a product of bad observation or wishful thinking, or both.

What else, besides a myth, disappears simply because the people who embodied it ceased to believe in it?

And yet there *was* that common ground. Whether the young were chanting, praying, trashing, fasting, or simply dropping out, the articulated purpose was to regain control of events, to transform the future's landscape. The counterculture's millenarian perspective was simultaneously its most obvious and most overlooked characteristic. The failure of journalists to place that characteristic in an historical framework was the result of two equally bad attitudes.

The first attitude was that of the Olympian, who neglected an historical perspective because he didn't want to dignify the antics of maniacs with anything so important as a reference to History. That is, because the counterculture was primarily cultural, rather than political, it did not seem to belong in the same paragraph with the state-centered events that we like to think is "the historical record."

The second attitude was that of the Romantic, who neglected an historical perspective because he felt that there was something "special" and unique about the counterculture. The origin of the Romantic's prejudice was in the wishful thought that *this* generation represented an *evolutionary* change, and so no historical comparison could have any relevance.

When the countercultural myth lost its credibility, when the movement(s) died of widespread disbelief, the first group said, "I told you so." The wisdom of their neglect was confirmed by the movements' disintegration. But, in viewing the upheavals of the Sixties as a decade's quirk, and nothing more, the Olympians missed the age entirely.

The second group, which advocated the speciality of the "younger generation," suffered the fate of every Romantic: disillusionment. The younger generation passed into early middle age. In their wake they left the acid tests, bellbottoms, be-ins, and naïvetés, the Hula-Hoops of their adolescence, and it was these things that the Romantic most admired. And they'd been left behind, the detritus of an era. As a generation, the generation had died.

What did not go away, however, were the people who'd made up that generation. Neither did the circumstances or conditions which caused them to act in the way that they had. If anything, those circumstances worsened.

It's this "residue," these leftover people, that constitutes the counterculture's contemporary relevance, the relevance which a dead myth can sometimes have for the present. For the first time in more than four hundred years, nations have rocked with millenarian sentiments and "new" ideologies. Failing to ask why that is the case is to make a mistake about both history *and* the future: the 1960s foreshadowed tomorrow as artfully as a playwright anticipates the last act in his first. While the "countercultural" forms of millenarian agitation have, for the most part, been discarded in the Seventies, the perspective which animated those forms is still very much with us. Even a powersucker like Billy Graham has noticed. As he told a White House prayer breakfast in December, 1973, "Almost everyone I talk to seems to sense that a hurricane, of cataclysmic proportions, is about to break on the world."

2. Ellul, Fuller, Skinner, Stent, Bell, Cayce, the Mormons, and That Whole Crowd

Essential to any millenarian outlook is a belief that the planet is about to be absolutely and irrevocably changed, whether for good or evil. That view, as I've suggested, is widely held and diffuse, but specific examples are readily at hand.

Jacques Ellul,[2] for instance, instructs us that *"la technique"* is an irresistible force whose end is the inevitable and complete dehumanization of society. "Complete dehumanization" is not an exaggeration. Ellul expects that, in the future, mankind will consist of genetically distilled technician-slaveys in the service of a test-tube dictatorship that makes *Brave New World* sound like Camelot. In a sense, the French philosopher suggests that man is on the brink of becoming vestigial to the methods he created.

Gunther Stent[3] informs us that the world is on the brink of an ersatz "golden age" characterized by Polynesian self-indulgence, fortified by caloric surpluses, and moderated by a good-natured mindlessness. In the rich shit of the "golden age," billions of Archies and Veronicas will clone their way to the repugnant maturity of fat carrots with opposing thumbs.

Buckminster Fuller,[4] the age's incubus, describes in machinelike prose how man is on the edge of an evolutionary leap afforded by the maximization of efficient "livingry" made possible by strategic environmental design. A gentle megalomaniac transfixed by what must be the most banal "vision" in the history of intellection, Fuller promises a future in which mankind delivers Dymaxion toilets to intergalactic civilizations that may not, in fact, require such devices.

B. F. Skinner,[5] on the other hand, predicts global catastrophe unless a "technology of behavior" is developed and applied to mankind with the result that we move *Beyond Freedom and Dignity* toward a carefully engineered environment designed in accordance with what is known about the behavior of brainwashed fruit flies, decorticated monkeys, and maze-crazed mice. Ellul's nightmare is Skinner's dream: you *vill* be happy. And, if you aren't, perhaps it's time you were treated to a taste of hypothalamic massage, or, more simply, returned to the federally funded genetic vat. (I've never understood why someone of Skinner's intellectual hubris balked at calling his book *Toward Slavery and Humiliation*. After all, in order to "save" mankind from itself, he proposes the elimination of what he calls, with almost felonious discrimination, "man *qua* man.")

Another book, *The Energy Crisis*[6] (written a year before the first Arab oil embargo), predicts a worsening oil shortage leading to severe economic disruption, proliferating government controls on economic and social activities, depression, fascism, and eventually a world war for control of existing energy resources. As the book's authors remark, "The brain trusts can't save us—when we're out of energy we're out of heartbeat, not just breath."

Daniel K. Bell,[7] a crypto-millenarian at Harvard, doesn't think things are so bad. In fact, Bell thinks the outlook is A-Okay, providing only that all power is transferred to elites within the universities, battalions of technicians capable of solving anything that may arise. A technogogue of the worst sort, Bell denies the possibility of utopia, urging "the sober construction of social reality," but notes that ". . . the most important social change of our time is a process of direct and deliberate contrivance. Men now seek to anticipate change, measure the course of its direction and its impact, control it, and even shape it for predetermined ends. 'The transformation of society' is no longer an abstract phrase but a process in which governments are actively engaged on a highly conscious basis." (And, one is tempted to add, with almost no success whatsoever, as the War on Poverty, War on Inflation, and war in Vietnam have demonstrated.)

Still another writer, *William Ophuls*, cites disappearing world oil reserves as the catalyst of future cataclysm, and predicts "the inevitable coming of scarcity to societies predicated on abundance. Its consequences, almost equally inevitable, will be the end of political democracy and a drastic restriction of personal liberty." [8] As Ophuls notes, "Historic responses to scarcity have been conflict—wars fought to control resources, and oppression—great inequality of wealth and the political measures to maintain it . . . In a crowded world where only the most exquisite care will prevent the collapse of the technological society on which we all depend the grip of planning and social control will of necessity become more and more complete."

William Irwin Thompson is equally explicit. Writing in *At the Edge of History,* Thompson remarks that "As one disaster after another hits the earth between now and the year 2000, it will be possible for the scientists to effect a palace coup in the planet. In a state of panic and exhaustion brought on by the disasters, the people will have no other alternative but to look up to their saviors who can promise to keep . . . Earth working—at the price of absolute scientific control over environments and populations. If world famine, overpopulation, pollution, ecological catastrophes, and the patriotic use of nuclear weapons bring us to another Dark Age, then obviously another ecclesiastical structure will arise from the ashes of the old order." [9]

These are only a handful of random examples of *rational* thinkers who have systematized what amounts to a millenarian perspective. To their number we might add the Club of Rome, under whose auspices the bleak *Limits to Growth* report was drafted. That report suggested that a global catastrophe is inevitable if we do not impose limitations upon "development," population, and the use of natural resources.

If we leave the realm of (relatively rigorous) rational analysis for authors whose intellectual methods are rather informal (e.g., Tim Leary, Charles Reich, L. Ron Hubbard, Aldous Huxley, George Orwell, and hundreds of others), we find that the millenarian/apocalyptic view is virtually epidemic. Cataclysm and salvation are glimpsed in a kaleidoscope of forms. Going still further, beyond even the vocabulary of reason, to the realm of revelation, we come upon traditional millenarian movements, the Mormons, Christian Scientists, Jehovah's Witnesses, National Caucus of Labor Committees, the Black Muslims, Divine Lighters, Children of God, Stelle Group, Hare Krishna people, Process Church, and a host of smaller groups such as the United Family, Manson Family, Lyman Family, and God knows how many other "families." And then, of course, there's the late Edgar Cayce and a panoply of fundamentalist sects in the South.

Without passing judgment on the validity of any particular analysis, projection, or revelation, it's obvious that the times are ripe with dread and nervous anticipation.

This in itself is not particularly new. Literature has always been filled with visions of the millennium and apocalypse. What *is* new, however, is the relatively popular acceptance of this view—by intellectuals and just folks—and its frequent identification with science or a quasi-scientific rationale. For the first time, the doomsayer's vision comes equipped with economic tables, disaster flow charts, and social graphs.

3. Science and Salvation

Science has proven to be at least as prolific as religion in its identification of potentially apocalyptic scenarios. The priests tell us that God will punish us for our sins, and the technicians warn that nature will punish us for our stupidity. It comes, essentially, to the same thing. But among the possibilities in the latter category are:

- destruction of the ecosphere by air, land, and/or water pollution;
- genocide by pesticide;
- interruption of the food chain through loony development schemes;
- thermal buildup brought about by industrial emissions

leading to a "greenhouse effect" that will, perhaps within a few generations, devastate the climate, melt the poles, flood the land, et cetera;

- decimation by nuclear radiation, whether through war, faulty reactor design, or leakage from plutonium waste containers;
- oxygen starvation brought about by the destruction of green plant life;
- overpopulation, leading to mass famine;
- dispersal of strategic ozone concentrations in the upper atmosphere by supersonic aircraft, radiation, and/or chlorine gas emissions (mostly from spray cans);
- and, perhaps, the escape of lethal bugs from bio-warfare factories secretly operated by the military.

Indeed, a particularly grim scenario was only recently published in *The New Scientist*. According to the article, man is on the brink of an ironic extinction. What's going to kill us all, to quote the magazine's euphemism, is "animal rumination." It seems that the proliferation of farm and domestic animals as sources of protein and affection has resulted—animals being what they are and doing what they do—in an excessive release of methane gas. Lighter than air, methane rises into the upper atmosphere where it mixes with ozone to cause the decay of both. Depleting the ozone is nothing short of catastrophic because it functions as an ultraviolet screen, preventing the sun's most harmful rays from frying folks on the ground.

And that, according to *The New Scientist,* is the way that the world ends: not with a bang, not with a whimper, but with a . . . uh, cow fart.

Whether we place our faith in prophets such as "Moses David Berg," or our fears in herds of cattle breaking wind on the pampas, it's apparent that our collective mortality has never been so well publicized. And yet, it's impossible to ignore the fact that most people confront this panoply of impending disasters with a neutrality that verges on apathy. The equanimity of the majority in the face of catastrophe is obscure and unsettling, as if their skepticism is predicated as much upon indifference as optimism. Is it that people don't believe the doomsayers, or is it that they just don't care?

Understanding this neutrality is essential to anticipating the probable shape of any truly popular millenarian movement that may emerge in the near future. And there are, I think, several reasons that explain what seems to be a lethal complacency.

The first question to ask is: if people *do* believe the doomsayers, how would they be expected to act? The answer is that they would probably act in much the same way as if things were "normal." We might expect a noticeable increase in the number of people suddenly "getting religion," but otherwise it's unlikely that daily life would be much disrupted by the anticipation of apocalypse a decade hence. It's only in science fiction films that masses of people go haywire when confronted with the prospect of a collective death in the future. When Hitler announced his intention to slaughter the entire population of Germany for its failure to win the war, his threat was credible, widely disseminated, and . . . virtually ignored. Confronted with a situation beyond their control, the Germans acted in a very human way: they went about their daily business, securing enough bread to keep themselves and their families alive until Armageddon.

Apocalypse is simply *de trop*—overkill in the most literal sense. Once we've come to terms with our own demise, the certainty of our *personal* deaths, the end of the world has a diminished relevance. As Dylan Thomas wrote, "After the first death, there is no other." Unless we hold a religious conviction about the hereafter, thinking beyond our individual leave-taking is an act of selflessness that proceeds from the same impulse as philanthropy. Collective death is, contemptible as it sounds, a redundant fillip, a footnote asterisked upon our private tombstones.

There are, of course, some who will argue that Americans are not Germans: the popularity of the ecology movement, its widespread acceptance as a public good, suggests that

Americans are willing and able to unite in a rational campaign for collective rescue. But the truth is that public endorsement of ecological values—their acceptance beyond the universities and outside the professions—reflects an antilitter aesthetic rather than eschatological concern. People just don't want the joint crapped up with beer cans and echoing with sonic booms that break windows and wreck television reception. The ozone? Well . . .

Not only is ecocatastrophe existentially *de trop,* its credibility also demands a nearly Kierkegaardian leap of faith. The arguments of scientists and economists are quite beyond the understanding of those whose education has left the impression that Keynes is a brand of antacid tablet. Very few people are equipped to make purely *rational* judgments about the pronouncements of science. We've not been "educated" so much as trained for very specific jobs—and saving the world isn't one of them. The result is an affirmative agnosticism where science is concerned: we believe everything we're told if there is unanimity among the specialists and if the message is couched in the totalitarian prose style of "sciencese."

Consider, for instance, the following: *At altitudes above the ionosphere, the Coriolus Effect causes enantiomorphic hydrocarbon radicals to combine with inert gases, typically yielding a precipitate of aqueous sulfides.* That statement, gibberish from beginning to end, is equally as credible to the average high school grad as the assertion that the release of methane by "animal rumination" will deplete existing ozone concentrations to such an extent that the troposphere will be penetrated by extraordinary quantities of ultraviolet rays. What happens is that, where science is concerned, most people willingly suspend their disbelief in much the same way that they do with a novel: they both believe, and don't believe; the world described is somehow not their own, not really. The assertions of scientists may be true or false but, in either case, they have no popular impact. After all, scientists are the ones who tell us that space is curved, that matter is a wave rather than a solid, that parallel lines must inevitably meet, and that one of the four most fundamental particles of matter is the "charmed quark." Each of which seems to be a matter of fact, but one that the ordinary man or woman is compelled to treat as a fiction.

It is ironic and tragic that, as our knowledge expands, our ignorance increases. That is, the amount of sheer *data* available to man as a species is so enormous that even the most brilliant can digest no more than the most paltry fragment of that information. As those data proliferate, with studies of the *Bufa bufa bufa* frog and the pineal glands of Antarctic penguins, the fragment accessible to any of us diminishes exponentially. The price of our collective knowledge is, therefore, individual ignorance. The more *we* know, the less you and I understand. And that cliché, uttered so often with a self-congratulatory smirk, becomes harrowing because the sense of awakening mystery that made our past ignorance *inspired* is now gone. While we individually know less and less, we believe *as a matter of faith* that the answers *are* known: if not to us, then to someone or -thing. Our perspective thereby becomes that of the dogmatist whose ignorance is transformed into stupidity by an utter lack of curiosity. Reason, Science, and Progress are established as a religious trinity whose central mystery is the absence of mystery; banality achieves an iconic stature.

That people *do* make the leap of faith which science demands of them, that their agnosticism is positive and credulous, is demonstrated by the fact that scientific jargon is a terrific marketing device. Forced to choose between two gasolines, most people will opt for the one containing the special additive, THX-1138. And who wants an ordinary tape recorder when he can own the one advertised in *Rolling Stone,* the TEAC 3300S-2T with "permaflux heads, EQ circuits, and a hysteresis synchronous motor"? There's really no choice: people will take the hysteresis synchronous motor every time.

As William Irwin Thompson insists, and Daniel K. Bell implies, science and the scientist today occupy a position analogous in many ways to that of the Church and the priest in the Middle Ages. Both groups represent hierarchical perceptual elites closely allied to government, wrapped in (mathematical or theological) dogmas whose mysterious veracity most people cannot judge and must not doubt. Both groups promulgate mysteries while pretending to do the opposite: the unimportant difference between the two is that religion proposes God as the Prime Mover, while science substitutes Force. The authority of science and religion proceeds from the general consensus that each is a social good, a source of material or spiritual comfort. What's happened is that we've exchanged the religious idiom for a secular one, the Miracle of Lourdes for that of penicillin.

But there is a disadvantage to science where salvation is concerned. That is, if science identifies a mortal threat, only two solutions are possible. Either the threat will be neutralized by the efforts of specialists working through the night in remote laboratories (as usually happens in sci-fi films), or everyone will have to pull together. The first solution places our fates in the hands of a very few; the second solution places our fates in the hands of the many. Neither is acceptable because the anxieties which lead to the millenarian perspective, the dream of salvation, are inevitably the expression of an urge to gain control of one's *own* fate. Religion is therefore a more probable future millenarian vehicle because it suggests that salvation can be achieved by an individual act of faith. It's this aspect of religion—its solipsistic motif—that makes it so attractive to so many. Utopia and salvation are made accessible to the individual through his *own* initiative: he needn't rely upon the activities of priests or physicists, or depend upon the goodwill or common sense of his fellow men. The Kingdom of Heaven is, as advertised, *within,* and not contingent upon any computer readout or referendum ballot.

Whatever shape future millenarian movements may take, they will have to overcome a widespread and deep-seated reluctance to accept the doomsayer's message—because doomsayers have even less credibility than presidents. There are a variety of reasons why this is so, not the least of which is the fact that everyone who has predicted the end of the world has so far been proven wrong. A second reason is that unpleasant news tends to be disbelieved until proof (rather than simple evidence) is offered: this is clearly impossible when the news refers to a prediction. A third reason is that many contemporary "doomsayers" identify their eschatological ends with the machinations of technology; since technology is closely identified with American "know-how"—since it is, as it were, *our baby*—doomsaying is inherently unpatriotic. As Marx pointed out, the ruling ideas of any time and place are the ideas of the ruling class. And in the American Seventies, the ruling class is a managerial elite whose *idée fixe* is Progress.

Most important of all, the doomsayer inevitably appears as a kind of hustler. Speaking of an apocalyptic end, whether predicated upon rational or religious argument, he conveys an impression of wishful thinking. That is, what the doomsayer really says is that catastrophe will befall us *unless we change our ways in accordance with his instructions*. Whether the cause of the anticipated apocalypse is said to be sodomy or ozone depletion, the doomsayer is also and always the salvationist. He knows the way out and demands that people follow his instructions; he's a person who pretends to be *absolutely* right and, whatever his motivation, his task is such that he must function as a cosmic blackmailer. His message is therefore always the same: "Do what I say, *or else*."

Still, large numbers of people *have* overcome their natural bias against the doomsayer, as the countercultural upheavals and the proliferation of chiliastic sects prove.

4. Millenarian Preconditions: Signes of the Times

Formerly, millenarian eschatology was the sole province of religious dissidents. It tended to emerge at times and places that had a variety of characteristics in common. Norman Cohn, the subject's Boswell, writes that "the social situations in which outbreaks of revolutionary millenarianism occurred were in fact remarkably uniform . . . The areas in which the age-old prophecies about the Last Days took on a new, revolutionary meaning and a new, explosive force were *the areas which were becoming seriously over-populated and were involved in a process of rapid economic and social change.*" [10]

Writing about European sects in the Middle Ages, Cohn points out that militant eschatology was mostly unaccepted until economic developments overthrew the customs and routine that dominated life around the manor. Encouraged by a new mercantilism, contact between different European communities mushroomed: cultures mingled, integrated, or were swamped by one another. Serfdom, battered by the conversion of agricultural lands to sheep pastures, went into a precipitous decline. Millions were uprooted and there began a massive emigration from the countryside to the cities. For their own parts, the cities suffered from too rapid growth, overpopulation, crime, and an increasingly frustrated populace.

Forced from their land, families and communities were shattered. The traditional labor shortage that provided the serf with financial security did not prevail in the cities, where, more often than not, he and his labor were superfluous. Community ties, and the mutual aid that was characteristic of the manor, were replaced by a new isolation and the fierce competition for work. Traditional skills were rendered obsolete. At the same time, institutions which had once offered succor or solace to the poor (e.g., the Church) had hardened into bureaucracies operating largely in the interests of the most powerful.

While the cities were heaven for the *nouveau riche* (of whom there were not a few), they were Bedlams for the poor. The same mercantilism and industrialization that enriched some people enormously created envy, disillusionment, and resentment among the frustrated and suddenly disinherited masses. Social disorientation, inequality, frustration, and anxiety were endemic to the age.

The growth of the revolutionary messianic sects can be attributed to those factors rather than, as is sometimes supposed, to poverty and ignorance per se. The poor were used to being poor: what they could not cope with was *change*. And, as for the intellectuals, many of them were among the first to enlist in the ranks of the millenarians.

What triggered the actual *emergence* of the messianic sects, however, was the sudden introduction of wholly unusual circumstances (such as the Black Death) which were both beyond the people's control and outside their ordinary experience.

As Cohn notes, "If the threat was sufficiently overwhelming, the disorientation sufficiently widespread and acute, there could arise a mass delusion of the most explosive kind. Thus, when the Black Death reached western Europe in 1348 it was at once concluded that some class of people must have introduced into the water-supply a poison concocted of spiders, frogs and lizards—all of them symbols of earth, dirt and the Devil—or else maybe of basilisk-flesh. As the plague continued and people grew more and more bewildered and desperate, suspicion swung now here, now there, lighting successively on the lepers, the poor, the rich, the clergy, before it came finally to rest on the Jews, who thereupon were almost exterminated.[11]

"Again and again," Cohn continues, "in situations of mass disorientation and anxiety, traditional beliefs about a future golden age or messianic kingdom came to serve as vehicles for social aspirations and animosities." [12]

For the poor of the Middle Ages, the world was a place of devastating instability: it was easy for the anxious to endorse the millenarian argument that the earth was in thrall to an immensely powerful, awesomely destructive force whose nature was more evil than corrupt, more demonic than human.

And the sects tended to have much in common. On the basis of divine recognitions miraculously revealed to their leader (frequently an apostate monk or unemployed clerk who pretended to the status of prophet, savior, or deity), the millenarians set for themselves a communal mission that intended nothing less than the total transformation of society. Occasionally murderous, often suicidal, and always elitist, the sects battled against existing institutions and the dogmas of the day.

Frequently despising the rich and denying the validity of private property, the millenarians were powerfully inclined toward a doctrine of mystical anarchism. Whether libertine or ascetic (there was seldom any middle ground), they envisioned a Kingdom of Heaven (internal or external) that would be brought about only through great suffering, sacrifice, and bloodshed.

In a passage that seems calculated to describe the counterculturati of the Sixties, Cohn discusses the Amaurians (eleventh century): "These voluntarily poor [people] formed a mobile, restless intelligentsia, members of which were constantly travelling along the trade routes from town to town, operating mostly underground and finding an audience and a following amongst the disoriented and anxious elements in urban society. They saw themselves as the only true imitators of the Apostles and indeed of Christ . . . But from the second half of the twelfth century onwards these multitudes of 'holy beggars' of both sexes showed themselves ready to assimilate any and every heretical doctrine that there was." [13] (It takes little effort to imagine the scene: scores of Amaurian freaks gathered on the tenement stoops of Londontown's Lower East Side, discussing Sufism, tossing Frisbees, and hustling the aristocracy for spare change, all this in Olde English.)

Common to many of the sects was the figure of the Antichrist, a ruler who "shall exalt himself, and magnify himself above every god." By signs and false wonders he will deceive the world. And the coming of the Antichrist was happily anticipated because it would herald the imminence of the final struggle before the establishment of the Kingdom of the Saints. Each generation preferred to believe that *it* had been born into the rule of the Antichrist, and there were always signs that confirmed that belief. As Cohn relates, "The signs included bad rulers, civil discord, war, drought, famine, plague, comets, sudden deaths of prominent persons and an increase in general sinfulness. . . ."[14]

If that list sounds familiar, it should. Taking each of the signs in order, we have—

Bad rulers: Nixon and Agnew will suffice as examples;

Civil discord: Wounded Knee, street crime, Watts, Kent State, and violent strikes;

War: besides the Damoclean nuclear umbrella which hangs over the land, there's the Mideast and Vietnam;

Drought: the Sahara, sub-Sahara, parts of Asia and the United States;

Famine: in Africa and Asia;

Plague: the complex of "civilized diseases" (e.g., cancer and heart disease);

Comets: Kohoutek may have proven bashful, but UFO sightings are on the increase and, in view of the awe in which such objects are held, can be said to occupy a mythic niche within the contemporary imagination, just as comets did in the imaginations of our ancestors;

Sudden deaths of prominent persons: our cup runneth over, and so do conspiracy theories about the spillage. The assassinations of JFK, RFK, and MLK complement the sudden deaths of such celebrities as James Dean, Marilyn Monroe, Sharon Tate, Bruce Lee, the Big Bopper, Buddy Holly, Mama Cass Elliott, Jim Croce, Jim Morrison, Otis Redding, Jimi Hendrix, Janis Joplin, Dorothy Hunt, and so on.

As for a "general increase in sinfulness," it was only a few years ago that the "Silent Majority" was whipped into a meringue of political hatred by condemnations of so-called "permissiveness."

It's clear that, as Cohn notes at the end of his book, ". . . it is the simple truth that, stripped of their original supernatural sanction, revolutionary millenarianism and mystical anarchism are with us still."[15] In some cases (but not all), the religious matrix has merely been replaced by a more secular idiom (e.g., Scientology).

5. The Unraveling of America: Charles Manson and Jan Bockelson

Today, social conditions in the West directly parallel, and sometimes duplicate, those which led to the emergence of revolutionary millenarianism in the medieval era (this is as true in Dahomey as it is in the United States*). Twentieth-century innovations in technology and technique (e.g., the ICBM and cybernetics, respectively) have dictated entirely new geopolitical and economic relationships between nations. Within each country, people experience a profound disorientation directly attributable to the acceleration, accumulation, and nature of social changes wrought within each person's lifetime by technical development(s). (Examples are ubiquitous. One of the most obvious, or grossest, is the automobile, whose means of production and popular use has revolutionized work-styles, redesigned the environment, and reshaped life-styles, cities, and the economies of whole nations.) Everywhere (thanks to radio, television, film, and jet flight) countries are being squeezed together in the claustrophobic confines of what amounts to a cultural Osterizer: the result is a mostly American blend, an international homogenization of customs and modes. (That this homogenization is resented is apparent to anyone who has reflected upon the sudden vitality of regional and ethnic chauvinism.)

As cultures mingle and merge, as technical innovation revamps daily life within each society, a sort of social vertigo results. Tourism (a wholly new phenomenon) severs the historical continuum, turning entire societies into servant pools and culture zoos. Families are fractured and scattered by the automobile, which, in making mobility feasible, makes movement economically imperative. Both traditional and newly learned skills are rapidly rendered obsolete by new techniques, products, and machinery. Television and the cinema deliver

---

* Good old Dahomey . . . on the whole, however, I'd rather be in Rio Muni.

images of spectacular wealth to those who can never achieve it, generating impossible consumer ideals that inevitably lead to vain hopes, frustration, and bitterness. The psychological effects of these phenomena are remarkably similar to the effects of mercantilism and the Plague in the Middle Ages (of course, the Plague killed millions—but then, so does the car). Citing these phenomena is not particularly original: on the contrary, one could line the walls of the Pentagon with books devoted to aspects of the various curses. What may be new, however, is the admission that we'll probably do nothing about any of these problems, lacking both will and means—and that, in fact, they will get worse, and never better. (I don't want to get too far ahead of my argument, but it seems only fair to warn the reader that I believe our situation to be Incurable . . . and that my concern is not with resolving that situation, or mending it, but is instead devoted to discovering a means of—simultaneously—living with it and overturning it.)*

The "situation" gets worse. Gagging on their own effluvia and pulsing with violent crime, the cities expand at a rate which urban planners predict will soon deliver the hundred-million megalopolis. The transition from present-day metropolis to the megalopolis of 2000 A.D. (assuming we reach that time) entails a tenfold increase in the population of the city and a projected *hundredfold increase in the city's size*. Eventually, we may expect the "ecumenopolis": "an interconnected stable urban network over the whole world." [16]

There's no reason to suspect that bigger is better or less complex. On the contrary. In a study of overlapping government units in large urban complexes, it was found that there are about 465 semi-independent governmental organizations in the San Francisco Bay area for a population of about four million people—roughly one governmental unit per ten thousand. Citing that study, planner John Platt notes, "The problem is to get these semi-independent government bodies interrelated so that initiating any new project does not require an almost infinite number of signatures, or so that one of

* This book's title is a clue to the means.

these bodies isn't doing something that another one is negating. This is a fantastic problem already at the four-million level: to extend this to the 100-million level is going to require new levels of organization and management."[17] Indeed, if the ratio remains constant, a megalopolis of a hundred million will be guided by the ministrations of about ten thousand different agencies. Commenting on this, biologist C. H. Waddington observed, "The possibility of an administrative jam-up occurring, so that some essential service just doesn't operate, would be enormous."[18] John Papaioannou concurred: "The next thirty years is going to be a [period of] continuous crisis."[19]

Indeed, twentieth-century "bigness" is a grim subject to contemplate since, on the social as much as on the molecular level, bigness entails complexity and that, in turn, implies fragility. As we become increasingly dependent upon the proper functioning of technical means and machines, those engines and processes also become increasingly dependent upon *each other*. One mechanism comes to rely upon and serve the next, creating a technical chain whose parts are so interdependent that any disruption of the chain is equivalent to total breakdown. Like a stone tossed into a pond, the disruption ripples outward in every direction.

As technology integrates itself, human tasks necessarily become increasingly specialized. At some point, the plurality of processes and machines becomes a system whose complex totality can be rationalized, or "comprehended," only by another machine. At that point, individual specialization has taken on the character of tunnel vision: the individual concentrates on his own task to the exclusion of everything else. He no longer even pretends to understand the system of which he's a part. The result is that his work, a fragment that may be wholly useless in itself (albeit essential to the system's functioning as a whole), is performed with only the most limited sense of responsibility. It's performed because higher authorities inscrutably insist upon its utility. In such circumstances, the consequences of one's labor are not one's own but belong instead to the (however vaguely defined) "higher authorities." As social psychiatrist Stanley Milgram has shown, it is this process, this alienation from the meaning of one's work, that results in ". . . a fragmentation of the total human act; no one is confronted with the consequences of his decision . . . The person who assumes responsibility has evaporated" [20] wherever work is performed by specialists. It's in this context that specialists such as Adolf Eichmann can, "with a clear conscience," shuffle papers sending millions of innocents to their deaths—he was, after all, merely a traffic manager striving for efficiency in compliance with orders from above.

The social disorientation caused by our technological drift corresponds very well to the disorientation generated by the economic and social vicissitudes of industrialization in the Middle Ages. The constancy of contemporary change requires so many major and minor adjustments by the individual that stasis is impossible and instability is the "natural" milieu—we're born into a plenum of ongoing cultural confusions.

And like the Middle Ages, ours is a time that is especially beset by the frustrations that accompany rapid cultural change. Overpopulation, the sudden obsolescence of skills, the disintegration of family and community ties, failing aspirations, ethnic clashes, and general bad vibes are with us to an extraordinary degree. Like beasts in a "behavioral sink," we suffer the physical and mental consequences of the social environment we've created—bad nerves, multiple addictions, anxiety, flash violence, and hormonal tremors.

It may be argued, of course, that one can make too much of the similarities between the present and the deep past. Ours is a noticeably more democratic and literate age, a time of real (if transient) prosperity. Those characteristics would seem to isolate us from history, rendering the present qualitatively different from the past, and immune to its examples. In fact, however, American "democracy," literacy, and "prosperity" are deceptively benevolent, properties that in no way guarantee a greater measure of freedom or dignity for anyone. On the contrary. As Dutch Provo Steve Davis sighed after winning a seat on the Amsterdam City Council, "No matter *who* you vote for—the government always gets in." * Commenting on the same phenomenon, expatriate novelist Gore Vidal remarked that the two-party system is a fraud since both parties are, in fact, wings of a single establishment, the "Property Party." Whether we vote for one wing or another is a moot enterprise since, in the end, our votes do nothing more than confirm the existing system (even if we vote "against" the wing in power). With similar results, literacy has also worked against the majority, reinforcing the *status quo flux* by rendering the mass of people more receptive to misinformation and social conditioning. Because our literacy is, for the most part, left fallow—useful in signing checks and in filling out job applications—Americans are not so much well informed as continuously advised. And, as to our "prosperity," it is no more equivalent to dignity and ease than literacy is to wisdom and tranquillity. Instead, American prosperity is contingent upon our subservience to an economic apparatus whose well-being requires that it perpetuate a continuum of needs; the price of our "prosperity" is sustained dissatisfaction, dependence upon a calculus of consumer addiction.

There was a time when most people were, like the trees, part of the land, resources owned by an aristocracy of blood and genes. That time was succeeded by an age in which the people were part of the factory equipment, machinery on permanent lease to an aristocracy of money. And that age was, in its turn, succeeded by an aristocracy of invisible means, a matrix of techniques, transmission belts, and "channels" whose authority is cruelly neutral and absolute—as absolute as the divine right of kings, and even harder to escape.

Things have not changed so meaningfully or much; for the most part, our afflictions have merely been rationalized.

It's in the context of the similarities of the present and the past that one comes to view the counterculture as a prelude of

---

* Davis, faithful to the anarchist principles of Provo, thereupon resigned his newly won office, and left for Spain.

millenarian things to come. Charles Manson's dune-buggy death squad loses its mystery upon comparison with earlier millenarian sects. Hoping to be a catalytic force in the inauguration of a bloodbath that would "purify" the world, Manson's entourage embraced poverty, attacked the rich, and undertook a nomadic life-style whose center was *ritually* brutal. Sadism, masochism, and humiliation, the protein of revolutionary millenarianism, fueled their mysticism. It's curious that, in view of the millions of words written about Manson, little or no attention was paid to the fact that his sect might easily have stepped right out of the thirteenth century. Reading Manson's "philosophy," one is struck by numerous passages that are virtually identical with the rhythms and sense of earlier peasant "prophets." His insistence upon material equality, the spiritual unity and ontic "oneness" of all people, is perhaps the most basic thematic complex in millenarian literature. That Manson's mystical beliefs should drive his band to murder is no contradiction. On the contrary, the killings were perfectly consistent with the articulated beliefs that Manson shared with so many of his generation. If we believe that *all men are one*—then murder is a kind of suicide, or amputation, a means of removing some unhealthy part of the body. If we also believe that reincarnation is certain, or that *life is eternal,* then slaughter is almost meaningless. And, if we believe that we can bring about the "Kingdom of Heaven" by serving as catalyst to Armageddon—then violence becomes a moral obligation. Manson preached all those things, and one of the great tragedies in the affair is that his acts were "wasted": recoiling from the butchery, we refused to take its author seriously, and so learned nothing about his motives, or those of his followers. Particularly disgusting, however, was the behavior of the New Left and countercultural writers who, after years of humming "Off the Pigs," trumpeted their disavowal of the Tate and La Bianca savagery. The idea, of course, was to preserve the vehicle of one's aspirations (the counterculture) by calling for the heads of those who'd taken one's rhetoric to heart and placed forks in the stomachs of the rich. The result was a shrill barrage from the counterculture's own establishment, an apostate condemnation reminiscent of nothing so much as "liberal" disavowals of "communism" during the 1950s. Indeed, the failure of the press (underground, overground, and sea level) to make clear the relationship between Manson's group and his counterparts in earlier centuries represented a twice-blown opportunity. Not only would such comment have made the present less opaque to its inhabitants, it would also have reached alpine heights of irony.

Compare, for instance, Manson's career with that of "the Munster revolutionary," Jan Bockelson. Four centuries prior to Manson's birth, Bockelson (like Manson, an impoverished bastard of great charm and persuasion) experienced a vision in which he, a prophet of divine authority, was to rule as King over the New Jerusalem. With the help of sycophants and various promoter-priests, Bockelson intrigued to convince the masses of Munster (and many other Germans) that his vision was inspired by God. Accomplishing this, he established the New Jerusalem within the fortifications of Munster. Forcing polygamy upon the townies, he took for himself more than a dozen wives and urged that the simple folk follow suit. Imposing a most severe austerity upon the people by means of confiscatory taxes, Bockelson justified his own luxury by explaining (as Manson often did) that he was "dead to the flesh" and therefore immune to luxury's effects. Soon, he added, the townspeople would also be dead to the flesh and, therefore, able to wear furs and drink from silver goblets. Meanwhile, Bockelson's pamphleteers were at work, explaining the special role of the Munsterfolk. Their message was simple: the people must go into the world bearing the Sword of Justice, and purifying the flock. "The glory of all the Saints is to wreak vengeance," they wrote. "Revenge without mercy must be taken of all who are marked with the Sign." After the slaughter of the rich and unholy, Christ would ordain a new kingdom for his saints, and all things would be held in common. Bockelson's goal was, like Manson's, "To kill all monks and priests and all rulers that there are in the world; for our king alone is the rightful ruler."

While egalitarian in its rhetoric, Bockelson's rule over Munster was as tyrannical as Manson's over the Spann Ranch. Followers who wavered in their faith or offerings, as well as captured enemies, were beheaded or hacked to pieces—often at public banquets. And, just as Manson was besieged in the desert by the state police, Bockelson was besieged in Munster. Eventually, the siege against Munster succeeded, and Bockelson was arrested. Like Manson, who was sentenced to death for the acts of his followers, Bockelson refused to recant (nor, for the most part, would his congregation). Penology being what it was in 1536, Bockelson was led from town to town in chains, exhibited as a kind of dancing bear. Having made their point, the proper authorities then returned the prophet to Munster, where, with his remaining honchos, the revolutionary was tortured to death with flaming irons.

My purpose, of course, is not to "defend" Manson, but to make some sense of him. His emergence, and the emergence of groups like his, suggest that we may be on the brink of an historical reenactment that could easily be bloody. Whether or not this is so, the Mansonoids may well serve as a Rosetta Stone for the times. Sects like his, and variations thereof, are born of conditions that are highly particularized. What some of those conditions are has already been related. What remains is to identify the "wholly unusual," all-effective circumstance that serves as midwife to all millenarian groups. In the Middle Ages it was the Plague. What might that circumstance be today?

6. Technical Fragility: Scenario from the "Fiery Flying Roll"

I suspect it will be the breakdown of the society's technical apparat, the resulting economic paralysis and the collapse of expectations.

The fragility of contemporary technique, its total dependence upon an increasing number of components, its accelerating *complexification*, increases the probable magnitude of any technical disruption we may experience. When anything is changed in such a whole-system as our own, everything is changed. Thus, an oil shortage or auto worker strike ripples through the entire culture, creating a chain reaction of gathering force, a reaction which cannot be isolated and contained, but which must be stopped. It seems reasonable to suppose that, as the whole-system's functioning comes to depend upon more and more parts, it becomes increasingly likely that the system will break down, assuming that the fragility of each part remains about the same. (It's in this context that Papaioannou predicts a period of continuing crisis.)

If breakdowns of this sort occur (and they will), then we may expect that the age's predisposition to millenarianism will flower in the humus of extraordinary events. What qualifies as an "extraordinary event" is any circumstance that is mysterious in origin, profound in effect, prolonged or chronic, and beyond the experience of the ordinary person. A severe epidemic, an economic catastrophe of Depression proportions, sudden shortages of commodities formerly taken for granted, an invasion of angels or UFOs—the nature of the event is unimportant so long as it takes people by surprise, perpetuates that surprise, and adversely disrupts their life-style in important ways.

If pressed to anticipate which event is most likely to generate the impending millenarian upheaval, I'd guess that it will result from the effects of a worsening energy shortage. Geologists agree that if European oil consumption continues to grow at its present rate, if America's consumption stays the same, if we discover oil at about the same rate that we have in the past—then the world will effectively be out of oil by 1995. Realities of Western economics dictate that alternative energy sources cannot be developed and put into popular usage prior to then. What this means is that the economies of most Western countries are relying upon the development of a technological *deus ex machina* that will somehow save us. Knowledgeable industrialists admit that they have little or no idea what that development will be, and privately doubt that—whatever it is—it can arrive in time to offset the depletion of the oil on which we depend. The program required to develop and implement such new technology demands research-and-development funds that private industry cannot afford to spend. Whether government is willing and able to do so remains to be seen. But if the energy "crisis" becomes an energy catastrophe, it's certain that the public mood will take a millenarian turn.

Some oil experts may disagree with the validity of the above scenario, but there is no reason to defend its probability at any length. It's simply one possibility among many. And, as we become more reliant upon the technical character of our environment, other possibilities for total disruption proliferate. Only religious nuts insist upon the monistic character of Apocalypse.

But, supposing something of this nature *did* take place, whether caused by an energy shortage, a climatic change, or some other event: what would happen?

It's probable that the upheaval resulting from such circumstances would conform in most ways to the traditional aspects of millenarianism. Sects would emerge proposing the immediate establishment of a protoegalitarian order, attacking existing institutions, searching for scapegoats, and defending themselves against the suppression that would certainly be applied.

In the United States, it's probable that a variety of such movements would develop—political, parascientific, and religious in character—in accord with people's intellectual biases. Thus we might expect the majority of *nouveau* millenarians to embrace a religious order of one kind or another. Some of these groups are likely to withdraw from the society, isolating themselves in rural retreats while they wait for everyone else to go down the technological tubes. Others will be more aggressive, proselytizing on the city streets, and perhaps adopting a neo-Luddite stance if the anticipated apocalypse is linked (in fact or imagination) to industry.

Intellectuals and rationalists from the middle and upper classes will be split between political and scientific associations. Utopian organizations tied to the insights or fantasies of theorists such as B. F. Skinner, Bucky Fuller, and L. Ron Hubbard will establish elitist enclaves for the salvation of their members.

Those whose paranoia takes political analysis as its context will commit themselves, in all probability, to a militant Marxism. In all its essentials, Marxist theory is nothing more—nor anything less—than an attempt to rationalize the millenarian urge with economic, class, and historical analysis: it is, in other words, an accommodation of revolutionary millenarianism to the Age of Reason and Industry.

Each of these groups will identify its own scapegoat. The religious orders are likely to take the same racist approach that was popular in the Middle Ages: minorities will be their targets. If all goes well, the utopians will do no more than punish inefficiency. Marxists will, of course, have no trouble identifying *their* enemies.

All of the above assumes that these groups will remain exclusive and separate, a situation that by no means needs to be the case. It's known, for instance, that the "Drummer of Niklashausen," an itinerant musician of the fifteenth century, was a poor and uneducated youth of questionable intelligence but great eloquence. Preaching repentance and apocalypse, after a vision of the Virgin had appeared to him, he attracted thousands of followers. Historians agree, however, that it wasn't until the youth fell under the influence of a hermit living nearby that he began to command *a movement*. It was the hermit, apparently, who was responsible for converting the youth's reformist doctrine into a volatile version of revolutionary millenarianism (the recluse is thought to have been active in mystical-anarchist movements before meeting the drummer boy). In woodcuts of that time, the Drummer of Niklashausen is often shown speaking to a crowd while the hermit whispers in his ear. (The youth was eventually burned at the stake after an unsuccessful peasant rebellion, and his ashes were promptly scattered by the authorities.)

Nor was this an isolated instance in the history of millenarianism. It seems that many reformist movements were "captured" by revolutionaries and transmogrified into militant egalitarian sects.

It's in this context that one wonders about (for example) the conversion of Rennie Davis and other New Left activists to the faith of the Guru Maharaj Ji, Lyn Marcus' NCLC, the Children of God, et cetera. It would be interesting to know if Mr. Davis is aware of the Drummer of Niklashausen's example, and if he is sometimes seen to whisper advice in the young guru's ear. Indeed, it would make a fine science fiction plot:

Shortages of strategic parts and materials (ball bearings, perhaps, and oil) caused by domestic strikes and foreign boycotts have resulted in the nearly total breakdown of essential services and the distribution of vital commodities. American houses are cold. The people are suddenly hungry. Epidemics begin. Incomprehension and confusion jitter the streets.

Disoriented by accelerating change and rampant insecurities, totally reliant upon the efficient functioning of a socio-economic system which no one wholly understands, the people respond to the new exigencies by enlisting in the ranks of diverse millenarian sects.

In Harlem, processions of black flagellants parade through the streets humming "A Love Supreme" and flicking each other with cattle prods. Downtown, hordes of the unemployed and dispossessed invade the roseate fortress of NYU and, after a vicious fire-fight, demolish the computers and lynch the science faculty in Washington Square. (Arabists escape into the Bleecker Street IRT station, and disappear toward Brooklyn on a commandeered train.) In Central Park, a community of militant Skinnerites, their eyes rinsed of dignity, defend their utopia from behind a maze of concertina wire, negatively reinforced by megavolts. Throughout Midtown

Manhattan, roving cults follow self-appointed messiahs into high-rise residential buildings in bloody forays to liquidate the rich. Meanwhile, in the Bronx, a half-witted white youth inspires multitudes to mayhem by revealing a "Negro-Jewish" plot to enslave the world by fluoridating water supplies and infiltrating Wonder Bread with BHT and calcium propionate.

Across the Hudson, Rennie Davis and an estimated 200,000 blissed-out "premies" have sealed off all bridges and tunnels leading into the city; aging New Leftists converted to the Divine Light use half-forgotten printing skills to mimeograph the Guru's latest admonition:

"I say (once more) deliver, deliver, my money which thou hast . . . to poor creeples, lazars, yea to rogues, thieves, whores, and cut-purses, who are flesh of thy flesh, and every whit as good as thy self in mine eye, who are ready to starve in plaguy Gaols, and nasty dungeons, or els by my selfe, saith the Lord, I will torment thee day and night, inwardly or outwardly, or both waies, my litle finger shall shortly be heavier on thee . . . than my loynes were on Pharaoh and the Egyptians in times of old . . . I inform you that I overturn, overturn, overturn . . . I am coming to Levell in good earnest, to Levell to some purpose, to Levell with a witnesse, to Levell the Hills with the Valleyes, and to lay the Mountaines low . . . You shall weep and howl for the miseries that are suddenly comming upon you; for your riches are corrupted and . . . the plague of God is in them. Your gold and silver, though you can't see it, is cankered, the rust of them is a witnesse against you . . . Come! give all to the poore and follow me, and you shall have treasure in heaven . . ."[21]

II. Breakthrough in the Gray Room

> Everything is going to become unimaginably worse, and never get better again.
>
> *Kurt Vonnegut, Jr.*

1. Preliminary Definitions: Technique and the Technical Phenomenon

"Your gold and silver, though you can't see it, is cankered. . . ." And so, one might add, is our carburetor and, in fact, almost everything else, from the potty chair to Exxon.

The millenarian upheavals of the late 1970s and early 1980s will have as their catalyst an economic catastrophe caused by a technical breakdown of massive dimensions.* The nature and necessity of that breakdown I intend to show, but, first, one must admit that there are certain problems with the discussion itself. Specifically, thought too has become "cankered."

If ideas have their seasons, this must be the dead of winter, an age which heaps contempt upon the amateur thinker, the visionary who declines to specialize. Large concepts are unfashionable and problems which do not submit to technical solutions (e.g., abstractions such as "alienation" and *angst*) are generally regarded as irrelevant, mythical, or poorly defined. That is, such problems seem to be the result of conceptual *non sequiturs*. Solving them requires only that one redefine the terms of their expression. In this way, for instance,

---

* As I'll indicate later on, the alternative to such a breakdown is a smoothly functioning society which, given existing problems that are not amenable to democratic solution, would resemble nothing so much as a martial apiary.

"dread" is seen to be a kind of psychometabolic dysfunction probably brought about by sociological factors; urban renewal, two weeks in Aruba, and four hundred milligrams of Dexedrine will solve immediately what Sartre could not resolve in years. Similarly, concepts which preoccupied philosophers for millennia (free will, skepticism, causality, and so forth) are today understood to be no more than syntactical blunders.

Since the advent of the Logical Positivists, traditional philosophical concerns have fallen into professional disrepute. Undergraduates curious about the nature of being are now referred to basic texts in quantum physics and molecular biology; those reckless enough to express an interest in something as general as "the human condition" will probably find themselves deported to the College of Pharmacy. In a sense, certain kinds of speculation have been banned or are, in any case, obstacles which the ambitious should avoid.

Like most other activities, thinking has become the province of technicians. And since the business of technicians is the rationalization of means, contemporary philosophy is devoted largely to the analysis of its own methods and the ways in which it gets work done. The answers which it seeks are critical solutions to methodological problems, preferably ones which have industrial applications. Thus, the most honored philosopher on the scene today is probably Saul Kripke, a young genius who made his bones over Copi's dead body by rationalizing modal logic. Problems of epistemology and consciousness are no longer subjects of ethereal speculation, but technical conundrums whose solutions are essential to the development of, as in Kripke's case, Next Generational computers.

The point is this: technique—*the most rationally efficient means of accomplishing an end*—is a dynamic, all-affective phenomenon which penetrates even the most remote and private areas of human activity, inevitably resulting in the ascendancy of means over ends. Philosophy, traditionally at a remove from the marketplace, is no exception. Its submission to the *phenomenon of technique—the ensemble of developing technical means*—has resulted in its evisceration: it becomes mechanical and critical, empty of vital contents.

Indeed, there are no exceptions to the consuming transformations wrought by the technical phenomenon, the pattern of our means. But before this subject is entered upon, it might be well to anticipate some of the objections that are certain to arise.

2. Alvin Toffler: Pimping for Progress

In a technical world, pessimism is the ultimate attitudinal sin because it denies the primacy and certainty of Progress. By "pessimism" I do not mean the simple identification of serious problems, or only that, but the concomitant assertion that there is nothing that can be done, or is likely to be done, to solve those problems. It is, in other words, one thing to say that democracy is threatened, and quite another to insist that totalitarianism is inevitable.

An indication of the contempt in which pessimists are held, particularly those whose forebodings relate to technique, is beautifully illustrated by Alvin Toffler, the *Future Shock* [22] magnate.

Mr. Toffler is an ideational apparatchik who thrives upon the dismissal of perceptions that are, while unpopular, of greater validity than any he has ever had on his own. In their place he substitutes a pantheon of technical potentials designed to dazzle and frighten us with the prospect of a future characterized by unlimited possibility. The rhetorical question underlying the entirety of his effort is contrived to elicit self-congratulatory yups from all who encounter it: Are we wise enough and brave enough to take a can-do attitude toward the future? Or are we a bunch of doomsaying ostriches, ninnies who cringe before majestic destinies?

Pimping for Progress, Toffler is almost bodacious.* In, for instance, an egregiously brief dismissal of what he calls the "orthodox social critics" (he names Kafka, Orwell, William Whyte, Herbert Marcuse, and Jacques Ellul) (!), Toffler tells us that bureaucracy is dying. "If we set our conceptual clichés aside," he promises, we will see that contemporary bureaucracy is evaporating in the pressure cooker of accelerating change. The "conceptual clichés" to which Toffler refers (with, I think, atavistic gall) constitute the lifework of men who are among the century's most brilliant social theorists. In a paragraph whose brevity is practically electric, Toffler reduces their complex perceptions to the simplistic thesis that mechanization and the ascendancy of technical expertise are demoting individuals to "faceless cogs" in the bureaucratic machine. Having thus distilled his antagonists' opus to such a limp and hackneyed summation, Toffler then reassures us by denying the argument's validity. He does so in the most oblique and elegant way, never bothering directly to address either the exquisite hallucinations of Kafka or the grinding insights of Ellul. Never mind about Whyte, Marcuse, Orwell, and that crowd—we're in the presence of a master chiropractor.

Toffler's concern with bureaucracy is intimate to his refutation of the "faceless cog" bugaboo. If he can show that bureaucracy is on the decline, to be replaced with what he calls "Ad-hocracy" (get it?), then the fears of "technophobes" like Kafka and Ellul can be disregarded.

His argument is simple and largely contingent upon definition. Bureaucracies, he says, are those organizational entities which are vertically structured, rigidly compartmentalized, and static. The coming Ad-hocracy, however, will be composed of organizations of task-force impermanence: they will be kinetic, functionally fluid, and more democratic in structure. The evi-

* Too late! Too late! As *Decadence* goes to the printers, Mr. Toffler has begun to question his own technophilia, the naïveté which underlies *Future Shock*. The February, 1975, issue of *Esquire* contains a fine article of his, a despairing meditation upon the possibility of eco-spasm. Great.

dence which Toffler cites for the impending rise of Ad-hocracy is the new frequency with which executives are changing jobs, the increasing redefinition of executive responsibility within private and public organizations, the sudden importance of disposable "project" groups within large organizations, and the accelerating necessity of bureaucracies to redesign their operational and structural styles in response to phenomena such as mergers and technical innovations.

Proceeding upon an indifferent definition and an ambiguous lump of evidence, Toffler then argues a syllogism whose basic premise is as wacky as its logic is impeccable:

1) Bureaucracy cannot survive change.
2) Bureaucracy is changing.
∴ 3) Bureaucracy cannot survive.

Obviously, the most important characteristics of bureaucracy have been entirely omitted from his definition. It's not the vertical structure that makes bureaucracy odious; it isn't its compartmentalization that makes it offensive; it isn't even its stasis, its penchant to endure. The most relevant characteristics of bureaucracy are its unresponsiveness to human concerns, its inclination to reduce both employees and clients to statistical ciphers.

The nature of bureaucracy is such that the organization's ostensible purposes and the individual's needs in relation to those purposes are both subordinated to the bureaucratic *means,* its red tape and "proper channels." *This* is what's so infuriating. The welfare client applying for medical aid is indifferent to the organizational peculiarities of the welfare bureaucracy. All the client's concerned about is that she or he seems to be adrift in a maze of inhuman dimensions. The simplest requests may require months of "processing" and, in any case, are likely to be granted only after the victim, or client, has been carted off for an autopsy.*

---

* This may sound like an exaggeration, but it's not. While a social worker in Chicago, I had a nice old lady on my "caseload," a real *grande dame* of the ghetto. All she wanted out of life, it seemed, was a new pillow. It

In any bureaucracy, responsibility is so diffused that, for all intents and purposes, it no longer exists. Whether that diffusion takes place vertically (as happens in a single organization) or horizontally (e.g., between different federal agencies) is irrelevant. What's important is that the buck stops nowhere—it is, instead, perpetually recycled.

Bureaucracy is more like a virus than a dinosaur, and far from the edge of extinction. The changes which Toffler describes are symptomatic of bureaucracy's health, rather than of any malaise which may afflict it. Its primary function is, like that of a virus, its own growth; and, again like a virus, it accommodates itself to the evolving characteristics of its host —the age in which it adheres. Its ability to adapt is legendary. Perhaps the most obvious example of contemporary bureaucracies are government and Ma Bell. Do we see the roles of Uncle Sam and Ma Bell diminishing? Do we find them becoming more responsive? Are they getting smaller? Is there, within either structure, a place where the buck can come to rest? Hardly. Each gets larger, slower, less responsive, more expensive, and more pervasive. When Toffler points to the phenomenon of merger, and the organizational shifts taking place within bureaucracies, he views it as evidence of their decline. In fact, however, it is evidence of their consolidation,

---

meant everything to her, having long since (with other caseworkers) become an *idée fixe*. Unfortunately, nothing could have been harder to obtain. She refused to lie about the fact that she already had "an existing pillow," as she put it, in reasonably good shape. What she wanted, therefore, was a three-dollar requisition for the purchase of what the Cook County Department of Public Aid called "a superfluous pillow." For months I tried to satisfy her obsession, but it seemed impossible. (As my supervisor explained it, "Sally gets a second pillow and, the next thing you know, they'll *all* want one. Do you have any idea how much that'd cost?") I even tried to give her the money myself, but she wouldn't hear of it. "I don't want charity," she said. "I want the Welfare to buy me that pillow *with an emergency donation*." Now, Sally's problem was that she had the highest blood pressure on the South Side: she quaked all the time, as if attached to a battery or lawnmower. Eventually, I got her doctor to prescribe a second pillow for her health. But, before the emergency check could come through, her heart blew up—a coronary while she slept. I quit a few days later.

entrenchment, and ability to adjust without changing in any meaningful human way.

That executives are switching jobs more frequently, and that those jobs are themselves being redefined, is not, as Toffler suggests, indicative of any humanizing trend. On the contrary, it suggests that human beings, like mechanical parts, are becoming ever more interchangeable, as are their roles—first came the universal joint and, shortly thereafter, the universal vice-president (management consultants call the phenomenon "interfacing").

What seems to be happening is that both white and blue collars are being phased out and replaced by a more efficient gray neckerchief manufactured in a single size designed to fit all. Bureaucracy is thriving on the nutriment of organizational techniques, and so are its consequences.

Dismissing as "technophobes and future-haters" those who are skeptical about the inevitability of Progress, Toffler would have us embrace technical innovation with the indiscriminate affection of Shmoos. In this regard, he's a premier example of the technocrat, firmly convinced that problems generated by the technical phenomenon can be resolved by purely technical means.

This is what makes Toffler representative, and it's why I discuss him here. His failure to investigate the nature and meanings of technique as a phenomenon, preferring to report upon technical artifacts and processes, guarantees the optimistic outcome of his inquiry. Because techniques are developed in order to solve problems and extend human possibilities, any technique considered in isolation must be seen as benevolent: it is *an answer*.

But studying the trees without reference to the forest is a useless pursuit. The transformations wrought by industrialization could not have been anticipated by someone whose attention was confined to, for instance, the steam engine's impact on the drainage of mines (its first application). Similarly, the probable shape of a future created by technicization cannot be anticipated by the study of any single technical process or means. What's necessary is a broader understanding of the phenomenon as a whole. If we know what technique is, in itself, and what it does, in general, we can guess the probable shape of tomorrow.

3. William Burroughs: Reflections on the Heavy Metal Kid

One of the best metaphorical descriptions of technique is contained in the novels of William Burroughs. In an interview with the *Paris Review,* Burroughs was asked what he meant when he wrote (in *Nova Express*)[23] that there had been a breakthrough in "the gray room."

"I see that as very much like the photographic darkroom where the reality photographs are actually produced," Burroughs replied. "Implicit in *Nova Express* is a theory that what we call reality is actually a movie. It's a film, what I call a biologic film. What has happened is that the underground and also the nova police have made a breakthrough past the guards and gotten into the darkroom where the films are processed, where they're in a position to expose negatives and prevent events from occurring. They're like police anywhere. All right, you've got a bad situation here in which the nova mob is about to blow up the planet. So the Heavy Metal Kid calls in the nova police. Once you get them in there, by God, they begin acting like any police. They're always an ambivalent agency. I recall once in South America that I complained to the police that a camera had been stolen and they ended up arresting me. I hadn't registered or something. In other words, once you get them on the scene they really start nosing around. Once the law starts asking questions, there's no end to it. For nova police, read technology, if you wish." [24]

The "gray room" is the scene of the crime, the place where reality is developed, where events are born or die. There is no doubt that Burroughs means the gray room to refer to the brain (which is, after all, a gray "room" of sorts). And, according to the author, the gray room has been invaded by the nova *mob,* a constellation of superpowers (nations and individuals, Russia and Henry Luce) whose unspeakable practices threaten to make the planet uninhabitable, to "blow it up." To stop that from happening, the Heavy Metal Kid invokes the nova *police.* Blasting their way into the gray room, they descend upon reality, taking charge of all the images and events, poking their noses into everything. No one is ever wholly innocent and, as the author's anecdote is intended to suggest, everyone ends up being busted. ("Once the law starts asking questions, there's no end to it.") Ultimately, the nova police are as bad as the nova mob. Each is addicted to control and any analysis of their operational styles yields the conclusion that each is nothing more than the mirror image of the other: the cop and the crook are one.

It's interesting that the nova police are called in by the Heavy Metal Kid. As Burroughs explains, "Heavy metal is sort of the ultimate expression of addiction . . . there's something actually metallic in addiction [such that] the final stage is not so much vegetable as mineral. It's increasingly inanimate, in any case. You see, as Dr. Benway said, I've now decided that junk is not green, but blue. . . ."[25] The Heavy Metal Kid is therefore the persona of absolute addiction. And the fact that he's talking to the nova police, that it's *he* who's calling them in, is bad news for everyone.

What Burroughs seems to be saying is that powerful cabals (the nova mob) have taken control of the citizenry's collective head (the gray room) and threaten to demolish the earth; our addictive nature (the Heavy Metal Kid) has invoked technology (the nova police) in an effort to save us. But technology, which satisfies our material cravings, is as dangerous as the nova mob itself. The former renders us inanimate, in bondage to the needs it creates, while the latter would enslave us outright. (In view of this analysis, it seems fair to say that Burroughs is the alter ego of Marcuse, albeit a very stoned Marcuse.)

It seems reasonable to ask how serious Burroughs is and, more importantly, how seriously he should be taken. His own testimony answers the first part: "I mean what I say to be taken literally, to make people aware of the true criminality of our times, to wise up the marks. All of my work is directed against those who are bent, through stupidity or design, on blowing up the planet or rendering it uninhabitable." [26] How seriously Burroughs should be taken is a separate question. His perceptions are expressed in metaphors, and the malignant forces he describes are given dramatic personae (e.g., Izzy the Push, Sammy the Butcher, Green Boy, and the Subliminal Kid) which obscure their ultimate banality. Burroughs' world is our own, but it's transformed by literature; it exists at a remove from "reality," its very clarity an obstacle to our belief in it. It's likely that we'd have more confidence in Burroughs' analysis if he wrote less well, or if his style huffed with the fake objectivity of the laboratory, if his metaphors were replaced with numbers, his insights with "data." In a sense, Burroughs comes too close to be believed.

We've begun to identify truth with instrumentation, to mistrust insights that cannot be measured, quantified, and mathematically expressed. We take the berserker's pride in the disciplined alienation of the lab, the "objectivity" of the scientist. We have the intellectual machismo to think about "the unthinkable," and applaud the elegance with which prospective global butchery is articulated in terms of "megadeaths." Clotted with acronyms (conceptual disguises of absolute neutrality) and verbs of strategic unfamiliarity, the literature of science and politics extends our human possibilities by making the grotesque appear innocuous.

Is there any meaningful difference between the maniacal experiments of Dr. Benway and the Lobotomy Kid (as described in *Naked Lunch*) and the federal "health" project recently exposed in the American South? (I refer to the project in which government physicians identified numbers of mostly illiterate blacks afflicated with syphilis. Under the pretense of administering treatment, the physicians recorded their patients' disintegration over a number of decades, administering placebos and carefully noting how their brains turned to pus, how blindness set in, and muscle control vanished—all in the interests of Science.)

I'm reminded of a passage in *Naked Lunch*.[27]

> "Come in and take a close look," says Benway. "You won't embarrass anybody."
>
> I walk over and stand in front of a man who is sitting on his bed. I look at the man's eyes. Nobody, nothing looks back.
>
> "IND's," says Benway, "Irreversible Neural Damage. Over-liberated, you might say . . . a drag on the industry."
>
> I pass a hand in front of the man's eyes.
>
> "Yes," says Benway, "they still have reflexes. Watch this." Benway takes a chocolate bar from his pocket, removes the wrapper and holds it in front of the man's nose. The man sniffs. His jaws begin to work. He makes snatching motions with his hands. Saliva drips from his mouth and hangs off his chin in long streams. His stomach rumbles. His whole body writhes in peristalsis. Benway steps back and holds up the chocolate. The man drops to his knees, throws back his head and barks. . . .
>
> "Jesus! These ID's got no class to them."
>
> Benway calls over the attendant who is sitting at one end of the ward reading a book of J. M. Barrie's plays.
>
> "Get these fucking ID's outa here. It's a bring down already. Bad for the tourist business."
>
> "What should I do with them?"
>
> "How in the fuck should I know? I'm a scientist. A *pure scientist*. Just get them outa here. I don't hafta look at them is all. They constitute an albatross."
>
> "But what? Where?"
>
> "Proper channels. Buzz the District Coordinator or whatever he calls himself . . . new title every week. Doubt if he exists."
>
> Doctor Benway pauses at the door and looks back at the IND's. "Our failures," he says. "Well, it's all in the day's work."

If we fail to take our best writers as seriously as they deserve, we proceed at greater risk than is necessary. Authors such as Burroughs are simultaneously our finest reporters and our clearest oracles—their metaphors reveal the nature of the news with greater accuracy than any processed "objectivity" can do. If we disdain their reports as "mere fiction," we demonstrate the truth of what every carny hustler knows from a priori: the real mark doesn't want to be wised up. It cramps his style, imposes obligations he'd rather be without, and generally dismantles his entire identity. If he isn't a mark, what is he?

("Don't tell us! Don't tell us what's going down . . ."
"I don't wanna hear about that Coca-Cola thing! Enough, already! . . ."
"For God's sake, not the Cancer Deal!"
"Not the Green Deal—don't show us that!"
"Not the Orgasm Death—haven't you got any respect?"
"Not the Watergate, not the Wheat Deal, *not the ovens* . . ."
"For chrissake—give us some time to adjust!")
Adjust to what?

4. The Technical Chreod: Rationalizing the Ovaries

The technical phenomenon occupies about the same place in the collective consciousness that "the environment" did fifty years ago: we take it for granted because it's literally everywhere. Because it is so pervasive, a virtual plenum, it's practically invisible. The ecology movement overcame the invisibility of its subject because, in the 1960s, it became obvious that the natural environment was on the brink of an unnatural, catastrophic transformation. And so it is with the technical ecology: its dynamism is, and will be, overlooked until our attention is turned to it by the prospect of disaster. Admittedly, there is already some substantial (and justified) concern about particular techniques—offshore drilling, supersonic flight, insecticides, psychosurgery, behavior mod, and so forth. My concern here, however, is not with individual examples, but with the totality of technique.

A subject as broad as this might easily result in a study of encyclopedic dimensions. Jacques Ellul's *The Technological Society* and Siegfried Giedion's *Mechanization Takes Command* are massive, and profound, attempts to outline the subject's parameters.[28] My own effort is necessarily narrower, and even somewhat arbitrary. In this and the next two chapters I intend to consider the technical phenomenon only in so far as it is a determinant of those extraordinary conditions that give our discontents a millenarian shape.

Earlier, I made a beginning, defining *technique* (after Ellul) as "the most rationally efficient means of accomplishing an end." The *technical phenomenon* was described as the ensemble of developing contemporary techniques interacting with one another as an ecology, a kinetic closed system, an entity greater than the sum of its parts.

From these definitions it should be obvious that the technical phenomenon moves increasingly closer to the center of our lives as the twentieth century proceeds. Nothing is so private, or so remote, or even so trivial that technique is not applied to it. Lovemaking is an obvious example. If anything should defy rationalization by the technical phenomenon, balling would seem to be it. It's a virtually instinctual activity so personal that its public expression has traditionally been taboo. Moreover, how does one improve upon it? As usual, technique has an answer: in terms of efficiency, *more is better*. Specifically, the transition from the lambskin prophylactic to the Syntex pill is clearly a technical advance that's had profound effects upon the frequency, promiscuity, and circumstances of our lovemaking and relationships (trivializing both, perhaps). In addition, studies by scientists such as Masters and Johnson, and books by empiricists such as the Happy Hooker and "J," rationalize our approach to sex as scientifically as the Pill "rationalizes" women's hormonal systems, imposing a methodology of sensual efficiency upon our encounters. A little background music here, a strategic obscenity there, a dab of musk upon the ice cubes, a hit of grass, an exclamatory confession that one has neglected to don one's panties and then, after appropriate tactical foreplay and clitoral twanging —WHAMMO! Another victory for technique.

Any consideration of the technical phenomenon rapidly leads to the conclusion that it's a *chreod*. That is, a system whose components interact with each other in such a way that the system changes as time passes; and the interactions are of such a nature that the pathway of change is "buffered" from external influence by its internal rules or organization; if an outside force shoves the system in a direction contrary to its nature or rules, the system will *automatically* redirect itself along its natural path.[29] A chreod, in other words, is a system engaged in a process of self-transformation, which process is virtually impervious to permanent outside influences. A burning sun is one example. The decay of radioactive materials is another.

And a third example of such a system is the technical phenomenon itself. Its components are all the individual, developing techniques. They interact with each other in such a way that a technical advance in, for instance, the manufacture of transistors leads to a revolution in communications; this in turn generates innovations in, let us say, the teaching of foreign languages, which results in—and so on. The system changes in time, remaining closed, but kinetic and developmental. The "internal rules" or organization of the technical chreod proceed from the definition of technique: the natural path of the system as a whole is toward *the most efficient rationalization of all activity in every area of endeavor*. If an external force (e.g., an oil boycott) shoves the system away from this natural path toward a less efficient means (windmills as opposed to the internal combustion engine), the system will automatically redirect itself back toward the means of greatest efficiency. In this example, such a redirection would not necessarily mean a return to the internal combustion engine when the boycott ends. It might mean continuing improvement upon the windmill until it's more efficient than that engine, or the search for a technique (e.g., solar power) which hasn't yet been developed. In other words, while the chreod is sometimes forced to regress toward supposedly obsolescent techniques, its ultimate direction remains inevitably progressive. Indeed, most people are unable to distinguish between technical innovation and "progress."

The inevitability of technical innovation, or progress, proceeds from the fact that because technique is remembered, it is therefore cumulative (like mercury and DDT). (It's interesting to note that when techniques had accumulated to the point that no individual could recall them all, the printing press was invented; when print became overloaded to the extent that information could not be conveniently, or efficiently, retrieved, cybernetic data processing systems took over.) Techniques are not forgotten except in those extraordinary circumstances when whole civilizations, their languages and artifacts, are abolished by catastrophic events. Otherwise, techniques accumulate in symbiotic relationship, interacting and augmenting one another. The most rationally efficient means retains hegemony in any area of activity until it is improved or transcended (made obsolete) by a more efficient means.

There are only two limitations upon the technical chreod and they constitute the banks of the technical "canal." Those limitations are the restrictions of natural law and the availability of natural resources. The law of entropy, for instance, seems to preclude the development of a perpetual motion machine. Similarly, the depletion of existing oil reserves seems to limit the proliferation of techniques whose operations are contingent upon the availability of oil.

But man himself is unable to impose his will upon the chreod —only nature can.

True, some individuals, groups, and even nations have attempted to forgo the most efficient means to accomplish certain ends. Every neighborhood has an old man who curses the "motorcar" and cantankerously balks at central heating, preferring to use his outmoded Franklin stove. The Amish are a group which has made a conscious decision, based upon scripture, to limit their employment of sophisticated techniques. The United States and Russia are engaged in Strategic Arms Limitation Talks (SALT) whose ostensible purpose is to limit the development of some lethal technology.

It would seem, then, as if man has an important and effective voice in what techniques are developed and used. But this is an illusion. Technique is, as much as gold and diamonds, *capital*. Individuals can, through eccentricity, religious devotion, or exemplary act, forgo its use. But the effect of so doing is social isolation, as the cranky old man and the Amish realize. Increasingly, technique is the currency of social relations. In so far as we eschew it, we must withdraw from society. When whole nations attempt to limit individual techniques, as in the SALT talks, they quickly discover that they're engaged in placing limitations upon their wealth, upon the technical capital which governs the balance of power between nations. Any two, ten, or one hundred nations may reach such an agreement (always remaining wary of duplicity and unforeseen technical developments), but so long as any single capable nation refuses to sign such accords, the agreement constitutes eventual surrender to the abstaining party. Similarly, while environmentalists have delayed (or prevented) development of the American SST, Russia, England, and France have proceeded apace in its technical realization. This in itself might seem to be a small, but important, victory for the environmentalists but, in fact, it's only small. The scuttling of the SST was seen to be necessary because its workings represented a global threat: ozone depletion and a redirection of the jet stream (which the SST threatens) do not honor national boundaries, whatever the wisdom of American conservationists. The technical phenomenon will, therefore, proceed unchecked so long as any individual or nation seeks an advantage over another. That is, the phenomenon is as old and enduring as competition.

5. From "I Ching" to "The Whole Earth Catalog"

Another group which many believe sought to limit technique, to forgo it in their private lives, were the cultural radicals of the 1960s. Many abandoned the cities for rural enclaves, or chose to wander in Europe and Latin America, in each case leaving contemporary technology as far behind as possible. But their protestations about the "plasticity" of the society, its commercialization and materialism, were not rejections of technique per se. On the contrary. The counterculture, or large segments of it, was largely in tune with the technical chreod, perhaps even anticipating its directions.

A generation is known at least partly by the books which it embraces: the "Lost Generation" of the 1920s and 1930s finds itself fully evoked in the work of Fitzgerald and Hemingway, particularly in *The Great Gatsby* and *The Sun Also Rises*. If we consider the generation of the Sixties in those same terms, we encounter several books which that generation embraced more or less in direct accord with its own developing consciousness. Those books are the *I Ching, The Lord of the Rings,* and *The Whole Earth Catalog*. In that order.*

The progression from an opus of oracular divination to a trilogy of unremitting fantasy to a final preoccupation with a catalogue of available technical means is surprising in that it precisely recapitulates man's developing intellectual history. It's as if a generation felt it necessary to start all over again and, in the course of a decade, worked its way from prehistory to the beginning of the Industrial Age. (Science follows on the heels of technique: that is, the lyre is antecedent to the formulae of Pythagoras.)

By 1970, the cultural radicals of the Sixties had moved from magic to technique, and embraced the latter with the enthusiasm of the postwar Japanese, the only difference being

---

* Obviously, not everybody was on the same trip, but this progression seems to have held true for most of the people I've known or encountered.

that they ignored prevalent techniques and concentrated upon those which were undeveloped or "obsolete." Immersed in the verities of the dome, the zome, the loom, the potter's wheel and Snap-On Tools, their "radicalism" disintegrated when, after a decade's striving, they effectively returned to the brink of the present. Culturally, they'd come full circle: from yarrow stalks to the chain saw.

Earlier, I said that the young may have "anticipated" the technical chreod's direction. In their return to more primitive artifacts and techniques—the log cabin, yurt, and windmill —the young acted out their pessimism about the continuing viability of "progress," and sought to regain a measure of independence through what amounted to a nostalgic renaissance of technical obsolescence. It seemed to many that rural isolation and nomadic wandering were more prudent and rewarding than urban indulgence. The handicraft revival begun during the 1960s was a manifestation of that pessimism. It would be better, the young seemed to say, to make one's own clothes and pots and houses than to rely upon what seemed to be a doomed system. Indeed, it's interesting that the word most often used to describe the handmade houses of the young was "shelter" rather than "home." It was an awkward (and therefore thoughtful) choice of words for kids who were, for the most part, apostate exiles from suburbia. Shelter is a word that bristles with defensiveness. Besides conveying a sentimental whiff of the old frontier, its virtues and values, shelter denotes a shield or barrier against attack and danger. A "home" is a place in which one lives; a "pad" a place from which one springs (sexually, perhaps); but a shelter is a place in which one *endures*. We might dismiss this emphasis upon shelter, endurance, and the simple things as a manifestation of "peasant envy," but that would be a mistake.

Survival was one of the most unrelenting themes of the counterculture (as we'd expect to be the case in a millenarian subculture). Somehow, in the midst of all the affluence that the most powerful nation in the planet's history could muster, the young headed for the woods, the yurt, and the butter churn. That was not a rejection of materialism, as many believed—or not only that. It was evidence that some had glimpsed a fire in the future.

The emergence of the ecology movement was coincident with the renaissance of handicrafts and the young's "ruralization." It articulated the pessimism which informed the other phenomena, and those who were involved in one movement tended to be interested in the other. Ostensibly, ecology is concerned with the natural environment; in practice and as a movement, however, its business is to impose limitations upon the application of techniques. While the ecologists sometimes propose new ways (or old ways) of getting things done, their social role is primarily one of restraint. But restraining technique is practically an impossibility, and the ecology movement is a good example of that fact. Briefly, the movement is a lost cause. It is so because it's quite unable to confront its real adversary—technique as a chreod or complex. In directing its critical attentions to specific techniques, the movement overlooks the technical phenomenon as a whole. The result is, at best, a series of pyrrhic victories on highly discrete issues, which victories only serve to divert attention from the overpowering, ubiquitous *fact of technique* and to create the illusion that something meaningful is being done, that people are still in control. In practice, the ecology movement abets the ascendancy of technique by identifying its least rational manifestations, thereby paving the way for further technicization. Admittedly, the cadres of the movement have a distinctly populist flavor; as a group they tend to be liberal young humanists whose aesthetic concerns for The Environment are amplified by a large dose of *angst*. But a sentimental regard for the whale and an appreciation of nature at its wildest are not the arguments which the movement takes into court. On the contrary, its strategy is almost wholly shaped by the arguments of scientists and technicians who take a position of rational dissent vis-à-vis the application of individual techniques. Actually, this isn't so much a strategy as it is an abdication. The ecologists, in choosing the courts for their arena of struggle, confront technique on its own grounds: efficiency, safety, and legality become the criteria of the movement, just as they are the criteria by which technique measures itself (legality and safety are merely facets of efficiency). What's been surrendered is the irrational animus of the movement, its entire *raison d'être:* conditioned to the sanctity of Progress, Due Process, efficiency, and reason, ecologists are forced to jettison from their legal briefs such vague nouns as freedom, dignity, beauty, and tranquillity. These are conditions which defy quantification—we cannot measure the weight of dignity, the breadth of freedom, the wave lengths of beauty, or the dimensions of tranquillity. The closest we can come (in court) is to discuss property rights, health factors, industrial density, and decibel levels. But these are only tangentially related to the actual concerns of those active in the movement. And the result is that even individual techniques (let alone the phenomenon as a whole) are immune to criticisms based upon values which, because they defy measurement, are legally invisible. What cannot be measured can neither be increased nor diminished: arguments pertaining to such qualities (assuming they exist at all) are necessarily irrelevant to reasoned judgments. Indeed, if the ecology movement recognized that its adversary is the technical phenomenon as a whole rather than, for instance, flip-top cans, it would immediately realize the folly of its legal strategy.

The judiciary is as much a technical means as is, for instance, fractional distillation (which, in fact, the judicial process resembles quite closely). It's not so rational and not so efficient as distillation, but it's the most rationally efficient means *currently available* in its particular area of activity. And, while the judiciary is dedicated to Justice, its dedication extends only to the degree to which that concept can be rationally defined, or quantified—an eye for an eye, a tooth for a tooth. Even that arithmetical injunction, however, is subordinated by the courts to Due Process and The Law, systems which our technical ingenuousness has allowed to become values. If a court must choose between what is just and what is legal (a circumstance that is by no means unusual), it must inevitably opt for the latter or have its decision overturned on appeal. And, even as engineering depends upon the ironically misnomered "prior art" to determine its future directions, the courts depend upon "precedent" to determine theirs. Because it defies rational analysis, Justice is necessarily one of the first things to be sacrificed in the deliberations of the courts—indeed, judges' instructions to their juries often make this quite explicit. Clearly, if Justice were a central value of the courts, the judiciary would have outlawed "plea bargaining" long ago, and "precedent" would be merely advisory rather than determinant.

My purpose here, however, is not to criticize the courts for being unjust or the ecology movement for being a patsy. My intention is simply to show that even the most obvious and popular attempts at limiting technique tend to be defeated by the technical phenomenon as a whole. The ecology movement, in choosing a strategy which accuses individual techniques of technical crimes before what amount to Technical Courts, is converted (unwittingly) into the service of the phenomenon it opposes. The SALT talks stagnate, or proceed toward cosmetic concord with no hope of meaningful agreement, because parties to the disagreement cannot predict future innovation nor the behavior of nations so "underdeveloped" that an Armageddon capability represents a social advance—that is, Russia and the United States are literally at the mercy of their own genius and others' ambitions, both of which are functions of technical progress. Where technical refusal *is* effected, as with the Amish and some freaks, the result is isolation, suspicion, and ridicule. And, where technical withdrawal *does* occur, as with the youngs' retreat to handicrafts and the farm, the process is more an expression of millenarian anxiety and discontent than it is a sign of returning to control. The young are simply betting that sophisticated technology is, like the society as a whole, on the verge of collapse and that what was obsolete yesterday will be the only available means tomorrow.

III. Freedom as Epilepsy

> A minimum of unconsciousness is necessary if one wants to stay inside history. To act is one thing; to know one is acting is another. When lucidity invests the action, insinuates itself into it, action is undone and, with it, prejudice, whose function consists, precisely, in subordinating, in enslaving consciousness to action.
>
> E. M. Cioran [30]

1. The Black Hole of Technique: The Inventor as Midwife

As a phenomenon, technique is a disaster . . . irresistible and infinitely impoverishing. As a closed, kinetic system, or chreod, technique obeys its own internal laws, impervious to external influences. What makes the phenomenon irresistible is its *tendency toward completion,* the heartbeat of its *logic.*

Because techniques are never lost, only superseded, their accumulation is ineluctable. And since each technique represents "a better way" of doing something, any activity which enters the technical domain never leaves it. Indeed, it's as if the activity had entered a kind of Black Hole, a nonspace from which there is no escape. Returning to a less efficient means is, on a social level at least, unthinkable. Technique cannot retreat any more than a burning fuse can return along the path of its incineration. Its only possibilities are the extension of its domain and, theoretically, stasis. But stasis is impossible in any economy predicated upon a continuum of rising expectations: there will always be a market for a better mousetrap, and its inventor will always be rewarded. Thus, the technical phenomenon necessarily *progresses,* moving forward through the improvement of individual techniques, and in every other direction as those techniques are given new applications or adapted to activities which formerly seemed immune to mechanization and rationalization. It tends toward completeness: absolute efficiency and ubiquity.

There is one qualification that might be added to the above, however. While whole societies cannot willingly return to a less efficient means of doing anything, individuals sometimes do. But whenever they do so intentionally, it's because they have deliberately removed themselves from a competitive milieu. And, in so far as their society is organized in terms of competition, their willful act must isolate them (providing, of course, that the inefficient activity is an important part of their lives).

Tending toward completion, therefore, the technical phenomenon resists outside influence by extending its domain and eliminating all such influence. In this way, the tendency toward completion is equivalent to a tendency toward autonomy: increasingly, the primary influence upon the technical phenomenon is the phenomenon itself. It's very nearly the only game in town.

Moving toward hegemony and self-control, the chreod accelerates, much as a river gathers speed when the obstacles in its path have been removed. The changes engendered in the course of the chreod are, by virtue of their rational common source, synergistic: the result is that each change tends to replicate exponentially, and the impression created is one of mind-stunning acceleration—everything seems to move faster. Nothing remains the same. Technique consolidates itself, remaking the world in its own image of absolute efficiency.

Some may insist that the major influence upon technique is not technique itself, but man. It is he who creates the means, he who uses them and he who defines their purposes. Clearly, then, the technical phenomenon is within his control.

Whatever its apparent common sense, however, that argument is multiply false.

First, the technical phenomenon is not "simply" the aggregate of existing techniques. It is a *gestalt,* an entity greater that the sum of its parts. As a phenomenon it has effects which do not derive from any single component, but from the entirety of its components. And, while men "create" individual techniques, they do not "create" the phenomenon —its existence emerges as a side effect of the techniques themselves. It is an inevitable effect, but the technical innovator is no more responsible for it than the inventor of the wheel is responsible for traffic accidents.

When something is inevitable, there is no responsibility and no creativity. The possibility of any technical innovation is inherent in the aggregate of the techniques which precede it. The inventor serves as midwife to a possibility which he *delivers* but did not "create." Because technique is rational in nature, it follows a logical development; one step leads to another with compelling force. To say that an inventor is a creator in the same sense that a poet is is simply false. While all poetic possibilities are in some sense inherent in the language and in the alphabet, their emergence as poetry is not determined by any rational process, nor is the creation of any poem inevitable (which is merely to say that poems aren't highways). On the contrary, the value and excellence of poetry are largely functions of its irrational nature and its most mysterious qualities. (E.g., the speech of Polonius to his son in *Hamlet* is a poetic tour de force *in spite* of its reasonableness and moderation; the genius of Shakespeare is demonstrated by his ability to transform the message of a shmuck such as Polonius with verbal magic, to overcome the crippling good sense of his character.) There's nothing "necessary" about poetry or any other art, and we can easily imagine a world in which art has no place—however impoverished such a world might be. One poem, sculpture, or painting does not *lead* to another: it's finished; it goes nowhere; it is. There's simply no "progress" in art, only in technique. And, while there are obvious differences between ages and artists, the most recent poem or painting is not necessarily the best. When we talk about the beauty of an artistic work, we talk in terms of its "magic" rather than its "engineering." (Critics, of course, discuss "structure," "economy," and "advances" in the arts, but their work is more quixotic than artistic. Attempting to impose rational analysis upon the hocus-pocus of creation, they're enmeshed in a contradiction that cannot be resolved.)

So people do not create technique, they deliver it. Not only that, but the deliveries take place almost automatically in any society which does not intentionally penalize the innovator.* That is, innovation is independent of the innovator in so far as it can be said that if A had not invented X, B would have. The truth of a statement like that, involving "if" and "would," is impossible to prove, but one need only observe how frequently it happens that independent researchers isolated from one another frequently come upon the same discovery at about the same time, often publishing their findings in journals that appear within a few days of each other. The certainty of technical innovation is no longer at the whim of genius: one can *depend* upon it. Suggestion boxes for workers, patent protection for inventors, tax breaks for corporation-sponsored research, tax supports funding university experiments, and market advantages which tend to accrue to the most efficient producer—all these, and hundreds of other incentives, guarantee that the technical phenomenon will never run out of fuel. The fact that man "creates" technique in some distorted sense of the verb falsely implies a control which man does not have.

2. You Are What You Drive: "Brewster McCloud" and Aztec Sacrifice

There is another characteristic of invention which demonstrates the absence of human control. Specifically, an invention is transformed by common use; it becomes something

---

* Which is, upon reflection, a good idea: define inventors as "technopaths" and impose fines upon them for each discovery they make. "Repeaters" should be locked up.

other than what the inventor intended or predicted as soon as it makes the journey from the laboratory to the outside world. Because it's impossible to assess all the implications and applications that any innovation or invention will have, it's meaningless to speak of human control where technical progress is concerned. Almost any technique, from surgical transplant operations to the transmission of holographic images, will serve to demonstrate that fact, but the automobile probably offers the most obvious and grotesque evidence.

When first invented, the car was an efficient means of private transportation, a means which promised to integrate the country by bringing distant points relatively closer together. But, in the transition from laboratory singularity to market hegemony, the automobile underwent a profound change. In the space of fifty years, it took virtual command of the society, affecting everything and everyone within it. In doing so, it defeated the end for which it had been devised, and degenerated from a luxury to a necessity. Designed to liberate us from the tyranny of distance, to bring people together and to increase the efficiency with which goods and services are delivered, it ended by imprisoning its beneficiaries, pushing people apart, scattering families and imposing new geographical limitations upon the classes: to be poor in the automotive age is to be immobile in a way that the poor have never been before—in shrinking distance, the car pushed everything farther apart, effectively stranding those who could not own one.

The popular availability of the car destroyed the cities by opening the way for suburban development and the exodus of the affluent to the countryside. As the middle classes absconded to the sticks in their traveling machines, urban areas increasingly became reservations for the very rich (who could afford to pay for their "security") and for the very poor (who couldn't afford to leave). Concentrating the nation's most exotic imbalances in wealth and education in precisely those places where the media themselves are concentrated, the automobile was instrumental in provoking both the conditions for urban uprisings (in the 1960s) and a distorted image of the country as a whole.

Mass transit systems which were essential to the young, the old, the handicapped, and the poor were ruined or their development deferred in recognition of the car's growing importance: while the urban rich might not own a car, they could always hail one that was for hire. As for the others . . . well, they could walk, grab a bus, or risk a ride on the festering subways.

Exhaust emissions and the paving of vast rural tracts (coupled with a new demand for cheap single-family dwellings outside the cities) deranged the ecology and depleted environmental quality. America sprawled and gasped but, by the time anyone asked whether it was worth it, it was too late: there was no turning back. The future had been invented.

Diminishing the relevance of distance, the automobile demolished the nuclear center of every community it touched. New towns, cities, and urbs evolved in ways and places that lacked all reference to tradition. The organic sense of being-in-a-community was erased as the automobile sundered the society into geographical compartments, explicit areas devoted to single activities: work, play, buying, eating, medicine, and even burial. The shopping center, recreation center, medical center, sports complex, and mass cemetery neatly subdivided people's lives into segments—rational, functional, and isolated. Displaying all the sensibility of rain-forest primitives, we encouraged the old to remove themselves to the desert, where, with shuffleboard, air conditioning, and new boomtowns based upon the certainty of high residential turnover, they went and died. The automobile made it possible.

Just as the serf was forced from his land by the demand for increased sheep pasturage, the twentieth-century farmer was driven from his small holdings by the gasoline-fired internal combustion engine—the tractor-car with a hoe, baler, or thresher attached. Prior to the gas engine, agriculture's dependence upon manual labor had defied rationalization; after the automobile's advent and its technical spin-offs, farming became "agribusiness" with the result that hillbillies and hayseeds everywhere repeated the migration to the cities begun five centuries before by their medieval counterparts.

There isn't anything that the automobile hasn't changed. Cultural activities and patterns relating to sex and to the family, to entertainment, sports, business, and worship have been radically revised or wholly devised by the car's invention. Drive-in restaurants, theaters, churches, banks, whorehouses, and mortuaries have promised to reshape the way we eat, play, pray, do business, get laid, and get buried. Architecture is increasingly at the service of the automobile.

The car has taken command, penetrating not only our daily existence, but our histories and fantasies as well. For those born after 1935, any discussion of adolescence is likely to return to the 1951 Chevy, Merc, Studebaker, and Ford; to cruising for girls, dragging, crossing the county line for beers, and tuning in to AM Top-Forty music while "parking" with a member of the opposite sex. Where we once had "roots," we now have wheels.

The car's central place in our fantasies is realized on quiz shows where the "contestants" undergo orgasmic shudders in anticipation of owning a new car. In films such as *Bullit, Duel,* and *Brewster McCloud* the automobile is given an actual persona and rightly assumes its place as the real "star" of the century. As a symbol, the car is more powerful than the cross or the ankh: increasingly, our identities are expressed in terms of the vehicles we own. We are what we drive. Whether we hang a skull from the rearview mirror or put bumper stickers on the trunk, the automobile expresses our loves, hates, religious and political beliefs ("Honk twice if you love Jesus!").

In small matters such as courtship and big ones such as foreign policy, our dependency upon the car is nearly total. Tactical warfare was transformed by it, and so was recreation. Our relationship to other countries is ever more a function of their relationship to our oil needs, which are, in turn, closely related to our reliance upon the car. In the present, one of the worst punishments which the society can impose upon a citizen is to suspend his driving privileges: to do so amounts to social amputation.

Is any of this within our control? Was it ever and, if so, in what sense of the word "control"? The Aztecs sacrificed hundreds every year to a deity that supposedly conferred power. We sacrifice fifty thousand people a year, and mangle another million, in behalf of a device which lays waste to the cities, ruins the air, denatures our experience, scatters families, and generally sees to it that Yeats is correct when he says that things fly apart. If insanity has its "circles," like Dante's Inferno, who is closer to the center that will not hold: we or the Aztecs?

The automobile is what we have instead of the Black Death.

3. Alphaville versus Betaville

To say that we create technique is a misperception. To say that we use it, implying control, is an arrogant delusion—comparable, in fact, to the slave's insistence that the plantation exists for him because, without him, the plantation could not exist.

We have no choice but to deliver technique into the world. Family automobiles have engines which will take them to speeds in excess of 120 miles per hour (more than twice the national limit)—not because that speed is safe, legal, or desirable, but because it is possible (technically and economically). Since it can be done, it must be done. Similarly, military tacticians develop softball-size nuclear bombs because such development is feasible, not because those bombs are necessary or in any way desirable: on the contrary, "tactical" nuclear weapons, *because* they're manageable and limited in their effects, negate the deterrent value which is the primary justification for having a nuclear arsenal in the first place. The *in*flexibility of "nuclear response" is what makes both the

United States and Russia impervious to attack; as soon as either country develops a flexible response, its continuing existence comes into question.

There seems to be an existential necessity inherent in every technical possibility. Just as Sir Edmund Hillary climbed Mount Everest because it was there, we climb the technical mountain because *it* is there. Almost without exception, human ends and values vanish into the shadow cast by the ascendancy of technical means. In terms of both national priorities and personal tastes, it is the means rather than the end which has social importance. We travel to the moon because it's technically possible to do so, because it demonstrates our know-how and furthers technical progress—it's irrelevant to point out that money used for that project would have been much better spent on earthbound social programs. Just as the technical means determine our national priorities, they determine our personal tastes as well. Americans actually prefer grunjy wines, tasteless beer, glutinous bread, processed "cheese food," and fishy chicken. They prefer it because advertising techniques have bombed their taste buds into oblivion, an aggression made necessary by the fact that the most efficient means of producing those (and many other) commodities inevitably cast considerations of taste and nutrition by the wayside.

We do not create, use, or define the purposes of "our" techniques. On the contrary, we are transformed, used, and directed by the possibilities of technique.

And yet, however abundant the evidence for that assertion, the idea is still very difficult to accept. It seems to imply that the technical phenomenon is informed with a quasi-sentient intentionality—that it is, in some sense, animate and purposive—when obviously technique has no existence independent of man and is, in fact, a dead thing. Moreover, it's extremely difficult to condemn any technique in particular since all techniques (from anesthesia to woodworking) are, by definition, useful to man.

These are powerful gut objections to my argument, and

their commonsense force is such that we almost inevitably conclude that technique, while it may create some problems (germ warfare, pollution, nuclear bombs, et cetera), is manageable and beneficial if only we apply wisdom to its use. But common sense is often in error.

To the argument that technique has no intentionality and so cannot recreate man, use him, or redefine his purposes, William Burroughs is at least metaphorically accurate when he compares "technology" to an alien life form. A viral parasite, perhaps, or an incubus within its human host. If this metaphor is too eccentric, we could say instead that the technical phenomenon has a "natural" animus and moves toward its ultimate objective in the same way that a river moves. It obeys laws inherent to itself and to the world around it; in doing so, it follows a path that could not be otherwise. There's nothing extraordinary or supernatural in this. The inanimate world has always "acted" upon mankind in definite, if insensible, ways. Earthquakes, ocean currents, tides, and typhoons remain outside our control. The only difference between these natural forces and the technical phenomenon is that man is "responsible" for the latter. But once that phenomenon is set into motion, it's no more within his control than is the orbit of Uranus.

To the objection that every technique is useful, there can be no real response, as I've indicated earlier. The traditional argument advanced by most pessimists is wholly inadequate. It says that man's use of technique is an act of force which, in seeking to master or coerce the world, inevitably puts him in disharmony with it. To "prove" the point such pessimists invariably cite the most emotionally provocative (and atypical) examples of technique. Thus, Philip Slater writes: "It is absurd, therefore, to talk of using technology for good or evil, just as it is absurd to talk of using a bomb constructively. The impulse that goes into designing, building, and dropping a bomb is inherently destructive, and the technological impulse by the same token is inherently anti-organic and life hating." [81]

Nonsense. More often than not, the "impulse" which goes into the creation of techniques is, if not life-neutral, life-loving. Only the Brainiacs of *Superman* comics deliberately devise destructive techniques for "life-hating" purposes. The Salk vaccine, anesthesia, and the violin are all examples of "technology" and each owes its creation to an affirmation of life and to the best impulses in man. Even the Bomb was devised by men who believed it constituted the most efficient means to end the slaughter in Europe and Asia with a minimal loss of life—we remember Einstein, Oppenheimer, and Heisenberg as humanists, not as destructive maniacs.

The traditional argument against technique, as articulated by Slater, displays a fantastic pantheism whose origins go back to notions of original sin and the Garden of Eden. The argument seems to be that technique is responsible for the destruction of Paradise: a world in which man and nature coexisted in perfect harmony. And yet, a world without technique, even if possible, would not be paradise. It would, on the contrary, be a druidical milieu raped by disease, ignorance, discomfort, and monotonous, unproductive labor. In a world devoid of techniques we would sit around waiting for lightning to strike a tree and warm our children.

The answer which the pantheists propose is to strike a balance between the technical and druidical universes. But this returns us to the second objection mentioned above: it is difficult to condemn any technique because it is, by definition, useful. And this fact is what makes the technical phenomenon unstoppable: each part of it is, in some sense of the word, *good*. Indeed, its goodness is its *raison d'être:* it constitutes "a better way." The result is that interference with any *part* of the phenomenon is unjustifiable. The ill effects generated by the phenomenon as a whole are gradual and subtle: the loss of freedom, dignity, meaning, creativity, and tranquillity. Technical side effects such as smog are examples of inefficiency and are, therefore, contrary to the very nature of technique: technical progress will overcome them. The future which technique proposes is not, therefore, the one displayed in Godard's *Alphaville:* a clanking, choking rattletrap of a planet. It is, instead, a streamlined world as antiseptic and painless as it is anaerobic—a cosmic Intensive Care Ward. Betaville, rather than Alphaville.

4. The "Standard of Living" versus the "Quality of Life"

A balance between technique and nature is impossible: they contradict each other. McLuhan is partly correct when he compares the technical "extensions of man" to the nervous system.[32] But the comparison would be more precise if those "extensions" were described in terms of the *autonomic nervous system,* over which we've little or no control.

At the center of the relationship between man and the technical phenomenon is a void, an emptiness where we'd expect to find control. But there can be no control without choice and, where technique is concerned, we have no choice but to use it. As the most rationally efficacious means toward any end, technique negates choice in much the same way that a logical syllogism inevitably leads to a single conclusion: the rationally correct one.

Confronted with several options we may *decide* upon a particular one but, in so far as that decision is made rationally, there is no choice involved, only a process of discovery, of mechanical determination. A computer could make the same decision—in fact, given the same information, a computer *would* make the same decision. It seems valuable to distinguish between the "freedom" of a machine *to decide* and the freedom of a human being *to choose.* Behaviorists may prefer to blur that distinction, or to deny it. But it must be obvious that a machine is "free" only within the limitations of its program, whereas a person is "free" in a more absolute sense— he can contravene his "program" by acting irrationally, choosing to disregard his best or most selfish interests, and thereby overturning the appropriately termed "dictates of reason."

It seems clear, therefore, that as the world becomes increasingly technicized the number of choices available to us become fewer (even as our decisions are made to multiply). As technique penetrates all areas of human (and inhuman) activity, we're more and more often compelled to decide in its favor.

And, in so far as our choices are limited, so is our freedom. It's useless to speak of one without invoking the other. When an individual has no choice in a matter he's neither free nor in control of himself. It doesn't matter that, within the context of his situation, he's called upon to decide between alternative courses: a judge or jury must also make decisions, but they're not *free* within their situation—they do not *choose* innocence or guilt, but discover or decide it. Their only responsibility is legal and intellectual: to make a correct determination according to the "dictates" of the law.

Freedom and control, choice and responsibility are, if not synonymous, at least concomitant. If any one element is missing, so are the others. A man with a gun at his head has no choice but to follow the dictates of the gunman; he's not free and, therefore, has no responsibility for his acts. Even the law recognizes the distinction between a hostage and an accomplice.

Technique is such a gun. And what it shoots is money, the ultimate technical denominator, the final measure of efficiency.

There's nothing democratic about reason or its products. Just as logic dictates solutions, technique dictates the means. Through its expansiveness, technique rationalizes the world with the result that our choices and actions become increasingly automatic. Driving toward hegemony in everything, technique rationalizes not only each activity, but *each part* of each activity, fragmenting and segmenting all areas of endeavor. In doing so, it limits the individual to increasingly narrow, or specialized, roles. The result is impotence and, as a secondary consequence, a failing sense of responsibility.* As a cog in

---

* As we'll see, this secondary consequence is of profound importance in that it's strategic to the radical nature of decadence.

the means, the individual's responsibility is limited by, and to, his particular task: thus, the auto worker is not responsible for (proud of, or particularly interested in) the car "he" produces; in the same way a mass murderer might insist that he is merely an expediter of human traffic.

Controlling the means with which an end is accomplished or a thing is produced, technique increasingly determines both what's accomplished and what's produced; we go where it takes us, and use what it provides. Indeed, its very reasonableness limits our choices in its favor; and, in so far as it does so, it also limits both our responsibility and our freedom. Technique is authority in motion, and the fact that we embrace it willingly, clearly, and perhaps inevitably does not make it any less totalitarian.

There may seem to be a contradiction in all of this. That is, as technique removes obstacles, it necessarily increases our possibilities. It is through technique that we can count to a thousand, cross oceans, make music, and eavesdrop electronically. And the fact that technique increases our possibilities—multiplying the number of things we can do—seems to imply that it must also increase our freedom.

The contradiction, however, is more apparent than real. For every concert hall there is a jail, for every violin there is a gun: technique is used as often to coerce us, and to limit our activities, as it is to free us. After a while, the coercion becomes a part of our second nature: we wait for the stoplight to turn green even when there are no cars in sight; in school we learn to think and not think at the sound of a bell; threatened by "City Hall," we acquiesce in the knowledge that it's a seamless entity which individual needs cannot penetrate. Silence, once the most natural condition in the world, constitutes a disturbance today; white noise becomes necessary for sleep, and sleep itself is measured out through the uncompromising sanity of the alarm clock.

Moreover, technique increases our possibilities only in so far as we decide to *use* it and, when we do, we act not freely, but rationally, surrendering our autonomy to the method or machine that's used. (As I intend to show, reason and freedom are mutually exclusive.) The relationship between freedom and possibility seems indirect at best. The twentieth-century factory worker is certainly no "freer" than the Iroquois Indian was a thousand years ago, even though the former has vastly more possibilities available to him. We've simply moved from being at the mercy of nature to being at the mercy of the machine and the system which it serves.

It's sometimes argued that technique frees us by diminishing our labors and increasing our leisure time. But there is little evidence that any such thing actually happens. All technique does is to make our work more "productive," but this in itself doesn't entail any increase in leisure. A man with a tractor can do the work of ten, but the tractor's invention did not free 90 percent of the nation's farmers. What it did was to make many agricultural workers redundant, forcing them to find other work or starve. They were not so much freed as abandoned. (Another argument in favor of technique is that it improves the "quality of life" by raising the "standard of living." This is certainly valid up to the point that visceral needs are satisfied but, beyond that point, it seems that quantitative increases in the standard of living entail sacrifices that diminish the quality of life. Most middle-class Americans implicitly recognize that fact when, during their allotted vacations, they "go native," spending their leisure time in the same way that Polynesians formerly spent their *entire* lives—hunting, fishing, swimming, and goofing.) *

The relationship between technique and leisure is ephemeral in any society that has moved beyond the hunting and gathering stage. Technique either trivializes labor or dehumanizes it. When the worker (machinist, housewife, or farmer) is not replaced by a more efficient means, his task is transformed in such a way that Man-the-Maker becomes Man-the-Inspector (or Man-the-Made)—an organism whose only task is mechanical, the turning of a screw, checking of a dial, or pushing of a button. This is not labor saving, but labor negat-

---

* At least, I like to think that's how they spent their lives.

ing. The automatic dishwasher "liberates" the housewife from a tiresome chore, but it doesn't make her "free": it only gives her less to do.

5. Charles Whitman, Lordstown, and the Disease of Reason

Freedom is an objective condition.
Either you have it or you don't. The appearance of freedom, such as that generated by technique's cascade of proliferating decisions, is a mere chimera: believing that we're free does not make us so. Rousseau understood:

> Let the child believe that he is always in control, though it is always you who really controls. There is no subjugation so perfect as that which keeps the appearance of freedom, for in that way one captures volition itself. The poor baby, knowing nothing, able to do nothing, having learned nothing, is he not at your mercy? Can you not arrange everything in the world which surrounds him? Can you not influence him as you wish? His work, his play, his pleasures, his pains, are not all these in your hands and without his knowing? Doubtless he ought to do only what he wants; but he ought to want to do only what you want him to do; he ought not to take a step which you have not foreseen; he ought not to open his mouth without your knowing what he will say.[33]

In so far as our actions are determined by a program independent of our will, we aren't free—whether our acquiescence to that program is conscious or not. The manipulated child, the junky, and the fanatic who submits to a cause that is "larger than himself," allowing *its* directions to determine his own, are equally enslaved, however good or bad the parent, addiction, or cause may be.

It might seem perverse to suggest that a person may be an accomplice to his own enslavement, but the fact is that behavior of this kind is the norm rather than the exception. It could hardly be otherwise.

When a person decides to act in the "most reasonable way," he submits his fate to the determinations of a process whose laws are wholly outside his own control. He has, in effect, "thrown up his hands," however "reasonable" it was for him to do so. Whatever "freedom" is, clearly it must entail *choice;* and choice, of course, entails some process of *deliberation.* Once we accept these entailments, however, we're led to an unhappy conclusion: rational deliberations preclude the possibility of free action. They do so because the nature of rational deliberation is *discovery* rather than choice. Confronted with a set of alternatives, we consider each element in relation to every other. Weighing the probable outcomes of the various alternatives, considering them in view of our priorities and goals, we arrive at the one course of action which is, so far as we can determine, the most reasonable one for us to undertake. We've discovered the best way of accomplishing our ends. That is to say, Reason has revealed what amounts to fate.

There is in this process an illusion of choice. But, in fact, the only choice involved has been made before the process of deliberation was begun: that is, if our reasoning attempt is sincere, we've decided *in advance* to comply with the demands of Reason. Choice is no more a part of this process than it is a part of arithmetic: confronted with an arithmetical problem, we do not choose the answer—but discover it.

This isn't meant to be a particularly exotic argument. Its truth is recognized, at least subconsciously, by most people, and its colloquial expressions are many. "Sorry I'm late. *I had no choice.* The car broke down and, unless I wanted to leave it in the middle of the road, I had to get a tow truck; that took time." Even while we excuse unwanted actions that have rationalizations that we can understand, we nevertheless have contempt for those whose actions are inevitably reasonable. The person who never takes a chance, who never gambles or defies the odds, the person who is wholly without spontaneity —is less than human, an automaton or drudge. We have contempt for those who are *too* predictable.

It's in this context that we may come to speak of "the disease of Reason," a pathology that saps our will. E. M. Cioran has written movingly about the illness:

> When the feeble are legion, they charm you, they crush you: what means is there of struggling against a continent of abulics? . . . Reason: the rust of our vitality. It is the madman in us who forces us into adventure; once he abandons us, we are lost; everything depends on him, even our vegetative life; it is he who invites us, who obliges us to breathe, and it is also he who forces our blood to venture through our veins. Once he withdraws, we are alone indeed! We cannot be *normal* and *alive* at the same time. . . . Once I become reasonable, everything intimidates me; I slide toward absence. . . . An individual, like a people, like a continent, dies out when he shrinks from both rash plans and rash acts, when, instead of taking risks and hurling himself toward being, he cowers within it, takes refuge there: a metaphysics of regressions, a retreat to the primordial! [34]

Obviously, this isn't a "rigorous" philosophical argument anent causal determinism. And it needn't be. Whether or not we decide that all action is determined, we nevertheless act as if we are free or have the potential of being free. Moreover, even if all action is determined, it's clear in a colloquial sense that some persons are more "free" than others. Most important, our belief in freedom is so strong that *we act upon it.* Even if our actions are determined, they are determined in part by our belief that they are not determined. That is, beset with the divine illusion that we are, or can be, "free," we sometimes act to affirm that freedom. And when we do, we act unreasonably, defiantly and, in a sense, against ourselves.

The disease of Reason, however, is a disease of motive. It requires a central focus, or value, without which reason is immobile. To the scientist and logician, truth is the ultimate authority, and all intellection is bent toward its discovery. Existentially, though, all acts are equally "true" or real. To *act* reasonably we require values which are, of necessity, independent of "truth" or "falsity"—values which are in some way "stipulated." Money will do. Ethics will do. In fact, anything will suffice. All that's required is our submission to the absolute authority of the value. Once that's accomplished, we act "reasonably," orderly, and predictably. (Which is to say that in so far as people have values, they aren't free.)

It seems, therefore, that there are only two circumstances under which a person acts freely: when the outcome of the act is utterly meaningless to him (when he's indifferent), and when he intentionally acts in an irrational way.

Choosing to eat either of two identical beans is an act that involves a choice, but not a decision. Because the result is irrelevant to the doing, the chooser acts freely; he picks without motive, without thinking . . . almost convulsively, almost as if in an epileptic spasm.

In the second circumstance, the individual chooses to act in an unreasonable way. He revolts and behaves in a fashion that contradicts his own values, whether those values are conditioned by society or, in some way, "freely chosen." This circumstance, because it's unreasonable by definition, is somewhat difficult to imagine. If we look for an example we're likely to be confounded by our own thought processes. The temptation is to ask, "What would *cause* someone to do such a thing?" And, once we ask that question, we lose all hope of finding an answer.

And yet, examples of this "second circumstance" abound. In Camus' *The Stranger,* a clerk whose entire life has been an accumulation of submissions to the social order is freed by his literally "senseless" act of murdering two people on a beach. He guns them down for no reason, and the very futility of the gesture is what releases him. He acts with the intentionality of an explosion, and the gesture's only "purpose" is the gesture's release. The Stranger is a being in utter revolt, and what makes him "strange" is the freedom that separates him from other men.

Examples of this second circumstance are not confined to literature, though it's only in literature that we can speak with certainty about a figure's motives or their lack. But certainly Charles Whitman's trip to the Texas tower had much in common with the Stranger's stroll along the beach. (That Whitman had a brain tumor is an irrelevant fact which only seems to explain his acts. In actuality, there's no *demonstrable* connection between his illness and his killing spree.) And so do many other "senseless" crimes, from vandalism to auto theft to murder. In fact, a few weeks spent reading police reports is sufficient to convince anyone that a substantial number of crimes, if not most, are largely committed *because* they're crimes—rather than in spite of that fact.

The irrational gesture, however, is more often banal than criminal. The baby who fights to stay awake, squalling against sleep, and the housewife or husband who absconds in the family station wagon never to be seen again, are persons whose independence is preserved or achieved through rebellion. Even more typically, the worker wakes one morning and says "No." He stays in bed, listens to music, or goes fishing. But what he does is more or less irrelevant; it's what he doesn't do—the reasonable thing—that makes his gesture meaningful.

So long as rebellions of this kind remain singular and personal, confined to Missing Persons reports and films like *Five Easy Pieces,* the social effects are minimal. But collective rebellion is very much in the contemporary works. Laborers at Ford's Lordstown plant, the *summa* of industrial efficiency, confounded both management and their own union when they repeatedly rejected company offers toward the settlement of their strike. What the bosses and union leaders couldn't understand, or reconcile, was the workers' *attitude:* their grievances proceeded from the very nature of the plant itself, and management was correct when they charged that the workers were being "unreasonable." They were. That was the whole point. Efficiency had been maximized to such an extent, and with so little regard for the employees' human needs, that employment within the factory required the workers to surrender their humanity at the gates. The plant was a purgatory of absolute sanity: what was not essential to the means of production was effectively ruled out by the plant's organization and design. All that was required (or allowed) of the workers was, in most cases, the exercise of a single muscle: one man placed a bolt, the next added a nut, a third tightened the nut, and so on down "the line."

In a sense, the workers didn't exist within the factory: all that was present was a set of particularized muscles, to which human beings were inconveniently attached, performing highly discrete tasks which precluded both the exercise of judgment and the experience of even mild satisfaction or pride in their performance. Ultimately, management and labor arrived at the only possible agreement: the workers were given raises and benefits of sufficient magnitude that absenteeism was effectively subsidized by the company. But even with this detente having been reached, sabotage continued at the plant as the workers struck back at the machines they hated.

Gerald Piel, publisher of *Scientific American,* has said:

> The new development of our technology is the replacement of human beings by automatic controls and by the computer that ultimately integrates the functions of the automatic control units at each point in the productive process. The human muscle began to be disengaged from the productive process at least a hundred years ago. Now the human mind is being disengaged.

Piel's roseate analysis sounds as if it *ought* to be correct, but the facts suggest that it isn't. For more than a hundred years human muscles have indeed been disengaged from the productive process, but the human being has not: if his replacement is total, he must find other work; if it's less than total, all that can be said is that less is required of him, and less of him is required. Whereas he formerly had a series of tasks to perform, requiring a variety of movements, muscles, and skills, he today has only one or two things to do, and "skills" are seldom required for any of them. This isn't liberation, as Piel suggests, but mere mechanization—a process which reduces the worker from human being to inhuman muscle. Cybernation, the subject of Piel's comments, has roughly the same effect on an ideational level that automation has on a physical one.

Commenting on the division of labor entailed by mechanization, Siegfried Giedion writes:

> The worker cannot manufacture a product from start to finish; from the standpoint of the consumer the product becomes increasingly difficult to master. When the motor of his car fails, the owner often does not know which part is causing the trouble; an elevator strike can paralyze the whole life of New York. As a result, the individual becomes increasingly dependent on production and on society as a whole, and relations are far more complex and interlocked than in any earlier society. This is one reason why today man is overpowered by means.[35]

Later, the historian adds:

> Never has mankind possessed so many instruments for abolishing slavery. But the promises of a better life have not been kept. All we have to show so far is a rather disquieting inability to organize the world, or even to organize ourselves. Future generations will perhaps designate this period as one of mechanized barbarism, the most repulsive barbarism of all.[36]

(Giedion's use of the qualifying word "perhaps" is not meant to question his own assessment of the present, but to allow for the possibility that future generations will themselves be reduced to a level of "mechanized barbarism" that exceeds even our own and so may not have the will or wisdom to understand either their own plight or our own.)

The mechanization of which Giedion speaks (what I call "technicization") is an ongoing process, a dynamic that proceeds toward the complete transformation of all and everything. Through a seemingly infinite subdivision of labor, the technical phenomenon renders each individual increasingly dependent upon the smooth functioning of the society as a whole. By himself, the individual is able to do less and less. The complexity of goods and services, and the processes required to produce them, are such that we find ourselves more and more at the mercy of our means—means whose operations we don't understand and whose operators we do not know. The cooperativeness and predictability of our fellow men become essential in almost everything we do: the society becomes so well integrated, so organic, that nearly every industry is in some way strategic to the whole. A strike, shortage, or breakdown in one economic sector is likely to generate a chain reaction throughout the entire economy. It is as if technicization pushes the society toward a kind of critical mass, simultaneously increasing both its power and its fragility.

The analysis that precedes any subdivision of labor seems to be a process of theft: it robs the work of its meaning, the worker of his pride, autonomy, and responsibility, and the environment of its human or benevolent characteristics. Nuclear technology provides an exotic example of the process.

E. L. Doctorow, writing about a missile silo in the Dakotas, says:

> It is not an impression of free men in a democratic society that you get from a visit to a launch-control capsule. As with the pilots on the flight line, the sense is definitely one of imprisonment. The steel doors are locked. The fluorescent lights are on all the time. The lights buzz and the air conditioners hum and the radio crackles and the teletype spits out its tape messages and the whole place mounts a constant assault on the privacy of the mind. At the exact locations of our nuclear-conscious technology is a total environment, one that has replaced all other landscapes and made irrelevant all considerations other than its own functioning. The men who guard us with our bombs live in airplanes or in underground capsules or in submarines—anywhere but on the face of the earth.[37]

In this utterly artificial environment (which sounds disturbingly like Times Square and Las Vegas), individuality has been effectively "designed out" of the surroundings; the soldier-workers' identities have been completely submerged in their relationships to the technical world that they serve. It's well-known that, supposedly to guard against the possibility of an *espontáneo* starting World War III, a number of disparate operations have to be performed almost simultaneously in order to launch a missile. Two men have to turn keys placed in locks twelve feet apart; another man must activate a mechanism by pressing a button while the keys are being turned; other operations have to be performed by other people elsewhere, and even if the missile is launched, it can be exploded "harmlessly" by monitoring teams working in other locations. But this fail-safe procedure probably has a more devious purpose than to prevent a mistaken launching: specifically, the procedure seems to have been designed for the express purpose of diffusing all sense of responsibility on the parts of those who may be called upon to irradiate millions. In this case, the division of labor guarantees the desired result—that, upon the proper command, no missile-silo moralists will develop ethical objections to genocide and refuse to do their parts. By dividing the procedure into so many petty tasks, no one (or group) can be said to have been charged with the responsibility of launching *anything*. At most it might be said that Private Jones turned a key; so did Lieutenant Smith; Corporal Stein pressed a button; Captain Miller opened a door; Colonel Felafel stuck a tape into a computer; and General Babbit did nothing but *decline* to stimulate the "self-destruct" mechanism. Who dropped the Bomb? No one. It fell from the air, by itself almost, almost figuratively.

IV. Gizmo and Siege

> One never knows, do one?
>
> *Fats Waller*

1. The "EM's" Quarters; the Technical Police

Just as the military provides a fine example of the rationalization of *labor* (in its missile installations), it will also serve as a paradigm of the rationalization of *leisure*.

While not a particularly leisure-oriented organization, today's "Action Army" frequently anticipates developments in the civilian sphere. More than Californians or any other so-called "trend setters," the military represents a cultural vanguard in that its access to the most advanced techniques is total—and, moreover, it has the motive, capital, and manpower to put those techniques into effect long before anyone else. Indeed, the way in which the Army solves its problems today is the way in which the larger society will solve its problems tomorrow.

Consider, then, the following remarks made at a press conference by an associate of an architectural firm which had been awarded a contract for the redesign of the Enlisted Man's quarters: [38]

Jack L. Bedingfield, the speaker, first notes that "The enlisted man, or EM, has characteristics—just the way all of us here in this room do." His prologue over, Bedingfield then goes on to itemize, in masterful technocratic fashion, the "characteristics of the EM, breaking him down into a set of convenient stereotypes: Physical Man, Professional Military Man, Psychological Man, Social Man, and Spiritual Man. As Social Man, Bedingfield says, "the EM needs facilities and spaces which allow him to establish beneficial social relationships/activities." In reference to Spiritual Man, the military architect points to a subheading entitled "Identity/Individual" and remarks that "the living spaces and facilities should allow each EM to maintain his identity/individualism." The planner then reveals that "each EM has a basic set of activities which occur within the living spaces" and that "each activity has a corresponding set of positions. Positions generate environmental surfaces and spaces necessary to maintain activities." (So much for the Mind/Body problem.) Two of those environmental surfaces, according to Bedingfield, are "surfaces for sitting and reclining positions." How to satisfy the EM's need for such environmental surfaces? The planner reveals that the best means of providing them is to include a "chair" and a "bed" within the "living spaces."

Lest anyone doubt the flexibility of technical expertise, the planners established under the category "Positions" that "activities with similar positions and privacy/community can be grouped into sets of compatible activities termed Activity Groups" and "activities in compatible sets can occur on the same surfaces and simultaneously with other activities of that set." This apparently means that the enlisted man can use the same *environmental surface* (e.g., a chair) in his capacity as *Social Man* (talking-in-the-chair) and *Spiritual Man* (meditating-in-the-chair).

If Bedingfield is somewhat obfuscatory in his method, a book provided at the press conference clears matters up. Describing the methodology applied to the redesign of the EM's quarters, the book states (their caps):

> THE CRITERIA AND PRIORITIES ESTABLISHED IN THE PROGRAM INFORMATION [the study of the enlisted man] THEN PROVIDED THE NECESSARY RELATIONSHIPS WHICH WERE USED TO DEVELOP GROUPS OF ELEMENTS. THESE GROUPS ARE FORMED BASED ON AN ORDERED HIERARCHY OF ELEMENTS

WHICH ESTABLISHES, AT EACH LEVEL IN THE SCOPE OR SCALE OF THE COMPLETE ENVIRONMENTAL PACKAGE, BASIC FUNCTIONAL CLUSTERS OR SETS OF ELEMENTS. THESE CLUSTERS ARE INTEGRAL AND SELF-CONTAINED AT THEIR PARTICULAR SCALE, AND EACH IS MADE UP OF INTEGRAL SMALLER SCALED SETS. THEY BECOME PARTS OF LARGER GROUPINGS BY THE ADDITION OF NEW ELEMENTS INTO A SET OF SEVERAL IDENTICAL CLUSTERS. THE DIAGRAM OF ELEMENTS AND THEIR RELATIONSHIPS AND SUBSEQUENT GROUPS IS IDENTIFIED AS THE ELEMENTAL RELATIONSHIPS DIAGRAM.

The diagram referred to consists of a series of circles with arrows sticking out of them, pointing toward one or another circle. Each circle is labeled ("enlisted man," "activities," "property," "storage facilities," "environmental systems," et cetera).

I quote this protofascistic nonsense not merely to point out the tautological roots of technique's rational analysis (after all, it's not news that activity takes place in space), but to provide an example of the way in which leisure and "living" activities are subjected by the planners to the same "divisioning" that has reduced labor to a kind of mechanical mindlessness.

The tendency of technique is toward the rationalization and control of *all* activity, acting either directly upon the individual (e.g., by lobotomy or "schooling") or indirectly, through the reordering of his environment—the limitations, punishments, and rewards *designed into* the world around him. The logic of the most efficient means, and the multiplication toward ubiquity of those means, persuade us to make more and more decisions in favor of technique. The result is that our actions become increasingly *automatic* and therefore predictable; the possibilities offered by technique come to determine both what we want and how we get it. In this way, spontaneity becomes an indulgence requiring *an effort,* and nonconformity, in view of our collective interdependence, takes on the aspect of a threat. Behavior that's variant comes to be seen as deviant, with the implication that it is also antisocial. It's obvious that, as the culture comes to depend to an ever greater extent upon mechanical methods and machinery, it becomes increasingly mechanical and machinelike: those parts, or people, which do not "mesh" with the whole tend to foul it up. They must, therefore, be removed, isolated, or rehabilitated in such a way that they will make a better "fit."

In any supertechnicized society the "social contract" is not a contract at all, but a subpoena. Without recourse to a frontier, we're drafted at birth into a culture whose expansion is as certain as the efficacy of our techniques. We have no choice in our socialization and, for perhaps the first time in history, there is no escape and no dream of escape. A would-be exile who, upon learning that he does not love America, decides to leave will probably be disappointed no matter where he goes. In Europe, Latin America, and Asia—indeed, even at the Poles—primitive and not so primitive societies are all engaged in remaking their cultures in accord with the possibilities afforded by technical expertise. In so far as the United States is in the vanguard of technical development, that is only to say that those societies are becoming "Americanized." The rapidity with which that Americanization takes place is lightlike, but unsurprising. For a culture to make the transition from the Stone Age to the present, only two things are necessary: it must learn to want the products of technique and it must have something to offer in exchange for those products. This second condition, however, is purely formal: any group of people constitutes a market and, even if it's landless, has its labor to offer in exchange. Therefore, once the *want* is created and the needs inculcated, nothing need be discovered or understood, merely imported.

Technique's rational character guarantees its expansion by virtue of its suitability for imitation. This inevitably leads to the homogenization of each culture in itself and, eventually, of all cultures taken together. In this way, technique eliminates frontiers.

One result of these tendencies is to transform every society, whether melting pot or not, into a kind of social pressure cooker. In the absence of a frontier, society's discontents have nowhere to go. Pressure of this sort creates a kind of social claustrophobia which, if it isn't released in rebellion or neutralized by fantasy, leads to neurosis or disintegration, individually or collectively. This innate volatility, coupled with the extravagant value placed upon conformity in deference to our interdependence, suggests that a technicized society has an outsized need for police.

Internal pressures, however, are only one cause of a technicized society's unusually large police needs. Even more important is the need to regulate the use of technique. Since each means is an embodiment of power, almost every technical innovation is attended by the creation of laws to govern its use, administrators to oversee those laws, or an increase in police personnel to enforce new applications of already existing laws. The correlation between technique's proliferation and an expanding police apparatus is eloquently demonstrated by the automobile. Since the car's invention, police departments everywhere have grown far beyond what might be expected from population increase alone. Indeed, the FBI owes its very existence to the automobile, having been created in an effort to control those interstate crimes which the car made possible. Today, a majority of state and local police are occupied almost entirely with some element of traffic control; traditional crime prevention and investigation activities take up an ever-diminishing *proportion* of a police department's time.*

Radio, television, and the computer would make the same point about technique's tendency to enlarge a society's enforcement apparatus. So would the advent of atomic energy and the airplane, as well as innovations in food processing, packaging, and pharmacology. Technique demands regulation, and meeting that demand requires an expansion of the enforcement bureaucracy. The FCC, FAA, AEC, FDA, and related inspectorate bureaucracies are essentially police

---

* Television tends to obscure this fact. But anyone who's worked as a policeman or (as in the author's case) worked beside policemen (as a crime reporter) can confirm the observation. Arrest and investigation take up a relatively small part of most policemen's time.

agencies operating in a purely technical context. They are, in a sense, *technical police* (white-collar cops) charged with controlling behavior as it relates to the particular means within each agency's jurisdiction.

2. Problems of Technology Assessment

In the preceding chapters, I've tried to identify the most salient characteristics of the technical phenomenon, suggest its directions, and note some of its entailments. I've attempted to show that technique proceeds irresistibly toward completeness; that its hegemony in all spheres is virtually undeniable; and that its proliferation necessarily diminishes our freedom by reducing the number of choices available to us. What this has to do with the apocalyptic perception, enlistment in the millenarian cause, and decadence I intend to make clear. But there are still some aspects of the technical phenomenon which demand to be recognized before we can move on.

For instance: since the technical phenomenon homogenizes and integrates each part of every society, it proceeds toward a seemingly infinite complexity—an absolute symbiosis of existing and anticipated methods. Because that integrated complexity entails fragility, the society's future viability seems to be contingent upon the establishment of social controls that are, by virtue of their necessary scope and authority, clinically fascistic. Anything less than routine perfection will result in collective catastrophe. B. F. Skinner is probably right when he suggests that we must choose between freedom and order.

The productive power which technique confers reduces its beneficiaries to what Norman Mailer calls "the Wad"—superfluous automata whose human discontents have no release but in rebellion or through the narcotic trance afforded by television and other mechanisms of fantasy.

And yet, there's a problem and some irony involved with

any analysis of the dangers inherent in the technical phenomenon. The irony proceeds from the fact that writing itself is a technique and analysis is nothing more than reason in motion. In order to prepare a rational critique of the technical phenomenon we must embrace it, imitate its methods, and (at least indirectly) affirm its efficiency. This is roughly comparable to hiring the Gestapo for the protection of a synagogue. Fighting fire with fire may be metaphorically valid, but anyone throwing matches at a burning building must be considered somewhat suspect. Yet what choice is there? We use the techniques that are available to us. The only alternative to a reasoned analysis of the phenomenon's dangers is to resort to some less efficient means—poetry, for instance. That poetry *is* a less "efficient means" must be obvious. Poets have been railing for centuries against technique (in one form or another), and with what result? Their perceptions are, when not completely ignored, misunderstood or buried with a grain of salt. One would think that, in any sane society, publication of *The Waste Land, Howl,* or *Ucanhavyerfuckincityback* * would be enough to stimulate policy debates within government. And yet, of course, the society is less sane than rational, less human than purposive, and so the poets are mostly ignored when they are not wholly destroyed.

The *problem* with writing about the technical phenomenon is similar to the one faced by the bridge commander of the *Titanic*. Suddenly, an overwhelming matter of fact heaves into view; it's clearly unavoidable and its dimensions are as lethal as they are extraordinary. What one does depends on one's inclinations. There's the temptation to grab a lifejacket, scream "Iceberg!" and jump overboard. The problem with this is that the other passengers are liable to stand around saying, "What'd he say?" "I don't know, something about Glenn Miller—the hell with it." Or one might, as the cobra does with the mongoose, become inspired and entranced by the prospect of thanatopsis, setting out to chart its every pe-

---

* The author of this remarkable book, D. A. Levy, committed suicide in the city that was its subject, Cleveland, at the end of the Sixties.

culiarity and detail, its size, shape, composition, direction, speed, history, and so forth. But, by the time you got to shape, you'd be under water and your pen wouldn't work. The only alternative by which one may emerge with *both* ass and honor intact is to focus public attention on the phenomenon and, while proceeding in an orderly fashion to the nearest lifeboat, suggest some of its most obvious consequences: if they bother to look up and around themselves, to pay attention, others will understand the force of the observation. "Iceberg. Drowning. Death. 'Bye."

This is what I've tried to do with the technical phenomenon. The subject is so large, fateful, and grotesque that a definitive understanding, however curious and convenient it might be, is better left to historians who may work at a comfortable remove from the subject.

The technical phenomenon is the overwhelming fact of the twentieth century. Its consequences are certain and plain to see. The desirability of placing some sort of limitation upon it is obvious to almost everyone, including the technicians themselves. To cope with the fact that more "advanced" technology does not necessarily lead to a more livable society, a specialized discipline has recently been found. That discipline is Technology Assessment, or TA. A good definition of TA is offered by Joseph Coates, an official at the United States National Science Foundation. It is, he says:

> the systematic study of the secondary and higher order effects or impacts on society of a present or proposed application of technology. In its fullest form it should anticipate, forecast, and evaluate the impacts of the technological intrusion on all sectors of society, including the economic, environmental, social, political, legal, and institutional components.[39]

TA isn't a new idea: corporations have practiced a form of TA ever since they began buying up patents and suppressing inventions which threatened to put their own products out of business. Marketing techniques are often a form of technological assessment, and science fiction writers have been practicing a sort of informal TA for more than a hundred years. But, while TA isn't a new idea, it *is* a new discipline. Most of its adherents have so far been preoccupied with establishing the discipline's methodology rather than in making actual assessments; professional TA societies have only begun to form; and the first government agency concerned with TA wasn't established until 1972—that's the Office of Technology Assessment (OTA), an advisory arm of the United States Congress.

The problems with TA are numerous and, it seems, insurmountable. Foremost is the fact that TA concerns itself with specific innovations rather than with the technical phenomenon as a whole. The result is that those effects which proceed from the technical *ecology* escape all assessment.

Secondly, TA is unable to cope with the fact that the popular use of any technique changes its nature in such a way that early assessments become obsolete very quickly. Since the practice of TA is almost always on a "project" basis, only a single assessment or group of assessments is made, and then the technique is either scrapped or put into operation. Once a technique is introduced into the mainstream of the cultural economy, it can't be recalled without catastrophic effect. (We might, for instance, decide that the automobile was a good idea that just didn't work out in practice; eliminating the car from our lives at this point, however, would amount to national suicide.) Indeed, even this idea is purely theoretical since it rather brashly assumes that those making the assessments will be heeded or given the power to abort the birth of any technique they disapprove of or find dangerous.

A third problem with TA is that scientists and technicians are steeped in a quantitative bias. If something isn't measurable, it doesn't exist or isn't worth bothering about. Thus, intangibles seldom find any defensible place within technological assessment. And if they are mentioned, their weight is subordinate to that of almost any quantitative factor.

A fourth problem with Technology Assessment is the very complexity of the task. Our techniques are so well integrated with themselves and with every aspect of the society that judging the impact of a particular innovation involves calculations of exponentially huge proportions, even if the intangible factors are disregarded. The "secondary and higher order impacts" of, for instance, medical transplants or advanced telecommunications are simply not amenable to *general* assessment. The impacts are too many and too diverse. The effects of truly revolutionary technology can only be accurately assessed by in-depth studies of the technology's relationship to a specific area of human experience—for example, the effect of laser communications technology on the prevention of violent crime in urban areas.

Yet another problem with Technology Assessment is the assessors themselves. With only a few exceptions, their entire professional lives, training and experience have been dedicated to wiping out every vestige of imagination that they ever possessed. As specialists, they necessarily have a narrow viewpoint. The result is that they're extremely uncomfortable with interdisciplinary approaches and wholly incapable of extradisciplinary approaches. Technique's impacts are felt in a multitude of dimensions, whereas the technicians are trained to think in a single one. They have, in other words, the brains for Technology Assessment, but not the minds.

Finally, TA is peculiarly susceptible to economic and political persuasion. A technician who points out that a particular device or method is not worth developing may find himself, as happened to one civil servant who criticized the C-5A transport plane, transferred to a post in Bangkok, there to supervise a PX bowling alley. In any case, technique's power makes it overwhelmingly seductive to the state. As Emilio Daddario, motive force behind the creation of the United States Office of Technology Assessment, makes clear, the business of TA is the *expansion* of technique, and not its limitation. "I never felt there was a need to clamp down on technology," Daddario explains. "Just the opposite: I wanted to show that the problems of society cannot be solved by stepping back but by pushing ahead, by using more technology rather than less, by not being fearful—that it was just a matter of *how* you use technology and under what conditions." [40]
The OTA (which has counterparts in West Germany, Britain,

and Japan) is therefore, according to its founder, an agency whose purpose is to maximize the efficiency of technical development.

Daddario sounds curiously like Alvin Toffler, even down to the technogogic suggestion that those who would limit technique are "stepping back" and "being fearful." Never mind whether a step backward might not also be a step in the right direction: it's "backward," and since it isn't forward, it can't be Progress. Ever since the Bomb painted Hiroshima with cancer, technophiles have tended to wear their rationality as a kind of mental bumper sticker, an advertisement of their intellectual machismo. To question the all-benevolent aspect of rationality and technique is to demonstrate a lack of courage, an unwillingness to "face reality," and similar eristic garbage. In the United States, where automobiles are named after predators, less than absolute confidence in the supremacy of (American) know-how is unpatriotic and evidence of probable faggotry. Moreover, it is not enough to think, as Herman Kahn does, about the so-called "unthinkable." The experts, like Lord Raglan, would have us put the unthinkable into practice: "Forward . . . into the valley of death . . ."

What will save us, they promise, is more technology. It may be that a new device will lay waste to our psyches, system, or society but, if it also increases productivity, it should be put into use. A percentage of the increased production profits can always be funneled into a special R and D project to find an antidote to the malaise our productivity creates. Technique, we're told, will solve itself.

3. The Mystique of Reason (A Report on an Encounter between Dr. Frankenstein and Mr. Nader)

This is the mystique of reason, a faith as inscrutable and as exacting as Zoroaster's. It demands an unquestioning belief in the omnipotence of technology and in the benevolence of technical evolution. It flatly denies the validity of any other faith and promulgates its world view as the only truth. It promises salvation from want, from confusion, and, most important of all, from ring around the collar. Organized in an almost ecclesiastical hierarchy of mechanics, lab assistants, technicians, Ph.D.s, and Novelists, the church of science is so well married to the ship of state that the latter passes the collection plate for the former. Miracles are daily performed in the service of technique, extravagant public displays, moon landings and saturation bombings designed to persuade the believer of his wisdom and the skeptic of his folly. In this sanctum rationality is the only state of grace—all else is the work ob de debbil.

It is a masculine religion and the proof and preservation of that characteristic is guaranteed by the fact that its hierarchy is almost entirely male. Women aren't *supposed* to like it: in so far as a woman succeeds among the grease and gears of technique, her femininity (resting almost entirely in the eye of the beholder) is diminished. Just as a man's incompetence with tools, or mistrust of technique, places a question mark against his masculinity, a woman's success with those same tools renders her somehow manlike. It is as if the woman's monopoly on the creation of life is intentionally balanced by man's monopoly over the means of (economic) production. A woman who can wield a wrench, fix a faucet, or program a computer is a threat to her male counterpart, diminishing his value (and hers) in his own eyes. It's interesting—and probably without any relevance whatsoever—that women's penetration of the technical establishment occurred at precisely the same time that men took the first steps toward creating life in the laboratory.

Tools are what men bear instead of children. The illusion that we control absolutely the things that we create is an inherently masculine delusion: women are disabused of that fantasy from the moment that they give birth and enter natal servitude. The recognition that humankind may fall victim to its own rational ingenuity is a romantic and feminine realization whose most mythic expression is found in Mary Shelley's *Frankenstein.*

It would be interesting to know what would have happened if the Technology Assessors had interrogated Dr. Frankenstein about his amazing creation.

"You say this thing costs how much to build, Frankenstein?"

"That's *Dr.* Frankenstein . . . Oh, I think we could bring it in for a few thousand petrodollars, depending on demand, and . . ."

"And?"

"*And* the availability of bodies."

"Of course. Speaking of which, we're told that there are some, uhhh, bugs in the mechanism."

"Yes, well, the instrument—I call it the 'instrument,' incidentally—tends to rape, rob, pillage, burn, and murder at will. At least, I think it's at 'will.' No way to tell, really."

"We understand you've been getting some flak from the environmentalists on that score."

"Mnnn . . . Nader and his little band of technophobes are blathering for an injunction against us, but we think we've got most of the bugs ironed out. The problem is that the prototype's just too darn big—about eight feet tall—and ugly as sin. What we're going to do with future production models is to use midgets, give 'em clerical collars and, with an assist from the boys over in plastic surgery, have 'em all look like Spencer Tracy. We'll get a terrific PR boost out of that, and I don't think we'll have any more instrument-connected rapes or pillaging. Of course, fire is something else again. For some reason these mothers just naturally tend to be vicious—"

"The Joint Chiefs have some thoughts on that."

"Yes. I know they do. We've gotten some marvelous cooperation from the gang at the Pentagon and—well, I'm confident we can work something out."

"You haven't come up with a name for the instrument. At least, that's our understanding."

"Right. That's a job for the market-research team. They're testing a number of different names: Robby Robo, the Little Liberator—you know, stuff that'll grab the housewife. We're hitting the household-chores angle pretty hard, frankly."

"I see."

"Yeah, well, it's all a matter of finding the right buttons to push. . . ."

The technician is one whose consciousness has been raped by rationality. His bias toward "objectivity" is so profound that his identity no longer counts. As a technician, he recognizes only one kind of problem: that which can be solved by further applications of technique. "Problems" which are not amenable to rational analysis and, therefore, to technical solution are not, in the technician's mind, problems per se, but delusions of an hysterical nature.

And yet, these are precisely the problems which serrate the present. Since the counterculture's evaporation in the early 1970s, two national cultural trends have emerged: a collective nostalgia that seemingly knows no bounds, and an equally collective persecution complex. Each is peculiarly American.

4. Nostalgia and Persecution

American nostalgia has almost nothing to do with *home*-sickness (as the word's roots would imply). It is instead a kind of time-nausea, an almost impersonal sense of loss whose focus is temporal rather than geographical. Adults whose entire lives have been spent in the cities are somehow *nostalgic* for a countryside and a way of life that they never knew; the fashions and music of the Forties are *de rigueur* for trendies in their twenties; cereals, soft drinks, furniture, films, and television shows succeeded in the marketplace by virtue of their faked connection with a past that is selectively remembered or wholly manufactured. Whatever the object of ersatz recognition—Heartland Cereal, *Happy Days,* or the "first drugstore" in which Coca-Cola was sold—it is the past itself, its imperviousness to change, that conjures with our collective melancholy.

The observation that "you can't go home again" used to be a figurative truth that had to do with people. Today the observation is literally true and has less to do with people than with "home." A visit to the house in which one lived as a child or adolescent is likely to be an empty return: it isn't there any more. Searching for some physical evidence of our own past, some proof that we not only are but have also *been,* we find nothing or fragments: a tattered baseball card, valentine or photograph, the detritus of an age preserved by accident, slippage behind the refrigerator and stove. The temptation is to revalue all such souvenirs, to make newly precious anything that claims a connection with a past that Progress has expropriated. Amputated from the anonymous histories of our private lives, we accept the Disney version of ourselves: edges are smoothed, textures softened, demons reduced to a manageable size. In this way we wax "nostalgic" at *The Waltons,* those celluloid ghosts of a genial Depression, and nod with a collective sense of sadness and loss. The subject of our wistfulness is, more often than not, a lie, a memory manufactured to meet the demand for memories. Our loss is so total that we cannot even recall what it is that has been lost, but whore after antiquity—*anyone's* antiquity—for its own sake, holding a common electronic wake for whatever is old or is said to be old.

There is in this national nostalgia the suggestion of a drowning man going down for the third time. Cut off from the future by a sense of impending catastrophe, submerged in a present whose aspect is pure menace, we accept a bowdlerized past with uncritical remorse, luxuriating in the bathetic strobe of deceits flashing by one after another. It's not our lives that pass before our eyes in the moment of anticipated eclipse, but a paraparade tuned to the oom-pah-pah of reminiscence.

Even as we cherish the remorse generated by nostalgia, so do we embrace the righteousness which our sense of persecution affords. By the common agreement of its citizens, the United States is today a nation of victims. Any characteristic or eccentricity which deviates from an abstract, statistical norm qualifies one for membership in one liberation movement or another. It's almost impossible to escape inclusion in some convenient category of the oppressed. To be black, brown, red, female, gay, young, poor, old, short, fat, or ugly is to be a victim. If these categories are inappropriate, the individual may file his claim to oppression through membership in some religious, regional, ethnic, or vocational minority. If one still lacks the proper credentials, that in itself is sufficient certification of one's victimization since those who are not said to be oppressed as a minority are said be oppressed as a majority —the so-called "silent majority," or middle-American Wad. It isn't necessary to have a *personal* experience of persecution to qualify for the condition of oppressee—an empathetic reference to a history of *ancestral oppression* will suffice. Indeed, even a rich, male, Anglo-Saxon, heterosexual, middle-aged Presbyterian landlord from Manhattan can qualify as a victim by identifying himself as a *consumer.*

My intention here is not to dismiss these groups' claims, nor to question the reality of their sufferings. On the contrary. While some are more oppressed than others, each has sufficient reason to complain. It may sound facetious to lump the short and the ugly with the blacks, but it would only sound that way to those who are neither. Ultimately, only those who suffer can judge the extent to which they suffer.

What's strange about this, however, is the astonishing multiplication of identifiable "oppressed minorities" in recent years. Increasingly, individuals tend to define themselves, by word and by life-style, in terms of that quality which is "responsible" for their victimization: cultural nationalism, ethnic chauvinism, and feminism are all expressions of the same sensibility. Formerly, minorities did everything possible to diminish the characteristics which separated them from the majority: blacks straightened their hair, gays cowered in closets, the old acted young, the young acted old, the poor bought Cadillacs (on time), and immigrants struggled with their syntax and pronunciation.

But during the 1960s, all this began to change. Black nationalism inaugurated the change, but it was quickly imitated by any group which could, through some stretch of the imagination, claim to be victimized by virtue of its singular identity —which singularity and victimization, real or imagined, was then flaunted. It became a matter of pride.

Belonging to a minority became, at the end of the 1960s, a cultural imperative. Minority status not only conferred a special social standing, but transformed each person's daily existence with a new meaning: to be black, to be old, to be young, Italian, Indian, or gay was, for the first time, *enough*. In so far as one belonged to a minority one was a victim and, given the nature of that role, one had no other social responsibility than to survive. Minority status, because it defined the individual in terms of his victimization, provided the confused with a clear-cut role and also rendered the society intelligible: it was out to fuck us.

Minority characteristics became the object of exaggeration by the minority itself, and a bizarre competition developed *between* minorities as one group sought to "out-nigger" the other. While the blacks could point to four centuries of slavery and humiliation, women trumpeted that they held the longest continuous record of oppression (variously estimated at between four and nine thousand years).

Through this prism of persecution, the ordinary state of affairs appeared to be a vast conspiracy of *them* against *us*. The focus of the conspiracy shifted, depending on which group one happened to belong to: blacks were oppressed by whites, women were oppressed by men, the old were oppressed by the young, the young were oppressed by the old, the consumer was oppressed by the big corporations, the big corporations were oppressed by government, gays were oppressed by straights, and everyone was oppressed by the state—which someone else had elected. America was in a conspiracy against itself.

It was as if, on some subterranean psychic level, Americans individually arrived at a collective apostasy, disaffiliating themselves from each other. Some sang "The Star-Spangled Banner" and others sang "We Shall Overcome," but, whatever the lyrics, there seemed to be an underlying melodic disclaimer, a distant hum recognizable as "It Ain't Me Babe."

5. "Fag-Waves of Mexican Dope and Chicom Ideology"

Technique's independent evolution, its flirtations with a phalanx of disasters and grotesqueries, causes us to turn from a future that is both opaque and ominous. Technicization blasts away at our traditions, recreates our mental and physical landscapes in its own rational image, and abolishes all evidence of a *personal* past. Our nostalgia, and the remorse that informs it, are corollaries of Progress itself, a temporal melancholy chugged from the locomotive of current events.

In this web of remorse and gears nothing is so natural as paranoia and a sense of oppression. Confronted with technique's drive toward homogenization of culture, we seek exemption, opting out of our collectivity through tribalization. Any singularity of perspective or inheritance—homosexuality, womanhood, blackness, or whatever—is sufficient to define a tribe and sustain an individual. If, for some reason, tribalization is uncongenial, the only alternatives to narcosis and surrender are madness, decadence, isolation, or rebellion.

Technicization renders us helpless. Our mutual dependence on each other, a function of the specialization which technique requires, demands from us a conformity so complete as to verge upon the inorganic. America's tribalization is a reaction against that, against the tendency to reduce each person to a statistical stuff, a mathematical expression of a social being. Minorities represent friction in a societal machine geared to "normalcy"; the fact that a majority of Americans feel persecuted and disenfranchised is merely a consequence of a statistical curiosity—the average never quite fits anyone. Since a democratic society relates to itself in terms of its majorities and averages, everyone is more or less out of whack with his own culture and institutions. In so far as we fail to conform to a statistical normalcy in a technicized society, we're "discriminated" against. And, if we *do* conform, we reduce ourselves to a vegetative anonymity. The alternatives therefore seem to be persecution or hibernation.

The counterculture of the Sixties explored the "other" alternatives: madness, decadence, isolation, and rebellion. Its emergence was an early expression of a discontent that now spans generations. In its earliest incarnation, the counterculture was a phenomenon without a name, a rebellion against the consequences of technicization: its spontaneity was uncalculated, its intellect apolitical, and its thrust almost wholly cultural. It lacked self-consciousness and, therefore, ideology. The body snatchers of the Left, exploiting the abattoir of Vietnam for the purposes of recruitment, combined with the media, for whom ideas are commodities, to change all that, destroying whatever part of the phenomenon could not be co-opted or marketed.

I intend to take this argument up some pages hence, and don't want to anticipate it too much. But the "counterculture" has been so misunderstood that one can hardly refer to it without making some attempt, however brief, at a redefinition.

Briefly, the Civil Rights Movement, Vietnam, Watts, and the serial assassinations of the Sixties warped the counterculture into a counterpolitik. What began as a rejection of the barbarous conformity and cultural repression of the 1950s became, in the mid-Sixties, a movement toward political reform—a kind of New Deal in bellbottoms.

In its adolescence, the counterculture was not a movement but an upheaval, an uprising rather than a revolution. The children of the middle class, in twos and threes and finally in thousands, went AWOL from the Cold War consciousness of the Fifties. They had no demands, only a set of barely articulated rejections whose vagueness and generality must seem, in retrospect, incredibly naïve: no more bullshit, no more "plastic." At its beginning, what came to be called the "counterculture" was an unassociated constellation of individuals in search of authenticity. They had nothing in common but their bourgeois origins, which they hated, and what they loved—good times, music, dope, sex, and Lenny Bruce. If someone could toss in a vision on occasion, well, that was just perfect.

In 1960, the United States was an alloy of the worst elements of Sparta and of Rome. In the suburbs and cities, an individual's standard of living was an index to his human worth. Conspicuous consumption was a patriotic duty, a social imperative whose disregard constituted an invitation to unemployment and ostracism. The citizenry was united in the common purpose of living beyond their means, welded together by what they owned and by what they despised: commies, crabgrass, and kooks.

Even as America was Roman in its consumptive indulgences, it was Spartan in style. Ready to nuke and to be nuked, American men kept their hair cropped to a military brevity and dressed in the uniform appropriate to their vocational rank. Officers in the work force wore the ghostly raiment of gray flannel, carried "attaché cases" that were often empty, and wore white shirts of such uncompromising sameness that the collars were buttoned down to foil sartorial deviance. Indeed, almost everything was buttoned down in some way, including the American ass, whose inviolability was symbolically preserved in a fashion for trousers whose unique distinction was an extraneous buckle in the back, a kind of rear-end chastity belt. It may be coincidental but, in the twentieth century at least, American attitudes have usually been reflected in the neckwear of its men: in 1959, ties were pencil-thin, short, and humdrum in their restraint, a darker version of the GIs'.

Stalemated in Korea, Americans understood the lesson of preparedness. They'd not be taken off guard again and, in deference to that caution, its men retained the sartorial trappings of an army, ready at a moment's notice to exchange their gray suits for khakis. In the suburbs, families tended their private foxholes, fallout shelters stocked with food, water, and sufficient weaponry to repel both treacherous oriental hordes and radioactive neighbors.

If the cities and suburbs were fortresses for consumers who'd been conditioned to save the Free World through free spending, the universities were industrial boot camps, training grounds for the economy's replacement troops. It was here that the counterculture was born and, finally, died.

Hair grew to subversive lengths as disaffected youths shed their uniforms, exchanging their ass buckles for the catenary folds of Levi's stitching. Ties vanished. Buttons went unused. Pegged pants bloomed at the ankles as cuffs were taken off and, for the first time in a generation, young people felt a gust of air on their shins. Most dangerously, perhaps, the young abdicated from their apprenticeship to alcohol, rejecting the country's communal drug ("Juiceheads are the lowest") and, therefore, its gods. In the eyes of most Americans it didn't take a genius to realize that nests of eggheads had started a fagwave with Mexican dope and Chicom ideology.

It didn't last. Within a few years, the counterculture stumbled from emergence to decline. Twisted by historical events, made self-conscious by the media, and cajoled by an uncomprehending Left whose propaganda was all the more effective for its being true, the counterculture withered to the status of a mass cult, an eccentric majority within a minority Left.

What began as a spontaneous rejection of the culture's rationalized conformity, materialism, "plasticity," and atomic banality—all consequences of technique—degenerated into a conformity of a secondary order. By the time the decade wheezed to an end, the symbols and artifacts of a generation had been co-opted. A calculated spontaneity became *de rigueur,* long hair was à la mode, dope was chic, and youth was an industry whose spin-offs included enlightenment and revolution.

6. The Future: Why It Hasn't Any

The foregoing has been an attempt to outline the most important characteristics of the age's central phenomenon, technicization, and to indicate the relationship those characteristics have to some present-day malignancies and discontents. Whenever possible, I've avoided reference to specific methods and technologies, concentrating as much as possible on the phenomenon itself. I have, moreover, deliberately omitted reference to the many obvious benefits that techniques confer. As if these limitations are not enough, the argument neglects to make such important distinctions as the one between ritual and technique, and utterly fails to consider how we could live without techniques.

The argument is therefore general, unfair, incomplete, and decidedly unconstructive.

For all these deficiencies, however, it's still sufficient—though some notes on my method may be in order.

My neglect of specific techniques represents an effort to deal with certainties rather than variables. Every technique is a solution to a problem—it's power, and power is ambivalent. Whether a technique is used for good or ill depends upon the sense and motives of the person using it. It would be easy to anticipate a satanic scenario for the future, one based upon malevolent applications of genetic engineering, medical transplants, behavioral conditioning, cybernetics, and other provocative techniques. But there's no certainty in such a scenario. While any one of these techniques is capable of establishing hell upon the planet, it could do so only if it were misused, through stupidity or corrupt design. Technology advocates (such as Toffler) correctly understand that a mistrust of particular techniques is really a mistrust of the people using them. Certainly, technical or legislative safeguards could prevent the most obvious abuses of the technical arsenal. My argument, therefore, has sought to eliminate the human variable from the technical equation, treating the former as a hypothetical constant composed entirely of goodwill, good sense, and an ability to muddle through. My analysis, therefore, attempts to show that—even if we suppose all men to be wise and good—the technical phenomenon is, of itself, inevitably destructive.

Ignoring the obvious benefits of individual techniques seemed reasonable in view of their very obviousness. No one needs to be told that radiation therapy can be a good thing. My argument's unfairness owes its negativity to the fact that individual solutions, taken as a whole, have themselves become part of a larger (and probably insoluble) problem. (For example: social scientists at a series of seminars in Cuernavaca, Mexico, have arrived at some startling conclusions with regard to transportation and medicine. Concerning mass transportation, the seminars concluded that as vehicles exceed a certain "optimum" speed—twenty-five miles per hour—in common use, an individual actually devotes more of his time to getting from one place to another. Similarly, the seminar concluded that there is an inverse relationship between the technical sophistication of a country's medical plant and the general health of its population: that is, developing exotic health care systems—such as medical transplants—requires a disproportionate expenditure of public moneys on pathologies that only the rich can afford to cure, with the result that general health care suffers, becoming more expensive and less accessible to the larger population.)*

That my argument fails to propose ways in which man can live without techniques is even easier to explain. We can't. Technique is a kind of psychobiological imperative: we have no choice in the matter. My purpose, therefore, is not to propose remedies—there are none—but simply to see where it is that we seem to be going, and what's likely to happen when we get there. As E. M. Cioran puts it: ". . . you cannot

---

* Detailed information about these, and other controversial studies, and about the organization responsible for them, can be obtained from CIDOC, Centro Interculturales de Documentación, Cuernavaca, Morelos, Mexico.

treat destiny." All that's possible is "to keep abreast of the Incurable."

And keeping abreast of the Incurable is a spectator sport that leads one to imagine only two possible futures: one that works, and one that doesn't.

Of course, a future that "works" is one in which the evolution of technique has proceeded unchecked by natural catastrophe or the disappearance of strategic natural resources. Technical hegemony, in such a world, would be complete. All productive work, including services, would be automated. So absolutely integrated and complex would such a society be that even "specialization" would be impossible: human beings would understand nothing of the world around them, but relate to it in the same way that a Micronesian cargo cult relates to the technological litter around it. If complexity entails fragility, then the social machine will exact an excruciating predictability of the people it tends. Like everything else, the means of imposing that conformity will be fully integrated with the environment itself. A water supply doped with mild tranquilizers, a climate spellbound with negative ions, ubiquitous subliminal conditioning—all these things make Skinner's more sophisticated "technology of human behavior" unnecessary. In a future that works we'll be the wards of our expertise, our emotions managed and our happiness enforced by a public utility for good times. Because there would be no work to do, there would also be no leisure: as productivity is maximized by automation and technical innovation, consumption will have to be maximized as well. Using what the machines provide will be a full-time job. In a future that works, society will resemble both a mental ward and Kiwanis Club, its citizens backslapping their way through an Elysium of stunned incomprehension. Forced to choose between happiness and freedom, satiety and aspiration, the romantic and libertarian will find himself in a minority, a backwater of unreasonableness.

Fortunately, the future doesn't look nearly that "bright." Far more likely is that the evolution of technique will be interrupted by one catastrophe or another. Two means of interruption which seem to be the most probable are the disappearance of some strategic resource (e.g., oil) and the evolution of a metacrisis.

A technically integrated society, a Gizmo culture, is one in which each element in the means of production and the modes of consumption is linked to and dependent upon every other element. Nothing is less than strategic. A fluctuation in one sector induces a variation in a second area, which, in its turn, generates disruption in a third . . . and so on. The process is a chain reaction of crises leading to a prevailing metacrisis in which almost nothing works. In such circumstances, the Gizmo is effectively under "siege," as historian Arnold Toynbee has suggested.

Our own society is only approximately integrated. We *tend* toward complete technical integration because that's the most efficient way of doing things but, as we approach that absolute, breakdowns proliferate exponentially. The seriousness of those breakdowns—in terms of unemployment, hunger, and general suffering—is directly proportional to the degree of our interdependence and reliance upon technique.

To the extent that we depend upon a matrix of complicated techniques, we lack buffers. The society is more or less finely tuned, requiring constant care and tinkering, and responds to the slightest inputs or disturbances. A crisis situation becomes the norm (as has already happened in the United States).

Moreover, the *social* pressures of technicization represent a centrifugal force that causes any democracy to fly apart. As we disintegrate into embattled enclaves of persecuted minorities, a majority becomes impossible. And, without a majority, a democratic government cannot act—it has no will, and no authority. The result is political paralysis, impotent gestures, or oligarchy.

Without a majority to support and motivate its actions, the government's standard response becomes one of vacillation, with the consequence that existing crises are unmet, expand, and intensify. If the situation is not to deteriorate into chaos, power must be transferred to some neutral, apolitical group—an oligarchy of, for instance, technicians.

Italy and the United States are both examples of democracies unraveling in the absence of majorities. Each country moves from crisis to crisis in a state of seemingly permanent metacrisis. Lacking a popular mandate, incapable of imposing solutions, the elective branches of government are forced to transfer their decision-making powers to supposedly nonpartisan elites, task forces composed of experts ordained with the authority of "czars."

Technical problems are not, of course, amenable to democratic solution—they require rational decisions that contain no element of will. As technique expands into every cranny of our lives, our existence is rationalized. Our choices are increasingly limited as more and more decisions have to be made on a purely rational basis. The complexity of those decisions suggests that they must be made by experts. And the importance of those decisions, in view of the society's fragility, means that they must be made promptly and without extensive debate. A fully integrated technical society is therefore one that cannot afford to be democratic, to indulge itself in the luxuries of consultation, debate, and popular participation.

Our most probable future seems to be one of an ongoing metacrisis managed by an emerging power elite of technicians, terminating—as it must—in eventual technical collapse.

Only a single mismanaged crisis is necessary to reduce the society to a chaos from which it cannot recover, and only the most mystical technophile believes in both the infallibility of the technicians and the panacea of "expertise." Solutions require both time and the means of implementation: it is entirely possible that we will, in the next two decades, undergo a crisis whose dimensions are such that those means will be destroyed before the solution can be effected.

Of course, it's extremely unlikely that a shortage of strategic resources would arrive unexpectedly. Geologists and economic planners predict, for instance, that world oil supplies will be completely exhausted within thirty years. That's an optimistic assessment based on the highly improbable conditions that the world will continue to discover oil at the same rate that it has in the past, and that America's demand for oil will not increase. Unless we eliminate our reliance upon oil, therefore, less than thirty years separates the industrial world from a postindustrial Stone Age. At this point we have no viable substitute for oil. If such a substitute should be found, an even greater problem exists: how to convert an oil-dependent society to an alternative energy source without demolishing existing cultural and economic institutions. Can the conversion be carried out in time—or would it prove so awkward that the social order would collapse even as it was being saved? How much economic, and therefore political, upheaval would result from the attempts at transition? Could the conversion be carried out relatively gradually, or, in view of our technical integration, would it have to take place simultaneously in nearly every sphere of activity? Is this latter possibility real, or only theoretical? What industries, besides the petrochemical nexus, will be destroyed by oil's exhaustion? Can the loss of those industries be absorbed with anything less than chaos? Even as our society runs on oil, it's held together with plastic (a product of oil); will our depletion of the one entail a sacrifice of the other and, if so, will our withdrawal symptoms be merely severe, or fatal? If we have to choose between cars and plastics, which will we choose? Or will the choice, as seems likely, be made for us? Could we, in any case, live without our cars? (Probably not.) If not, could we live without plastic? (Probably not—and certainly not as an "industrial" nation.) If no efficient alternative is discovered to replace oil-based plastics and fuels, technical and social collapse would seem to be inevitable before the year 2000.

Other shortages are also inevitable, as the *Limits to Growth* report proves.

Confronted with such shortages, governments tend to act uniformly and predictably. Conveniently confusing the "state" with the "nation," governments assign the highest priority for survival to themselves. This usually entails that materials in short supply be allocated on a priority basis to the military and police. In that way, the existing order can be defended and, thereby, preserved.

Thus, our most probable future is one of escalating shortages managed by a technical elite from whose decisions there will be no appeal or referendum. Those decisions are likely to be enforced by a modern, fully supplied military/police apparatus whose task will be to maintain order among a populace undergoing increasingly brutal deprivations. We will, in other words, be escorted to a medieval future by the most sophisticated enforcement apparatus that the Law Enforcement Assistance Administration (LEAA) and the military can devise. The social upheavals certain to accompany this drift * toward primitivism will be futile and ironic: rocks will be thrown at ray guns, and dissidents will be asked to surrender their flints at the booking desks of centrally heated, air-conditioned jails.

The specter of an American population living in medieval conditions while SAC Stratofortresses guard the sky above them is admittedly quirky, but not entirely farfetched. The military, in any sizable society, is always kept in the technical vanguard of the culture—always the last to experience the effects of shortages. The Greeks, for instance, were noteworthy for generally refusing to apply their scientific knowledge to practical matters. They seem to have mistrusted technique, to have understood that technical applications upset the har-

---

* It would seem that plans already exist for coping [41] with the anticipated upheavals. At one Army think tank, the Institute for Land Combat, a team of experts—the Intelligence Threat Analysis Group (ITAG)—has identified at least 385 potential military conflicts which may come to pass by 1990. Of these, 145 could involve the United States. Of *those,* only ten have proven to be of sufficient interest that they required study in detail, with battle plans and tactics evolved through repeated "game" simulations. One of those ten is a war between the United States Army and American citizens on United States soil between 1990 and 1995. In a seemingly parallel study, the Office of Emergency Preparedness's Wartime Information Security Program (WISP), formerly headquartered at the University of Maryland under the command of Watergate's Colonel James McCord, has prepared "contingency plans" for canceling United States presidential elections, imposing censorship on the news media, and "rounding up" "radicals" and others who, under certain conditions, might constitute a "security" threat.

monious relationship between man and nature, or between man and himself. As a result, while their pursuit of knowledge continued without restraint, application of that knowledge was halted early on—except in matters that concerned the military. In war, the Greeks applied every technique they could get their hands on, at one point incinerating an invading fleet by arranging a set of concave mirrors in such a way that the sun's rays were intensified and projected with the heat of a blast furnace.

Whatever the actual shape of our collective future, large numbers of people are convinced that it will be uncongenial in the extreme. Technological breakdown (sudden or gradual), ecocatastrophe, behavioral fascism, nuclear duels, mass famines, economic chaos and resource depletion—the likelihood of any or all of these things coming to pass is open to debate. But *the fears* are real and they seem to derive from a single source: the technical carrot which Toffler dangles before us has taken on the aspect of *fatum*—one of our own creation, perhaps, but *fatum* nevertheless. At some point we stopped making history and allowed it to remake us.

The disease whose virus William Burroughs identifies as technology is one that causes impotence. We're caught up in a great national Gizmo and our pathology is such that we can do nothing except perhaps to improve the body through diet and exercise, to master the mind through meditation and analysis. Jogging through the parks, stuffing ourselves with Granola, listening for the sound of one hand clapping—all these are training exercises for a future Olympics in survival.

Our collective impotence before technique seems to inspire a defensive sleep (what Herman Kahn approvingly calls "the general relaxation") or an aggressive solipsism, a bathetic flexing of the physical and mental muscles. Half-baked or boiled Napoleons of one True Faith and another proclaim themselves everywhere—God, Prophet, Healer, and General. Never have we had so many, a nation of ultimate solutions. Covens clot in the vicinity of every ersatz insight; movements gather in persecuted queues that go nowhere; salvation boogies behind a thousand psychic corners, illuminated in the flash of specula, bathed in chants and primal screams. Existence becomes increasingly ceremonial, a dance to Reason, part homage, part exorcism.

As Nero might have said, "Different strokes for different folks."

AND THE DECADENT

V. The Unmaking of a Katakulchur

> And if anyone is threatened by advertising, air pollution, or the police, they should chant SMOKEY THE BEAR'S WAR SPELL:
>
> DROWN THEIR BUTTS
> CRUSH THEIR BUTTS
> DROWN THEIR BUTTS
> CRUSH THEIR BUTTS
>
> And SMOKEY THE BEAR will surely appear to put the enemy out with his vajra-shovel.
>
> *Smokey the Bear Sutra* [42]

1. "The Whole Earth Catalog"

It's in the context of technique, and its apocalyptic implications, that I've become obsessed with *The Whole Earth Catalog*,[43] admiring and despising it by turns and sometimes simultaneously.

It's the Last Will and Testament of the counterculture, its ultimate artifact. Between its covers is the material and spiritual biography of a generation that never was, a minority of cultural apocalyptics who congealed only long enough to create the illusion of "generation."

The Catalog is a hymn to consumption and technology. It's what the young had instead of the Vedas, and it seems likely that in some few hundred years, when we're unearthed by a future Schliemann, it will be studied with the intensity reserved for a Rosetta Stone—it, too, unlocks a culture.

No problem is too large for the Catalog to solve, no preoccupation too trivial for the book's concern. *Everything* is here, waiting only for the postage to be paid: enlightenment, socket wrenches, natural foods, survival tools, Alan Watts, methane digesters, *The Complete Encyclopedia of Needlework*, a pocket horn, an almanac, recipes, maps, China, the *I Ching*, and the Cannula Abortion.

Each is equally a commodity, a chapter in the Bible of a postindustrial cargo cult that *works*.

It's easy to disparage *The Whole Earth Catalog*. Its Sears, Roebuck approach to transcendence, its do-it-yourself survivalism and cloying sentimentality combine to make it a facile target for the critic. And yet, as a document, it's too important to dismiss on purely critical grounds. The Catalog is nothing less than a last-ditch attempt to consolidate all the fragmented aspects of a decade's millenarian discontents. It is a *Fiery Flying Roll* of sorts, an attempt to reorganize the countercultural diaspora into a movement, a social force with a single direction. Its operative theory seems to be that the young, like the old, have their roots in things rather than in places; what holds us together, it suggests, is a Social Contract that speaks less of "land and liberty" than of "ninety-day warranties," "replacement parts," and "the first ten thousand miles." We are what we use and will, therefore, be whatever it is that we may come to own.

Like *Mein Kampf* (which it in no other way resembles), the Catalog's task was an ambitious one—to unify a generation, a subnation of discontents, and, in doing so, to forge a movement. And yet, despite spectacular commercial successes, the Catalog seems to have been a failure. No movement has emerged from its pages, only another trend and scores of printed clones. What happened?

It's clear that the Catalog's failure was a function of the counterculture's degeneration: the publication simply arrived too late. The radical nostalgia that suffused its pages with pleas for what amounted to an actual return to the past, to the techniques and environments of long ago, was incapable of reaching a generation that, *as a generation,* had already been demolished.

2. Myth of Counterculture

The death, or disappearance, of the counterculture has been widely noticed (it could hardly be overlooked) but largely unexplained. Those who placed so much faith in its ascendancy, whose stake in the counterculture was as much professional as intellectual, have maintained a discreet silence on its demise. Their embarrassment seems to be that of someone who identifies "the wave of the future" only to realize later that the wave was an ebb tide.

And yet the counterculture deserves an obituary of length and respect. Youth was deified in the 1960s because hustlers and humanists alike glimpsed salvation at the countercultural shrine. When the worship ceased, the future had new reason to hold its breath—because yet another "last chance" had expired.

An autopsy of the dreams of the young would show that death resulted from a variety of ills that combined to cause a massive hemorrhaging of faith. Ultimately, the counterculture was found to be a myth, and skepticism killed it.

The *élan vital* of any myth derives from its credibility, its capacity to explain mysterious circumstances in such a way that people detect order, purpose, and direction in events that are otherwise baffling. Myth informs history with motivation and reassures us that events which are contiguous are also *connected* in a way that we can understand. In its explanatory role, myth fools us with an illusion that pretends to demystify the world. It is, in other words, a constructive (or comforting) hype.

The counterculture was such a hype. Its advocates (Roszak, Leary, Reich, Neville, and others) proposed the existence of a homogeneous American monolith—the counterculture—to explain the upheavals associated with the young during the 1960s. It was a successful myth: it inspired a sense of communality among the young, imparted an impression of purpose to otherwise confusing events, and generated a dynamic and optimistic view of the future. The anhydrous technocratic society, according to *OZ* editor Richard Neville, would give way to "a brotherhood of clowns; the lifestyle which unites a generation in love and laughter." [44] Only a short while after that prediction was made, however, the brotherhood of clowns had disbanded, trading in their false noses for rural isolation or a shot at what their elders swore was "the good life." The generation of "love and laughter" seemed to have joined the boobs and Babbits they'd earlier abhorred.

But did they really? Could any one of them ever go back to the foul-brained prescarcity formulations of the Fifties, to the second-car-second-home-second-wife romance of the Cold War? Had the counterculture reached *détente* with the larger society, or had it simply abandoned itself? Was there an accommodation between the generations, a surrender, or . . . or what?

It's here that myth's disservice becomes evident. In the end, it's found to explain nothing. Even worse, when the myth is finally abandoned, its skeleton lingers on, discouraging an inspection of the events which were its animus. The *impression* of understanding remains even after the actual explanation has been forgotten.

If we believe the myth of counterculture we're made to view the cultural upheavals of the 1960s as singularly irrelevant to the present and to the future. Supposedly set in motion by an alleged political aberration (the war in Vietnam), the counterculture is thought to have resigned its historical role when concord (or a semblance thereof) was achieved in Paris. The myth of counterculture further insists that the 1960s were uniquely ahistorical, a time that was born and died of its own contradictions. As a result, the only lessons to be learned from that period are military and political rather than cultural. As myth and label, therefore, the notion of "counterculture" isolates an important decade from our understanding.

In fact, of course, the war in Vietnam was not an aberration, an accident of foreign policy. America did not stumble into Asia, nor did the war spring fully grown from the forehead of a demon president. It grew, slowly and deliberately, over a period of years in the policy-making humus of the boardroom, think tanks, Pentagon, and banks. It was the product of perceptual elites whose domination of the contemporary scene had been decades in the making.

Moreover, the counterculture was never what it seemed to

be or even what it wanted to be. It was not homogeneous, not unidirectional, and not a response to the war in Vietnam. Its alliance with the New Left was mostly fictitious, a combination of cultural expedience and political propaganda. Indeed, for much of its life, the counterculture was not even particularly "counter," having early adopted a passive, withdrawn position vis-à-vis the larger society.

My interest in *The Whole Earth Catalog*, and in the tendency that inspired it, is neither that of the historian (for whom each is too recent) nor that of the journalist (for whom both are old news). As an apostate freak, my primary concern is with the future and with the certainty of our decay.

The 1960s were the watershed years of American culture, and they were ripe with signs and images of tomorrow. Divided along generational lines, trembling with war and with the hatred of war, it was a decade shaped by forces that were at once subtle and powerful. For the first time in history a generation came of age under the shadow of nuclear erasure and in the flickering light of television. Raised in the perceptual steambath of a mass culture, indoctrinated in the immediate gratification symbolized by electricity and in the disposable conveniences made possible by the assembly line and plastics, post-World War II babies were mutants of a technical environment that has no precedent.

Differences between the younger and older generations were deep and could not be diminished by topological metaphors that spoke calmly of temporary "gaps." The differences proceeded from profound discrepancies in the environmental heritage of each. Between one generation and the next there had been a technological transformation so thorough that the values and aspirations of each were nourished in literally different worlds. Periods of transition that had always separated innovations and insights were suddenly compacted into the brief span of years or months. Change had become the only constant, and the placid stream which Heraclitus claimed could not be violated twice was found to be a waterfall of brain-rinsing force.

The young, with their long hair and self-indulgent tilt toward metaphysics, came to be viewed as cultural aggressors, their elders seemingly oblivious to the fact that it was they, rather than their children, who were out of synch with a wired world. In a most peculiar way, the young were thought of as anachronisms, nineteenth-century humanists running "counter" to a cultural current that had already taken us to the moon. To many, it seemed as if the future would be dictated by a voice from the past, and to some that sounded like a good idea.

Those who were young in the Sixties, however, are now moving into the adolescence of their middle age, and the technical culture to which they ran "counter" is threatening to make this an American planet.

It won't do to dismiss the cultural upheavals of the past decade as isolated, self-limiting symptoms of a bygone era. Every historical climax results in a new act, and a careful scanning inevitably reveals that somewhere beneath the tumult of events the future is amply foreshadowed.

The Whole Earth Catalog—because it is the last message of a vanished tribe—is a particularly strategic clue to the recent past. Decoding that message requires an understanding of those who produced it and, in this case, that demands a refutation of the myth which enfolded them. To understand what happened in the Sixties and what's going on today (the Catalog tells all), it's necessary to exhume the bones of the counterculture. Once its myth is disposed of, we can have some clarity about our probable tomorrows. Otherwise, buried misconceptions will haunt us and the future will take us by surprise.

3. Beats and Freaks: From Job to Atlas to Noah

The counterculture is usually thought of as the evolutionary child of the Beat Generation. And yet the Beats had little in common with their supposed offspring. Indeed, in so far as the counterculture bore any direct relationship to their predecessors, it was one of repudiation rather than continuation.

To the Beats, Hip was the contemporary state of grace, a condition that was at once a style and a locale. As a style it was manifested in demurral, jazz, irony, and an oblique economy of movement, speech, and intention. As a place, it lay dead center between exhaustion and despair.

The Beats were not so much a generation as they were an alternative milieu, a subculture that apprenticed itself to the ghetto. It was a milieu that inhabited the claustrophobic space between two worlds, that of the oppressed and that of the straight, a space that separated universes without ever being a part of either. Concepts of revolution and reform were at the furthest peripheries of Beat awareness. Confrontation and engagement, the necessary manner of any *counter*culture or counterpolitic, seemed futile and absurd. Theirs was not merely an unwillingness to "fight City Hall" but a deeper reluctance that stemmed from the recognition that the American malaise was more than political—that the illness derived from the very springs of consciousness, from the glands which Luce fed and Disney milked.

To be Beat was to have surrendered all hope of salvation, to have accepted (with as much grace as possible) the certainty of one's own, and the world's, decay. In the face of what seemed to be a spiritual blackout, the most valued ability was a capacity to remain cool—to avoid panic, roll with it, and survive the dehumanizing banality of the times.

If the Beats recognized any dream of salvation, they identified it with experiential excess. To move easily between madness and exhaustion, to suffer and celebrate, to thrive at the extremities of existence, was the only path to . . . not salvation, but the most reasonable substitute, a kind of cathartic immunity. It was as if the spirit had to be burned down before one could be found worthy of the vision that would sanctify experience. It was in this context that Neal Cassidy sought to become pure Action, Jack Kerouac pursued the canonical image of his dead brother, and Allen Ginsberg poked pruriently in the earth for the ghosts of the fathers of Kansas.

The Beat ideal was a deliberate journey to the end of the road, and yet, in the hopelessness of that cul-de-sac, the Beats continued to search for the all-redeeming Vision. And that search took them *inward* on an exploration of their private biographies. There was no utopian Beat novel—the idea is a contradiction in terms. But there were dozens that reported back from the inner and outer precincts of individual satori. It was pure Blake: at the end of the road lay Roszak's end of the wasteland.

What the Beats pined for was an American dream that seemed to grow ever less accessible. In the quagmire of the 1950s, their despair proceeded from the belief that the American Babbitdom was viable and lasting. It seemed a despicable society, but one that "worked," and the fact that it seemed to work meant that there was no relief in sight. America stretched into the future, an infinitude of polyester Protestants.

The counterculture emerged as a rebuttal to the Beat Generation. Its rejection of the larger society was based upon the apocalyptic belief that it did *not* work, that, like Babylon, it was doomed. Where the Beats lived anecdotal lives of privacy and despair, the counterculture dreamed along social and utopian lines.

To come of age during the 1960s was to grow up with the conviction that the future would not be a mere extension of the present (as the Beats believed), but something basically different, an unrecognizable world. It doesn't matter very much that there was little agreement among the young on the nature of the world's impending transformation. Apocalyptics saw a future braised by nuclear disaster, ecological catastrophe, or technological disruption. Others imagined that an evolutionary leap in consciousness was under way, that the ultimate Intergalactic Dream Order would be established by technical means or spiritual high jumps. Those who inclined toward Marxian analysis anticipated a rationally arrived-at Millennium brought about by historical necessity and workers' disgruntlement.

Whatever the actual nature of the anticipated future, it

seemed certain to be an age in extremis—and only the young could deliver us from its evil. In this sense, their task was nothing less than the salvation of the world from catastrophe, and the creation of a transcendental (dis)order. I don't mean by this that every freak felt that the fate of the world depended upon him or her, but rather that each tended to agree that you were either "on the bus or off the bus," a part of the solution or a part of the problem.

Those who saw themselves as a part of the solution labored under a collective Atlas complex, whereas the Beats could be most closely identified with Job. Between Atlas and Job lay all the difference in the cosmos. While each had a kind of suffering in common with the other, that was their only meeting ground: Atlas was a god suffering for man; Job was a man who suffered for God.

The difference is explicit in the approach each group took toward their experiences. For the Beats, each life episode took place in the singular, and its relevance was of a personal sort. Within the counterculture, experience was "relevant" only in so far as it furthered a common vision or expressed a collective view—everything else was an "ego trip." The importance of, for instance, LSD rested upon the fact that it seemed capable of transporting the society as a whole to a new level of consciousness. The same was true of transcendental meditation, macrobiotics, and the other "systems" that flourished during the Sixties: each offered an experience that was infinitely repeatable by others; and, in sharing that experience (dropping acid or meditating), one engaged in a social act even if it took place in isolation.

The word "counterculture," however, is a misleading convenience at best. It suggests an aggressive, monolithic homogeneity among the young that did not, in fact, exist. Instead, what's called the counterculture was a loose agglomeration of sects, systems, and disengaged youths who didn't have enough in common to constitute a "movement" in any meaningful sense of the word. What the counterculture shared with itself was a set of rejections, a preoccupation with consciousness, a belief in exemplary action, and the certainty that the planet's fate rested upon the shoulders of the young. It did not constitute a "movement" because its numerous factions shared no single direction—only their collective Atlas complex.

If a single image of the counterculture is required it ought not to be that of an arrow aimed at the heart of the Plastic Society, but that of a wheel whose many spokes moved out in different directions from a central hub of disaffection. While the counterculturati were intolerant of the larger society, viewing middle age as a sin of commission, they were even less tolerant of one another. The macrobiotic, Weatherman, acid-head, Jesus freak and Whole Earth planner existed at iron removes from each other. While they all shared a belief that the world needed saving, each also claimed to have a monopoly on the Way.

The desperate nature of the counterculture's task was such that the relationships between different factions tended to be governed by a mutual fear and loathing. While alliances were sometimes possible between groups, antagonism was more typical. Examples of these internal confrontations abound in the takeovers of underground papers, in the frequent purges conducted in "community" institutions, and in the combat between different religious groups (those who've witnessed the fistfights—over begging turf—between the Jesus people and the Hare Krishna adherents along Telegraph Avenue will agree that the word "combat" isn't too strong).

The counterculture moved in a decidedly either/or world. What one group claimed was a part of the solution was, to a different faction, a part of the problem. Depending upon whom one talked to, the American malaise proceeded from a defect of the heart, mind, stomach, soul, vision, or genitalia. The analytical bias which the young shared was decidedly monistic, and the bias kept them apart—in fact, however, they were *all* right.

From its beginning, the counterculture was a conglomeration in transition. Not only did individual freaks tend to move from one metaphysic to another (e.g., from Zen to fundamentalism), but the nexus of dissent itself underwent profound changes in the course of the decade. Indeed, it seems that those changes are still going on.

If we look at the first and last days of the social explosion called counterculture, we find that a series of basic shifts takes place in the perspective of the young. The early Sixties seem to have been dominated by a dream of *collective* salvation, a sense of responsibility for others and for the society at large— what I've referred to as an Atlas complex. It was a time of tremendous hope when the young willingly bore the planet's future upon their shoulders, confident that institutions could be transformed, the cities remade, and new projects begun. That hope was mostly an urban phenomenon, rooted in the campus, in youth ghettos such as the Lower East Side, and in communities such as those in Berkeley and the Haight-Ashbury. If any single perspective dominated the young at that time, it was that of the mystic in search of a new reality. Books such as the *I Ching* and Leary's translation of the *Tibetan Book of the Dead* achieved enormous popularity. Drugs tended to be used as a means of exciting consciousness, encouraging visions, and as the catalyst in a form of ritual-sharing: joints were passed from one person to another with the solemnity that Catholics reserve for Holy Communion. "Enlightenment" was an almost public goal.

By the end of the decade, however, all of this was reversed. The Atlas complex had degenerated into a Noah fetish: salvation (of the world/society) was replaced by a preoccupation with *survival*—the catchword of the Seventies. It matters very little that "survival" in the future is today thought to be a function of superior consciousness (of God or of tools) rather than one of superior physical strength. It is still a matter of Darwin's "fittest" prevailing over the weaker. The urban identity of the early counterculture is similarly overturned in the transitions of the decade, as the freaks abandoned the cities for a more congenial countryside. The initial mysticism of the young is almost entirely repudiated by the rational approach of *The Whole Earth Catalog,* a swan-song sourcebook that provides "access to tools" and implicitly affirms the superiority of reason over belief. Technical sophistication—a knowledge of carpentry, pottery, computers, or agriculture—today occupies the same position in the minds of the young that a knowledge of arcana formerly did. Similarly, the role of drugs, and the kinds of drugs used, have also changed. When drugs are not avoided in the interests of the body's natural equilibrium, they tend to be taken for the purpose of tranquilizing consciousness rather than awakening it; in this regard, alcohol, downers, and Quaalude have largely replaced the use of hallucinogens and speed.

Obviously, generalizations like the above will contain numerous exceptions, especially when, as in this case, they're applied to something as diverse and multidirectional as the "counterculture." The shifts within a political movement are relatively easy to define: spokesmen are carefully identified, position papers issued, and actions taken collectively. In view of this, a history of, for instance, the New Left would be at least conccivable, whereas a history of the "counterculture" would have to be a collection of minihistories subsumed under a general notion of cultural upheaval. Nevertheless, in so far as the young shared a common identity in the Sixties, and a common transformation as the decade progressed, it seems to have proceeded along the general lines that I've indicated.

4. Tabular Transitions; Millenarian Discontents

A table illustrating those transitions, with the middle stage sketched in, makes it clear that the counterculture was dynamic rather than static, and that it went through at least three distinct phases. It's curious that, in their progression from mysticism to magic to tools, the young seem to have acted out the anthropologist's view of human history; what this probably means is simply that the young's initial rejection

A TABLE OF COUNTERCULTURAL TRANSITIONS

ESTIMATED TIME:	(1962)	(1965)	(1968)	(1971)	(1974)
SUBCULTURE:	Beat	Counterculture	Counterpolitic	Alternative Culture	Anticulture
MYTHIC FIGURE:	Job	Atlas	Che	Noah	Narcissus
FOCUS:	Salvation (of the soul)	Salvation (of the world)	Salvation (of Vietnam)	Survival (of the family)	Survival (of the self)
ORIENTATION:	Pantheism Transcendentalism	Idealism	Socialism	Pragmatism	Solipsism
AFFINITY:	Poetry	Philosophy	Scripture	Blueprints	Entertainment
EMPHASIS:	Travel	Play	Ritual	Expertise	
ASSOCIATION:	Generation	Movement	Faction	Enclave	Isolation
			Ritual-sharing	Hoarding	
TRIPS:	*Howl* *Coney Island of the Mind*	*The Psychedelic Experience* *I Ching*	*Lord of the Rings* *Dune*	*Stranger in a Strange Land*	*Whole Earth Catalog*
BIAS:	Experience	Philosophy	Fantasy	"Common Sense"	Cynicism
LOCALES:	The City	The Campus	Youth ghetto (e.g., Haight)	Retreat (e.g., Esalen)	Living room
DRUG:	Booze Grass	Acid Speed	Downers	Smack Alcohol	Quaalude
TENDENCY:		Aggression	Passivity Withdrawal	Paranoia	
INTENTION:		Hegemony	Coexistence No social intention		
MUSIC:	Jazz (dissonance)	Beatles (harmony)	Rolling Stones (aggression)	Alice Cooper (death)	None
PERSPECTIVE:	Apocalyptic	Millenarian		Radical Nostalgia	Radical Decadence

of the larger society was total—that they literally started all over again and, in the space of a decade, worked their way back to the present. That it took ten years for the counterculture to return full circle to its original point of departure is evidence of its failure. It went a long way, only to get nowhere.

As for the table itself, it shares the somewhat arbitrary nature of the counterculture: ideas and trends are artificially segregated in a way that only approximates reality. Things were never so clear-cut with the heterogeneous young, who mixed their fetishes and inclinations with the same enthusiasm that they mixed their drugs. Still, the table has a relaxed utility in that it offers a chronological perspective of the meandering consciousness of the decade's cultural freaks. While it probably wouldn't hold up too well if applied to the experience of any single person, it seems a fair description of hippies as a group. Another objection that might be raised against the table is that significance is attached to the success of particular books which were, after all, published in a certain, but arbitrary, order. The young could not very well have flipped for *Dune* prior to its publication, and so one may wonder why it seems important that its popularity was subsequent to that of the *I Ching,* and why those two books should be seen as part of a trend. Obviously, the table's construction rests upon the assumption that the popularity of particular commodities (such as rock bands and books) is not accidental, but a measure of the degree to which they confirm or reflect the desires, or cultural needs, of the people who buy them. In other words, the latter-day success of *The Whole Earth Catalog* could not have occurred five years earlier because the trend that it ultimately exploited was not yet present. That is, cultural trends are not *inspired* by commodities, but become identifiable through the popularity of commodities (e.g., our nostalgia is not a result of watching *The Waltons*—*The Waltons'* success simply makes our nostalgia apparent).

The purpose of the table is therefore modest—to make explicit the internal logic of the counterculture's transitions, to illustrate its flow toward the present. The shift in emphasis from salvation to survival, idealism to mechanism, city to country, Eastern philosophy to Western fundamentalism, and from mysticism to technical expertise identifies the young's evolution from an aggressive minority seeking hegemony to a passive subculture content with an alternative coexistence.

I won't belabor the table's usefulness any further except to note that the motive of world salvation is not very much different from that of personal survival. Both are informed by the anticipation of an impending disaster. Each is rooted in the apocalyptic vision.

And it's precisely this vision that provides the counterculture with its historical context (and future import).

As I indicated in Chapter I, the counterculture factions of the 1960s conform in extraordinary detail with the criteria which historians use to identify revolutionary millenarian sects. Those sects emerged in areas and situations whose characteristics were virtually uniform. When overpopulation occurred in conjunction with rapid economic and social change, the foundations for millenarian upheaval were laid. Whether that upheaval actually manifested itself depended upon the occurrence of some unusual event outside the ordinary experience of the people. In Europe, the Plague served as just such a catalyst: it struck indiscriminately and its nature was such that, as fact or threat, nothing could be done about it.

When the social and economic turbulence of an age is italicized by such a catastrophe, people of all classes gravitate toward membership in millenarian groups. Those groups, whose task is nothing less than the transformation of the world, have always tended to be hierarchical elites—with a holy figure, prophet or deity, at the top, and the initiates gathered at his feet. There's little doctrinal variation. Almost all hold that, after a period of blood and slaughter, war, plague, and famine, an egalitarian utopia will be established to last a thousand years or more. The mighty will be laid low, the poor elevated, the Antichrist and his servants purged from the globe. Most such groups believe that the Millennium will be established through the direct intervention of God, by way of a Second Coming, but others place their faith more directly in the masses themselves.

However precise these characteristics may be, they're nevertheless sufficiently flexible to include the most savage blood cult and the most pacific tribe.

In contemporary terms, it's clear that Hitler exploited both the historic conditions and the latent millenarian sentiments of the German people in his rise to power; it wasn't a coincidence that his propaganda spoke of a Reich that would last "a thousand years." And then, too, his use of the Jews as scapegoats and collective Antichrist had ample precedent in history.

The same conditions that have generated millenarian activity in the past have been gathering momentum for more than fifty years in the United States. The sweep of technological change is such that the society is transformed on a decade-to-decade basis. Traditional social patterns and supports (marriage, the family, the neighborhood, and the political ward) disintegrate under the impact of technical innovations such as the automobile, the Pill, the skyscraper, and cybernetics. Skills on which people depend for their livelihoods are rapidly rendered obsolete as more efficient means are found and proliferate. Cultural institutions (e.g., the nightclub, theater, and "sewing circle") are transformed or destroyed by mechanisms such as the television and the telephone.

Some, even most, of these changes may be good in themselves, but their cumulative force is disorienting and widely resented. There is a dilating sense of helplessness and a prevailing feeling that "we can't go on like this," that the national Gizmo is racing out of control and certain to crash.

That sensibility is articulated by all the individuals, groups, and organizations mentioned earlier (in Chapter I), but the same apocalyptic view has begun to infiltrate *popular* entertainments—suggesting that the view has found sufficient acceptance to constitute a commercially viable commodity: America *buys* the prospect of disaster. And not only in such "disaster films" as *The Towering Inferno, The Poseidon Ad-*

venture, and *Earthquake* (which have renewed a profitable Hollywood genre)—America also buys disaster in its better entertainments, in the work of such writers as Walker Percy, Kurt Vonnegut, Jr., Robert Stone, Rudolph Wurlitzer, Norman Mailer, Thomas Pynchon, and William Burroughs.

Today, premonitions of collective catastrophe border upon the banal.

If we compare contemporary and past millenarian thought, we find few significant differences. Perhaps the only unique aspect of present-day eschatology is its embrace of science. Formerly, the apocalyptic vision was predicated entirely upon religious faith. Today, utopia and the end of the world are equally accessible to the analytical imagination: the planetary disasters anticipated by the Club of Rome, and the fascist "utopia" prescribed by B. F. Skinner, are merely secularized echoes of hallucinations reported by the faithful of the Middle Ages. They are, in other words, rational possibilities that have fantastic precedents.

Virtually every faction of the counterculture had its medieval doppelgänger. Similarly, the cultural characteristics of the counterculture were reenactments of millenarian days gone by. The voluntary poverty of the young, their identification with the poor and the despised, their transcience, communalism, egalitarianism, and *pro publico* elitism are reflections of attitudes that were epidemic in the past. The same holds true for the Great Guru Search (culminating in Manson or Leary, it makes no difference), the contempt of the young for material things, their mixing of doctrines, rejection of convention, and alternating visions of Heaven and Hell. Indeed, the parallels are so close that one can even see a similarity between the ancient millenarians' identification of the Pope as Antichrist and the rhetoric which the young used to describe both Lyndon Johnson and Richard Nixon. Paranoia and the nurture of conspiracy theories are equally central to both the countercultural young and the millenarians of yesteryear, the only difference being that the State has largely taken over the role formerly accorded to Satan.

The anxieties of the Middle Ages are not much different from those of the present. The effects of mercantilism and sheep pasturage upon the manor communities are paralleled by the impacts of technical innovation upon the cities, neighborhoods, and factories.

Earlier, I noted that collective anxiety and social turmoil are not in themselves enough to spawn discontents of a millenarian nature. What's needed is a catalytic event, a special circumstance. In the 1960s that event seems to have been the war in Vietnam, and its cutting edge was the draft. When the draft ended, the counterculture seemed to lose its energy, much as the millenarian sects of the past rose and fell with the comings and goings of the Plague. If a date is to be placed upon the tombstone of the counterculture, it would have to be the day in which a volunteer army was established. On that morning, the aggressive drive of the young for hegemony dwindled to a cultural détente with the larger society. Ending the draft effectively transformed the counterculture into an alternative subculture. It was as if the Plague had been ended by a legislative decree.

Obviously, the foundations, or substrata, of the period's discontent did not crumble with the termination of the draft. All that's changed is that this particular manifestation of "plague" has (at least temporarily) vanished from the scene. It seems certain that it will return, perhaps in a different form —and when it does it will create yet another millenarian outburst. What form the future Plague will take is uncertain. All that's clear is that it will have to be something extraordinary and beyond popular control: the most likely candidates seem to be serious scarcities generated by economic malfeasance, technical breakdown, or the exhaustion of strategic natural resources—or even an actual plague (of cancer, perhaps) caused by ecological bungling. Any of these would be sufficient to create a new "counterculture"—that is, a nexus of millenarian sects—although future upheavals are unlikely to be tied to a particular age group.

Indeed, no less an authority on the future than Herman

Kahn predicts the reemergence of such sects. In his Hudson Institute study, *The Year 2000*, Kahn writes: [45]

> Among primitive societies placed in situations of great stress, the phenomenon of redemptive mass movements has been most nakedly magical and naive. The totalitarian movements of modern Europe have (or had) highly sophisticated rationales, although their ultimate objectives defied reason. But it could be argued that there is a common impulse in all of these, that the kind of social crises that produced them will deepen in Asia during the next thirty years, not be reduced, and to expect that we have seen the end of such movements even in the advanced societies of the West must constitute an act of faith in human reason and progress rather than an argument from evidence.

(It should be noted that Kahn's description of these movements as "totalitarian," and his associating them with "primitive societies," is unnecessarily restrictive.)

5. Ebbing of "The Plague"; New Left Co-optation

Millenarian sects are held together by the centripetal force of extraordinary events (e.g., the bubonic plague or the draft), even as the larger society is shattered by those same events. The hegemony that the millenarians seek, however, is rarely found. Often it happens that the negative animus which motivates the sects disappears: thus, the ebbing of the Plague in the Middle Ages, and the ending of the draft in the Sixties, struck at the motivation of millenarians in both eras. But disappearances of this sort do not destroy healthy movements, only flawed ones.

While the termination of the draft delivered the *coup de grâce* to the counterculture, more powerful forces had already sickened it to the point of death. Long before the draft ended, the young entered upon a series of decadent transitions (from Atlas to Noah to Narcissus) from which they could never have recovered.

What sapped the counterculture's early strength, reducing it to the eventual passivity of an alternative subculture, was the reciprocating sclerosis of a myopic Left and the media. Of the two, the Left's role was the most blunt and calculated. Exploiting Vietnam as an opportunity for recruitment, the Left sought to co-opt the counterculture, to reforge the latter's cultural discontents into the political framework ordained by Marx a century earlier.

It was an awkward, painful fit. The discontents of the (mostly middle-class) kids sprang from characteristics peculiar to the twentieth century's second half. The malaise that inspired the youth revolts of the Sixties had more to do with the spirit's rust that with any material dysfunction. It had to do with the autism engendered by an increasingly technical environment; with the anxieties sponsored by constant change; with the ersatz nature of mass-kulchural experience; * with the social impotence imposed on each individual by the society's technical integration and complexity; and with the saturative aspect of a wired society whose ubiquity affords no refuge and little relief. These cultural conditions, rather than the political dislocations of *kapital,* comprised the substratum of the young's discontent—a discontent galvanized by the catalytic events in Southeast Asia.

If the counterculture had been singularly American, it would be easy to mistakenly attribute its emergence and decline to the ebb and flow of the war in Vietnam—to insist that the war was the sum and source of the young's disaffection rather than, as I suggest, merely the cutting edge of a broader and very deep discontent. In fact, however, the coun-

---

* The substitution of the letter "k" for "c" in certain words was a commonplace in countercultural writing; everyone understood that the letter "k" indicated something bad about the noun which it infiltrated, though few could say exactly what. Ezra Pound was probably the first to make the substitution (in *Kulchur*), but the counterculture's use of the letter seems to have originated with the Dutch Provo movement. Robert Jasper Grootvelt began painting the letter "K" on cigarette advertisements in Amsterdam during 1964. It was an abbreviation of the Dutch spelling of the word "cancer." Later, the "K" was applied to a broader conception of the society's carcinogenic aspects, and eventually made its way to "Amerika."

terculture was not singularly American: virtually every technically developed society in the West underwent the same, or very similar, upheavals without the excuse of Vietnam. In Holland, England, France, Spain, Mexico, Argentina, West Germany, Japan, Brazil, Scandinavia, Greece, and Italy, the young regurgitated the culture their societies proposed. In each of those countries, native countercultures emerged.

What were the "catalytic events"? For the most part, they seem to have been a combination of sudden affluence and rapid technicization, a combination that effectively de-Europeanized and de-orientalized the countries in question, severing the people from their history and the young from the old. In Japan, Greece, and West Germany additional circumstances intervened: the imposition of, respectively, official apostasy, fascism, and partition.

If one wanted to estimate the number of "freaks" native to any particular country, all that was necessary was to observe the technical indicators; generally, the number of freaks was directly proportional to the number of television sets, automobiles, and radios in their homelands.

A perverse nationalism led most reporters, regardless of their other biases, to assume that (as with everything else) the counterculture began in the United States—that the young of other countries were merely imitating an American lunatic fringe or, depending on one's sympathies, a perceptual vanguard from the States. In fact, however, authentic countercultural movements appeared in other countries at about the same time, or prior to, their emergence in the United States. In Holland, for instance, the Provos completely anticipated the style and essence of their American counterparts and, in fact, virtually ordained the Yippies.

For the most part, the American Left ignored the international character of counterculture, preferring to view the youth upheavals as a direct, if eccentric, response to the war—and not much more than that. That viewpoint made politicization (a cynical synonym for co-optation) feasible and defensible, and preserved the chaste intellectual categories of the Left—

class analysis based upon economic argument and a dubious animism applied to History with a capital H. Thus, the cultural agitation of the young came to be seen as an essentially bourgeois outburst for political reform, a disaffection that might be reshaped into an even more constructive revolution by the Book.

This was the myopia of the Left in full flower. In the arrogant takeovers of underground newspapers, in the "politicization" of cultural institutions such as food co-ops, and in the Leninists' blatant subversion of organizations such as SDS, the Marxist Left demonstrated its appalling bad faith and dogmatism. For a hundred years or more the children of Marx apparently learned nothing but refinements on the theme of internal purges and new ways of defusing revolts which fell outside their longed-for monopoly on revolution.

Marx himself would have blanched to witness the counter-revolution carried out in his name. As he wrote in the *Eighteenth Brumaire of Louis Bonaparte:* [46]

> The tradition of all dead generations weighs like a nightmare on the brain of the living. And just when they seem to be engaged in revolutionizing themselves and things, in creating something entirely new, precisely in such epochs of revolutionary crisis they anxiously conjure up the spirits of the past to their service and borrow from them names, battle slogans and costumes in order to present the new scene of world history in this time-honored disguise and borrowed language. Thus Luther donned the mask of the Apostle Paul, the Revolution of 1789 to 1814 draped itself alternately as the Roman Republic and the Roman Empire, and the Revolution of 1848 knew nothing better than to parody, in turn, 1789 and the tradition of 1793 to 1795. . . . The social revolution of [the present] cannot draw its poetry from the past, but only from the future. It cannot begin with itself before it has stripped off all superstition in regard to the past. . . . In order to arrive at its content, the revolution . . . must let the dead bury their dead. There the phrase went beyond the content; here the content goes beyond the phrase.

So it is that the contemporary epoch of revolutionary crisis, if that's what all this messianic ferment is about, is draped in the curious costume of the October Revolution of 1917. In a country that hasn't had a proletarian majority for more than a hundred years, loony Leninists, and not a few Marxists, continue to speak of a "proletarian dictatorship"—which is exactly what it would be. The prole, someone without property who has nothing but his labor to sell, has vanished with the advent of mechanization, automation, and credit. Where he has not wholly disappeared from the scene, he remains as an anomaly whose curious status as an endangered species is likely to be rewarded by scholarships for his children to attend Harvard, and offers to write syndicated columns for the Hearst press. Technology has transformed America from a country to a Gizmo, an increasingly classless society, a Wad of gray-collar drones.

The Left's attempt to shoehorn the contemporary situation into the glass boot of nineteenth-century dialectical materialism would be bathetic if it were not so destructive of valuable energies. As it is, the observations of Marx are devalued by the tactics of his followers, by their paranoid defense of his scripture in the face of contradicting facts, and by their infatuation with centralized organization in a country whose cultural evisceration is largely the result of the centralization of power.

The political economics of Marx are simply inadequate as an explanation of the American present or as a program for its future. The labor unions and the electoral parties, in which he understandably placed so much faith, are sufficiently powerful to ameliorate the circumstances in which people live and toil, but are incapable of treating the *condition* of the people—which, as I've argued, is incurable. Cybernetics, electronics, mass education—the entirety of mass culture and its implications—were largely unanticipated by Marx and, with the exception of Marcuse and a handful of anarchists, have proven enigmatic to his heirs.

Today, the worker's primary responsibility—his *work*—is increasingly that of consumption, rather than production. To "seize the means of production" becomes increasingly irrelevant (because that's not where the power lies), and self-destructive (because the interruption entailed by such a seizure would, in view of our technical dependence, result in a breakdown of Humpty-Dumpty proportions). The public's appetite for material things, rather than its labor, constitutes the people's contemporary "kapital": it's this appetite that keeps the economy running and it is, in terms of political power, all that the worker has left to sell. To regain a measure of control, it would be necessary for the people to, as it were, "seize the means of consumption"—to obtain mastery over one's wants, the industries (e.g., advertising and education) which regulate them, and the currency apparatus (e.g., credit systems) which perpetuates and reinforces those wants. But we're as likely to see this happen as we are to see a blizzard in Kuwait.

The cultural malaise afflicting the people is an entirely different matter. The first generation to be conceived and raised to maturity within the mass-cultural lagoon rejected that culture with all the force that it could muster (for a while, at least). If the revolts of the 1960s hadn't been channeled into the futile politics of the Left, it seems possible that a real transformation of the society might have resulted—a "revolution," or metamorphosis, of expectations, an assault upon the very fabric and seams of the culture rather than an attack upon the culture's reflection in the political apparatus. Indeed, if one is inclined toward conspiracy theories, it may be tempting to believe that the answer to the question—Why are we in Vietnam?—is that our presence there offered an irrelevant Left the fulcrum needed to co-opt a truly dangerous mass phenomenon. (As with all conspiracy theories, this one wildly overestimates the perception and chutzpah of the bad guys.) Certainly, in the absence of the Vietnam diversion, the anti-authoritarian young would not have tolerated the rhetoric, puritanism, materialism, centralism, or totalitarian style of the Left. Everything we know about the counterculture's biases—

its lust for spontaneity, self-indulgence, irrationality, and mystical bent—suggests that it stood in natural opposition to the rational millenarianism of Marx.

6. Collective Narcissism: The Media Warp

The destruction of the counterculture cannot be wholly attributed to the Left, however. At least as devastating to the young was the media's impact on their identity. At some point in the transition from a counterculture to an alternative culture, the young passed through a warp of narcissism from which they could never have recovered.

Narcissism is a condition of infatuation, *a falling in love with reflection*—a mirror image of the self, perhaps, or of something else. When the reflection which obsesses one is an image or idea of one's self, one's narcissism is private and decadent (it being understood that "decadence" is a condition that has no necessary connection to "degeneration" or even, for that matter, to "decay"). When the obsessive reflection is of something *other than* the self—e.g., a movement—our narcissism is collective and inevitably wasting.

Collective narcissism entails an excruciating awareness, a dedication of the mind's faculties to the details of a thing which, because it is a mere reflection, is inherently insubstantial. And, because that reflection is of something other than the self, our infatuation is impersonal: our emotional investment in the image is unrepaid—it takes, but returns no dividends, and is therefore necessarily, and utterly, exhausting. Unless we become bored with the image, unless we learn to love it less than wholly, we become emptier and emptier, drifting toward an absolute vacuum of self, an Angeladavis of inexistence. Whatever personal remnants endure do so as contradictions, quirks, and flaws in the image and its medium. While it lasts, the collective narcissist's infatuation represents a surrender to the absolute authority of the image: it enslaves him, bending his personality to its warp, compelling an unrelenting conformity. And because the image is of something other than the self, autonomy recedes to the vanishing point; eventually, the collective image is the only source of "private" experience—we live through *it*. We live not at all.

Collective narcissism is an impersonation, a pretense at being. It is a condition that is at once monstrous and *ludic*—as if Charlton Heston were to cast himself in the role of Technology.

But this is perhaps overly abstract: narcissism, in its collective aspect, is merely consciousness carried to a pathological extreme and focused upon a point of insubstantiality. It is a love of fucking ghosts.

In the United States, ghost fucking is sponsored by the mass media—news, entertainment, and advertising—which compel us to observe, with the most meticulous attention, the details and sweep of our collective condition. I say "compel" because the observance is practically unavoidable and the images are, therefore, contagious. Only the most heroic attempt at absolute isolation will succeed in insulating anyone from the barrage of news, propaganda, and amusement that's directed every moment at everyone. The air trembles with dee-jay jive, music, weather reports, and ball scores. Living rooms glow with jokes and chatter, advertisements and announcements. The countryside is studded with billboards, gargantuan logos separating the trees with pitches for Levi's, underwear, and TWA. We know so much about each other, and so little about ourselves! Our triumphs and disasters are collectively experienced: the scene of the crime, the path of the tornado, the site of the new monument—each is visited and revisited, transmitted and received, over and over again. It is a net of reflected events, a corridor of mirrors in which even our intimacies are edited, standardized, and conveyed: warbling stomachs, indiscreet odors, throbbing heads, "irregularity," and ring around the collar, each is a node in our collective attention, a dazzle in our subconscious. The sophistication of our technology, its specialization and mechanical particularities, creates an environment of such complexity that we're physically paralyzed without one another. Our common stains and pains, our repeated glimpses into the glass gizzard of the Alka-Seltzer effigy, connect us on an even more visceral level.

Given all this, it would seem that homogeneity would be our curse, and yet the opposite is the case. Majorities have virtually ceased to exist (which, in so far as a working democracy is concerned, is similar to the plight of an automobile with square wheels). Threatened by the cultural Mix-Master of the media, we submit to its agitation with only the greatest reluctance. Our attention to ourselves is so constant, our narcissism so spellbound, that we develop an almost Proustian discrimination about each other and about what's left of our selves. Our "secret" languages—the dialects of blacks, cops, hippies, and hoods—are not at all secret, but the lingua franca of our entertainments. Categories convenient, or sufficient, in another age—black and white, rich and poor—are no longer adequate; like the socialists of Italy, we require access to a hundred different parties, and even they will not hold us all. We know too much about each other, or hold too firmly a bowdlerized notion of ourselves. It is as if all our mysteries were being constantly explained away, and what remains is nothing but a harried solipsism.

The media's destruction of the counterculture, a mere mote in our collective disintegration, took place without malice. The extraordinary attention paid to the young—their *newsworthiness*—demolished the spontaneity of their styles and acts. By the time the young hit the cover of *Time* (in 1967), they'd already begun to imitate an idea of themselves, to impersonate a collective reflection (interpreted by CBS). Suddenly (it seemed) the young had a context, a name, an explanation, and a standard to which their nonconformity was made to conform: the media told them who they were (or were supposed to be), what they wanted, and how they acted, and so there was no longer any need or way for the young to seek their own answers to the questions their behavior posed.

Their collective infatuation with images of each other demolished the autonomy of each individual and rendered private experience increasingly inaccessible. Because that infatuation was collective, and therefore "impersonal," it was necessarily exhausting—a lethal drain that could only be plugged by boredom, or avoided by means of defection from the image.

Just as Madison Avenue co-opted the slang of the young, the Garment District adopted their styles. Levi's and H.I.S., Ma Griffe and Hertz battled the competition with the slogans, catchwords, comics, and calligraphy of the young. What began as a rebellion became an industry. Falling in love with the ghost of Generation, materialized within the Toob and Paper, the young underwent the same decline as Alexander.

Collective narcissism, consciousness that passeth understanding, afflicted every aspect of their lives. What had begun as an unaffected response, a natural reaction, to the circumstances of the time degenerated into a social obligation. The spontaneity of the early Sixties evolved, in mid-decade, into a calculated perversity, a succession of increasingly limp wows. The casual dress of the early years, a rejection of fashion itself, became fashionable in itself. According to the prevailing influence of either the Left or Madison Avenue, the young clothed themselves in the alternating current of terminal peasant-envy and gypsy-fop: the drab uniform of work shirt and jeans (SEE! ELLIOTT GOULD IN *GETTING STRAIGHT*) shared the countercultural streets with a studied garishness, an explosion of psychedelic patches, bangles, spangles, and beads (THRILL TO! PETER FONDA IN *EASY RIDER*). In the same way, rock declined from the driving harmonies of the Beatles, the perceptual trellises of Dylan, into the posturing cock-rock of the Rolling Stones, the grotesqueries of Alice Cooper: music, once the highest expression of the vitality and art of the young, became a subsidiary to mere performance.

Even in their conceptual transitions, the young's unraveling was evident. The early mysticism, the preoccupation with Zen and difficult Eastern philosophies, gave way to an obsessive fascination with spiritual kitsch—ritual magic, Maharaj Ji, and the ooga-booga of Christian fundamentalism.

By 1970, the counterculture was an artifact in disarray, its sympathizers bored with their own imagery, and brought together only occasionally by nostalgic and narcissistic pseudo events such as the smoke-in, be-in, and rock festival. In a sense, those gatherings—which consisted largely of aimless milling punctuated by flash violence and the odd fuck—were honest: that was precisely what the scene had become. Bad music and boredom amid the mud and litter of a new decade.

7. The Sears, Roebuck of Postindustrial Cataclysm

The ubiquity of the media in the United States suggests that future social movement will, like the countercultural factions, be stimulated to a debilitating narcissism. As each such movement emerges, the television's eye raises it, quite rapidly, to celebrity status. And once that happens, the celebrity-movement has no choice but to play the part assigned to it. Imitating itself, performing in its own image, the movement's evolution is aborted and paralyzed. No longer dynamic, it ceases to become. It goes nowhere. It is not a movement at all. In this way, the media reduce contemporary history to a series of freeze-frames.

There's an obvious danger in this. By sapping the vitality of new social forces, the media exert a terminally conservative influence on the society—even when their "content" is "liberal" or (God save the mark) "revolutionary." While some movements are unquestionably destructive, and others culturally regenerative, all are more or less newsworthy. Thus, the good and the bad are equally denatured, and the *status quo* perpetuated. As a force for stagnation, the media serve as a kind of cultural formaldehyde.

Which returns us—not quite *ipso facto*—to *The Whole Earth Catalog*.

It is the embodiment of the recognition that the society is entered upon an unrelieved stagnation or disastrous course, that the only paths open to us lead nowhere or "down the tubes."

The Catalog's obsession with "survival tools" and its frontier eschatology demonstrate that even apocalypse can serve as the mandala of a new culture.

All catalogs have certain things in common. They are, for instance, responses to isolation, whether the customer's own or the manufacturer's. The early Montgomery Ward catalogs were designed as a mail-order solution to the separateness of rural and urban America. Their purpose was to bring underconsuming hicks into the consumer mainstream of the country and, in that way, to extend the buying habits of urbanites into the American heartland. The eclectic content of the early catalogs was a recognition of the diversity of our material wants and needs.

The Whole Earth Catalog, apart from its obvious eccentricities of style, differs from the Sears, Roebuck variety in strategic ways. It's not the intention of Stuart Brand and the catalogue's other creators to stimulate the buying impulses of their readers, but to bring about a convergence in consciousness. That convergence is accomplished by directing their readers' attention to selected commodities that have obvious cultural implications. *The Whole Earth Catalog*, in other words, seeks to suspend the cultural isolation of its readers by uniting them in the consideration of strategic commodities; more traditional catalogs seek merely to compensate for the purely physical isolation of their readership. Like the windmill described in the catalog, the Bar-B-Ques and riding lawnmowers advertised in the Monkey Ward opus embody a social ethic with a discrete set of values. The publications differ, however, in that the ethic advanced by Montgomery Ward (or Sears or Macy's) is tacitly held by all its readers, and taken for granted by all—whereas the Whole Earth people must engage in a more polemical, heuristic editorial task. The latter's readers have no single ethic in common, and it's therefore necessary to make explicit those values which the commodities reify. The result is a persuasive encyclopedia of things in conflict, a discourse among objects. If *The Whole Earth Catalog* had done nothing else but give voice to the inanimate parts of the world, it would still be an important book. But it does more.

Perusing a catalog is a kind of meditation upon what the world has to offer—which is to say, it's a way of discovering what we want as well as what we need. The real value of a catalog is its way of bringing about a kind of recognition, of creating or identifying wants that we didn't know we had. It is also a meditation upon our own condition, forcing us to evaluate what we can *afford* (financially, culturally, ecologically, and even metaphysically). By telling us what we want, a good catalog tells us who we are and where we're going. *The Whole Earth Catalog* is superb in these respects.

It is, more than anything else, a book to be *read*, not skimmed. While its ostensible business is to provide "access to tools," its real function is to provide access to those ideas of which the "tools" are mere symbols. While the purpose of most catalogs is to generate mail-order business, the business of *The Whole Earth Catalog* is to generate ideas about values. Certainly the Portola Institute isn't trying to become the Sears, Roebuck of the postindustrial cataclysm.

Like its predecessors, *The Whole Earth Catalog* is a premier example of what Siegfried Giedion calls "anonymous history." If we examine it closely, we can learn more about the past (and therefore more about the future) than from any self-conscious pronouncements. More than any other document available to us now, the catalog reifies the confusion and discontent of the recent past and present.

As a stream-of-consciousness meditation whose symbols and images are unified by their common stature as commodities, *The Whole Earth Catalog* is the closest thing we have to the Great American Novel. Its central character is the reader, a consumer in search of himself; its theme is survival in a hostile and precarious environment; and its style is both polemical and critical, a conglomeration of reviewed possibilities.

Nothing could be more appropriate to the age.

VI. Expatriate Rust

1. An Aside

The preceding pages have been devoted, almost entirely, to a diagnosis of the times, an analysis of a condition that's *collective*. In the course of that examination I've tried to show that, for reasons stated and implied, our situation is Incurable. The society seems bent upon a most rapid decline, devolving toward a fascist metastate, an antiutopia of technocratic barbarism. All that stands between that state's realization and the present is the probability of an industrial, economic, or ecological cataclysm—an intervention which, while it may "cure" the disease, seems likely to kill the patient in the process.

Usually, diagnosis is followed by prescription: there seems to be an obligation to balance one's negative judgments with a regimen designed to remedy the malaise that's been identified. When the condition is Incurable, however, the prescription must be limited. Since the patient can't be saved, the physician's arsenal is limited to anesthesia, placebos, and, perhaps, to some means of deferring the inevitable. In the present case, we have numerous means for ameliorating the pains associated with the disease: popular entertainments, mass delusions, religious convictions—the cupboard is stuffed with analgesics. While we have no known means of slowing what amounts to our destiny, we do have an armory of placebos, delusive procedures which, while having no substantial effect on the malaise itself, do no harm and may provide some comfort (e.g., the political process, which—while having no effect on technical evolution—fosters the illusion that we have some control over our fate, that we're *coping*).

Having said that, there's still some hope—not for the culture, but for each of us individually. Because, after all, an important distinction exists between the culture and those who live within it. The morbidity of the one does not entail the other's demise. It's this distinction that allows us to ponder, with less than galloping hearts, the failing life-signs of a free society. Secretly, each of us is convinced of a personal immunity: the culture's collapse may engulf us, or its mechanization may enslave us, but . . . we'll survive.

And it's true. People have always endured, no matter how great the collective catastrophe—endured, perhaps not as *a* people but, more simply, as folks. And, no matter how coercive the society becomes, nor how sophisticated its methods, there will always be some shit that some people will not eat—and, therefore, in our imaginations at least, we are forever free.

And yet, to endure, and remain free, will require a means of doing so, a strategy of survival or salvation. And since it's I who claim to have identified threats to both our freedom and endurance, the responsibility for proposing such a strategy would also seem to be mine. Well . . . now the bad news: I don't have one.

At least, not for our collective circumstance. More personally, however, solutions do exist, and some of them are rather obvious. It's in this area of prescription, though, that the writer is called upon to make certain confessions and, given the nature of his method, to abandon temporarily the authoritarian style that analysis seems to dictate.

Reader, I have a daughter . . . small, blonde, skinny, and infinitely fragile. I love her more than music and would rather see the continent of Asia disappear, with all its millions, than have any harm come to her. The idea that she might suffer more than the indignities of childhood, its scraped knees and bruised emotions, delivers me to the brink of a furious depression. I mention this because I'm intensely aware of the apparent contradiction that exists between the social predictions that I've made and the very *fact* of my two-year-old daughter. The reader has every reason to suspect the sincerity of a writer who, on the one hand, predicts fascism and cataclysm for his society and, on the other hand, conceives a child. Why would anyone who anticipates a future of smoke and iron willingly have children?

The "contradiction" is more apparent than real. Like almost everyone else, like you, I cling to an irrational belief in my own immunity and, perhaps willy-nilly, extend that imagined immunity to my family, to my friends, to—well, it goes wherever I want it to go.

It's a curiously schizophrenic perception. Looking out my window on this small-town street in Maine, I can see Mr. Shea shoveling snow from his sidewalk. He works silently, methodically, and, above all, privately. His world is enclosed. Down at Tat's Diner, where the hardware clerks and lobstermen gather for coffee, there's talk of Nixon, inflation, a nymphomaniac in Boothbay Harbor, and a local shooting. In the living room, my daughter plays with a binful of toys and my wife sits staring at a stack of unpaid bills and Christmas cards.

Each of these things—the toys, the bills, the snow, the nymphomaniac—is, in one way, more important than the prospect of a collective catastrophe waiting in the future. To the family of my murdered garbage man, for instance, the consequences of technical evolution are a joke in comparison to the grief they feel. Mention "mercantilism," the manor, and millenarian upheavals down at Tat's and you've got a fifty-fifty chance of getting punched or handed a free beer. And, with my wife pondering a *Final Notice!!!!* from the goddamn phone company, threats from various collection agencies, and our lack of snow tires, the "disease of Reason" hasn't got a chance—not in this house, not until William Morrow coughs up. After the phone bill's paid—*then* we'll talk about the disease of Reason.

I suspect that the same general circumstance applies to each of my readers. No matter how right I am, or how convincing, present-tense personal needs, whether petty or grand, take precedence over any collective condition facing us in the future.

The fact of the matter is that we do not live at the level I've been writing about. We live individually private lives within the society. We live in our living rooms and in our cars, in the diners and the streets, but we do not in any real sense live as a culture, a society, or a nation. Those things exist—they're more than mere ideas—but their destruction is not equivalent to our own, not necessarily. Individually, we're both infinitely less than the culture which surrounds us, and infinitely more. Less, because it subsumes us within its plenum. More, because it is we who animate *it*.

I make this point in order to excuse my inability to prescribe a remedy for our collective condition. Because that condition is Incurable, no remedy exists. Certainly our deterioration as a culture will have profound impacts on each of us as individuals. To deal with those impacts collectively would entail a social strategy aimed at saving a culture which, as I've argued, is beyond salvation. Such a game plan would, if I'm right, be doomed to failure.

What can be done, of course, is to suggest personal strategies—ways in which individuals can insulate themselves from the impending cultural trauma. There are, however, two problems with this.

The first is your identity. You know who I am: a cranky credit risk and protective father who writes books in Maine. But who are you? Senator, janitor, teenybopper, spook? Poet, clerk, carpenter, croupier, proctologist, cab driver, blacksmith, critic? A roller of fat cigars? A prisoner? A sailor? A —is someone reading this book in a missile silo? Don't do it!

I recant! I'm wrong about everything: America is forever . . .

I haven't a clue to your identity and am, therefore, forced to address some primal "reader stuff," a plasma of personality, a theory without properties. How can I prescribe, equally, for the bull dyke, bull babbit, and all the people beyond and in between? It's impossible. For all I know, you're reading this on horseback, in a diving bell near Goa, on an expedition through the Amazon . . . in search of Mu, perhaps.

If you and I, reader, were cultural twins, there would be no problem with prescription. But that's an arrogant assumption to make. And, in view of the fact that our identities are separate, I'll suggest no collective strategy. We are, in any case, beyond the help of movements. They continue to emerge, multiply, and subdivide, but they're of no real use, blinded by inevitably monistic analyses and bound to masturbatory narcissism by the news media's attention.

It seems more useful to estimate what people *will* do, collectively, than to polemicize about what they *ought* to do, individually. And yet the writer has an obligation. At some point, he must put up or shut up—his acts and plans must be made available to his readers because only in that existential context can his words be judged. What one does is, after all, the "final analysis."

The remainder of this book is therefore devoted to description, rather than prescription—a description of my own strategy, with its personal quirks and consequences, and a more purely predictive description of what's likely to happen on a collective level, in terms of consciousness and behavior, during this decade's last half and throughout the next.

2. Psychic Reflex

If our apocalyptic views are rationally arrived at, we face three categories of catastrophe: ecological, political, and industrial (or economic).

If we regard ecological catastrophe as inevitable, all strategies are useless: when the ozone goes, so do we, regardless of any precautions we may have taken. If we regard such a cataclysm as merely probable, rather than inevitable, then our strategy is necessarily one of prevention. The task is relatively simple: write to your congressman and tell him the species is threatened by _____* and that he must _____ or else. Depending on the size of his electoral mandate, he will either ignore your letter or explain that there's nothing he can do.

But ecological cataclysm is, in the practical terms of mapping personal strategies, the least of our worries. After all, such a cataclysm is likely only so long as the technically sophisticated societies continue to function "smoothly." If we have reason to believe (there's an obscure pun in there somewhere) that those societies will break down *before* nature has her coronary, then our strategic concerns must be cultural rather than ecological.

But which comes first? Political or industrial cataclysm? Fascism or rupture?

The question seems moot: there's no way to know. If we assume that Americans value the illusion of freedom, their "democratic heritage," then we must also assume that fascistic controls could come about only in two ways: with the acquiescence of the majority, or through some sort of *coup d'état*. The latter possibility is extremely remote: such a coup would have to win the acceptance of the state and federal bureaucracies, and that is most unlikely.[47] The acquiescence of the majority, however, is not so improbable. On the contrary, it's likely that Americans will, when the going gets tough, mandate fascism. They will do so because its economics, martial inclinations, and perverse nationalism will seem to constitute "a way out."

And that answers the question. Political cataclysm (viz., fascism) will come about as a response to the metacrisis gen-

---

* Fill in the blanks. Additional space available if necessary.

erated by technical evolution—industrial breakdowns (in consumption, production, supply, services, communications, and transportation) and economic dislocations.

Whether political cataclysm takes place in anticipation of worsening technical breakdowns (i.e., as a preventive measure) or subsequent to those breakdowns (i.e., as a curative), it seems wise to prepare for both. Because, of course, fascism never solved anything: accepting fascistic controls in order to prevent economic disorder is like drinking Drano to quiet a heart attack.

If we can't prevent these occurrences, then disengagement is the only meaningful strategy. We must separate ourselves from the society at large, thereby achieving immunity to its collapse. For many, that disengagement has already taken place. Its form, however, depends upon whether one believes the anticipated breakdown will be simple or complex—either political or economic, or political and economic.

If we believe that the threat is industrial collapse alone, then the most reasonable thing to do is to regain one's autonomy. Maine, Vermont, New Hampshire, Oregon, and Canada are filled with people engaged in a struggle to achieve more or less complete technical independence—to grow their own food, construct their own houses, make their own clothes, and establish their own water and energy systems. This may seem to be a merely nostalgic exercise, an existential aesthetic, but it's much more. Talking with those who've gone back to the land leaves one with the impression that most, if not all, are convinced that history is at its climax, that the industrial world is committing suicide. When they speak of "survival," their reference is less to the dangers of living in the woods than to what they believe is their *immunity* or rescue. They've left a sinking ship: their survival is already accomplished, so far as they're concerned.

The problem with this means of disengagement, however, is that it assumes that those who've abandoned the twentieth century will be left alone by that century (and its refugees) when the anticipated breakdown occurs. They ignore the probability of political interventions in their affairs, or dismiss those interventions with nods toward shotguns rusting on the cabins' walls. They've made their stand, agrarian Custers all.

Expatriation seems to be a more efficient strategy, a most thorough disengagement. To move beyond the reach of disruptive technologies, and beyond the iron whimsies of paranoid regimes, is the best insurance against an historical fire. Of course, it will do no good to find some sweet exile in Rome or London: the United States is, as it were, the ozone of "the Free World" and . . . when it goes, so do its satellites. As a strategy, expatriation insists upon one's removal from the overweaning influences of technique *and* from the jurisdiction of prefascistic societies.

That this is a personal, rather than a collective, strategy must be obvious. Imagine, though, if it were otherwise. America abandoned! Its 200,000,000 citizens scattered amid the islands of Indonesia, the Caribbean, and Fernando Poo. Bowls of porridge left uneaten on their tables. Radios humming with static. Automobiles forsaken in the roads, their doors open, lights on. Lawnmowers lurching mindlessly through suburban jungles. Subway doors opening and closing through eternity, discharging invisible passengers for the electrical duration. The United States—a cultural *Marie Celeste!* The mystery of Roatan multiplied ten millionfold! A nation of Donald Crowhursts, diving overboard, leaving it all behind, the wires, transistors, and faked logs!

And ! again!

But nah. Fat chance. We'll all be here when it blows. . . .

Well, not all of us, perhaps—but almost all. If we need a clue to the identity of the Seventies and Eighties we need only look at a handful of emerging trends, social vectors which have largely replaced those of the counterculture. While the state responds to the crises of technicization in its own way, there is a popular response as well, and its implications are much more important. Included in that response (to the Incurable) are the following:

A flight to authority (religious and/or demagogic), represented by the ballooning interest in overtly millenarian elites (Children of God, Process Church, Divine Light, Sun-Moonism, Scientology, et cetera).

A flight from the culture as a whole (manifested by the establishment of rural communes, enclaves such as Esalen and Lindesfarne, and by the sometimes lonely emigration of the young from the city to the woods).

Militant tribalization: the emergence of utopian "liberation" cults whose common characteristics are a sense of persecution and the belief that each is, by itself, a cultural, biological, or political elite.

The widespread apprenticeship to a variety of technical adepts whose disciplines (biofeedback, Silva Mind Control, transcendental meditation, Aikido, et cetera) promise to establish an individual's complete authority over himself and his environment.

An epidemic interest in crypto-messianic literature—the works of Erich von Däniken, Ludwig Pauwels, Jacques Bergier, Edgar Cayce, Ignatius Donnelly, various UFOlogists, seekers of Mu, and exponents of the "hollow earth" theory. Indeed, the list could be as long as one might want to make it (Immanuel Velikovsky ought to be included, for instance, and so should many works on the subject of Nazi Germany). That this literature is messianic, albeit in some cases clandestinely so, must be obvious. Each author is in search of a *deus ex machina,* an event capable of extricating us from the present. Whether extraterrestrials have visited us in the past, or in the present, makes no difference: the possibility of divine, or at least heavenly, intervention in our affairs is explicit in the work of von Däniken and the UFO buffs. A belief in the prior existence of supercivilizations such as Mu and Atlantis is merely a hope for their rediscovery and, more important, for the retrieval of their marvelous technologies (the Atlantean crystal power will save us yet). Ditto the Pyramidologists. And, of course, an affinity for "hidden continents" and hollow-earth theories is nothing more than a prayer for a new frontier, a place to begin all over again.

These are rather desperate intellectual measures, an index to the depth of the society's paranoia. ESP and "conspiracy" investigations, preoccupation with psychics such as Uri Geller and with the astrological arts—fear and impotence render us gullible, eager to grasp at any straw or, indeed, at any illusion of a straw. That this gullibility lends itself to the manipulation of demagogues is a fact that needn't be belabored: one need only refer to the popular delusions current in the Weimar Republic for a case history of prefascist fantasies. And if, as seems certain, economic conditions continue to worsen in the United States, then we may expect this popular response, this reckless seeking, to grow proportionately. As it is, millions of Americans are already off on an occultist bender, a brain-struck quest.

Meanwhile, the rest of us slide toward decadence, becoming accustomed to the perception that America is at her climax, that no *deus* is likely to intervene in the collective *machina*. The national Gizmo winds down, and we wind down with it. If we fail to embrace a cause—whether it's UFOs or Populism—decadence embraces us.

Earlier, I remarked that as individuals our experience is necessarily private and singular; the world "happens to us" at some particular address; matters of fact, sensations and events, occur to us in sequences that are—to each of us—unique, empirical daisy chains, discrete and unreplicated. Our lives are inevitably *factual*. But "culture" is not factual; it is, instead, the plenum in which all such "facts," each you and I, inhere. It is the *sum* of our facticity, an abstraction. A consequence of our individuality, of the uniqueness of all experience, is that any discussion of "culture" is bound to have an unreal quality, an apparent irrelevance. It applies to all of us in general and, therefore, to none of us in particular. Entering a discussion of culture requires each of us to surrender our personality, to subside into an undifferentiated categorical mass: Americans, Westerners, freaks—whatever culture we happen to discuss. That this surrender entails a sacrifice of concern, or a sacrifice in the urgency of one's concern, is clear.

That's why this book is meant to be, among other things, an examination of decadence but cannot help but be an example of that condition as well. We live *in* a culture but not *as* a culture. We can, therefore, consider the death of cultures, the unraveling of a nation, with relative calm and even with wit—while at the same time we may be utterly incapable of considering even the slightest injury to someone we love. And, if we can imagine such personal harms, we find nothing in them to joke about; the notion seems obscene.

And yet, that culture is an abstraction does not make us impervious, *in fact,* to its decline. On the contrary, culture invades our senses continually, infiltrating every junction of awareness and the subconscious. There's no escaping the depredations of cultural decline. Eventually, consciousness is reduced to ruins—individually and unanimously.

Decadence is the most general response to cultural decline. It's a psychic reflex that we're helpless to prevent, an autonomic shiver that the mind undertakes when the society begins to come unstuck. When a nation encounters obstacles which it cannot overcome, when contradictions are generated that cannot be resolved, when a culture's possibilities are exhausted —it declines. At that point decadence intervenes at the level of private experience: self-consciousness is elevated to an almost pathological intensity, a narcissistic awareness so extreme that it rattles one's connection to the self. We "step outside" our private identities and become the narrators of our own experience, committed to the omniscient observance of our individual demeanors. When decadence becomes epidemic, the decline which authored it accelerates, and the culture flies apart.

The technical chreod is the wellspring of America's decay, a Gordian net of contradictions. In the next few pages I intend to broach the subject of the resulting decadence, but to do so in a more personal way than the reader may have been led to expect. As I've said, decadence is private and factual, even when it's epidemic. Before a more general analysis can be enjoined, or a more complete definition attempted, it will be best to provide an *ad hominem* account. The author doesn't pretend to be immune to its invasion of consciousness and, in fact, a Catch-22 seems to be in force. That is, even the strategy of expatriation offers no exemption to the mind's subversion by a declining culture; if we leave that culture, its lacunae travel with us. The result is merely a variation on the theme, a nomadic version of decay.

3. Inertial Observers

There's a famous etching, done in the Middle Ages, that shows an old man kneeling upon the earth and poking his head through the celestial sphere. What he sees are heavenly wheels, gimbaled stars, and serrated spectra. He looks appropriately astonished.

For a long time this bearded gent seemed to me to be the perfect symbol of the questing philosopher. But, on reflection, I think he's just another tourist. The etching is hopelessly Platonic. Feet solidly entrenched in terra firma, the coot peeps with amazement at a kind of cosmic ballet *folklórico*. His impression of the earth's centrality is in no way contradicted by his observations of the Great Surround. On the contrary, the encircling void bolsters his illusion. If we question him about what he sees, his report on the universe will anticipate the message on a billion future postcards: "It's a big, weird, wonderful universe—but the earth's still the greatest little place around. Wish you were here."

The trouble with the old guy is that he never really leaves his observation post on earth. For that, we need Copernicus.

Copernicus was no tourist, but the first cosmic expatriate. Unlike the old philosopher, he stepped *outside* the system and, in looking back, learned more about heaven *and* earth than the philosopher could ever do. By leaving home, Copernicus put the whole world in its proper place. He came to know the solar system inside and out—which is, after all, the only way you can ever really "know" anything.

The Insider and the Outsider are equally ignorant. One has the "feel" of a thing and the other has a certain perspective, but, in so far as their positions are mutually exclusive, neither has any real understanding. That's why it's impossible for me to *know* what it is to be black, and also why it's so difficult for black people to *know* "where they're at." It's as if two trains are moving in relation to each other. Passengers in the dining cars of each train observe their counterparts and form opinions about each other's motion. But, no matter how carefully they observe, no matter how accurate their instruments, neither is able to agree or, in fact, come to any accurate conclusion. The passengers on the Chiliast Express insist that they're standing still and that the passengers on the other train are moving North at ten miles per hour. The passengers on the other train shake their heads, insisting that *they're* standing still and that the Chiliast Express is moving South at ten miles per hour. Both sides point out that, if *they* were moving, they'd know about it because their coffee would spill.

The only way to resolve the problem is for someone to step off one of the trains and take a look. Someone finally does and, much to his surprise, he's immediately mangled in an impact with a telephone pole. His deathbed telegram reads: "Don't anybody step off the train. I got *news* for you." If there'd been time he might have explained that both trains are moving in the same direction at speeds of eighty and ninety miles per hour, respectively.

Expatriates are the inertial observers of their former cultures. Having been on the Inside and having left, they are—like Copernicus or the victim from the train—in a good position to observe the real, or absolute, motions of the world they've abandoned. Like trains and planets, cultures also bear us along and, if we're to understand them, we must leave.

That leave-taking can sometimes exact a terrible toll, the same price a fish pays when, in beaching himself on dry land, he finally understands that there's *water* and that his whole life has been spent in it. Until then, while in the swim of things, so to speak, he'd never noticed.

To know your own mind you must, as Blake intimated, go out of it, and the same thing holds true for culture. The tourist's trip, however, will not suffice. Poking our heads through the celestial sphere while remaining earthbound can be "broadening"—it can "expand our horizons"—but it will not tell us how fast we're moving or in what direction. To find that out, we have to take a longer journey and sever all ties. In doing so, the expatriate finds an answer, but he also pays a price. He learns that America does in fact have "a condition," an evolving quirk of consciousness . . . *and he rusts with the realization.*

4. Ibiza and Racine

Ibiza is a Spanish island some six thousand miles off the (Great Lakes) coast of Racine, Wisconsin, but actually it's much farther away than that.

Six time zones separate Racine from the Balearic Islands and, in going from one place to the other, the traveler is powerfully aware that his trip has taken place as much in time as it has in space. It isn't the six hours that are gained or lost, but the transition in textures, a transition that spans centuries.

The meticulous lawns, smooth roads and factory smoke of Racine—its hamburger stands, station wagons, telephones, and televisions—give that place a feel and texture which is not to be found on Ibiza.

Not that Ibiza is so beautiful or natural that an artificial touch would deface an otherwise virginal condition. The island is jaundice-colored and rocky; a dump at its center cranks out eye-watering odors, and the narrow streets tremble with the roar of inefficient engines, the two-wheeled Edsels of Japan. Sewage shifts turgidly through the cobbled gutters, and a canopy of boredom, laziness, and fatigue hangs over everything.

I went to Ibiza for the same reason that Hillary says he climbed Everest: because it was *there*. Which was, in my case, just another way of saying that it wasn't here. America troubled me, and, having realized that I couldn't love the States, I took a bumper sticker's advice and left.

Nothing seems to happen on Ibiza. Expatriate residents are always astonished to find out that one of their number has, somehow and with clandestine energy, managed to gain notoriety—to murder or create. The presumption of innocence is profound in either case because entropy is the island's essence: things move, or wind down, at the pace of roots growing.

I don't know anyone on Ibiza who owns a telephone, and this is superficially surprising in view of the fact that conversation is the warp and woof of all activity there. You might think that because nothing seems to happen there is nothing to talk about. But the opposite is true. Small talk constitutes the island's exoskeleton, holding everyone together in the defensive privacy of inconsequential conversation. Great events and profundities tend to stun everyone into silence, and to mention either is to blunder, to breach the island's etiquette. Ibiza is a place where rather complicated people strive to succeed at being simple, to transcend the world of events by immersing themselves in insular trivia. If there seem to be no telephones on Ibiza, it's because the conversational fabric is a net of small silences, caesuras amid the inconsequential; and these silences, of course, cannot be endured in the absence of faces. They require a direct connection between speaker and listener. Telephones depend upon the coincidence of news and separation: on Ibiza, thirty miles of *nada* laid end to end, there is neither.

Even the light—the artificial light—is different on Ibiza. Few homes are equipped for electricity and the commercial establishments are zealous in their commitment to fluorescence. The result is that most houses tend to be dimly lighted with candles and kerosene, while the stores and restaurants shudder in the depleted glare of oscillating tubes suspended from fly-specked ceilings. One moves constantly between the lambent radiance of private places and the moronic whiteness of the commercial sector.

Like anywhere else in America, Racine has one light that serves all purposes. It is an empty, senseless light—the village idiot of illumination. It's the sort of light one might expect General Mills to manufacture: neutral, anonymous, too sweet and reticent—a sort of *buff* color. There are no wicks to clip nor any crystals to clean. It never needs to be refilled and, like the earth's core, it's always there, the forgotten foundation of everything.

I mention this business about light to emphasize the difference in textures between Ibiza and the American Anywhere. The same point could be made about color and the feel of things. Ibiza is all stucco and sand, cobblestones and grain; its colors are made from vivid dyes, cheap and primitive (even the girls prefer henna for their hair). Racine is dumb with pastels and things have an amnesiac softness common to synthetic fibers. Needless to say, Racine doesn't smell. Its inhabitants brush and spray with the best of them. The sewers, deep in the earth, foist no unwanted intimacies upon the antiseptic populace, but deliver their rank nutrition to the Lake in secrecy. Every so often—rather like a CIA scandal—a turd washes up on the beach, and the bathers avoid each other's eyes while the children scream.

It's impossible to forget that one is on Ibiza: every sense reports continuously its special connection to the world around it. Because everything is alien and unfamiliar, one's attention is *compelled*. This is one reason why it's so hard to "do" anything on the island. One is so involved with being, or being *there*, that only the most heroic act of will can wrench one out of the present and into that ambiguous zone in which the future can be considered and plans mapped out.

In fact, it's more complicated than that: acts come easily on Ibiza. It's strategies that're in short supply. Violence tends to explode, to happen without the reinforcement of a grudge. Impulse rules. People come and go without suitcases.

Racine has the opposite problem. Strategies are everywhere, as common as the disconnection of the strategists. Life is deferred, and the anonymous light, the blank textures and pastels, induce an almost Buddhistic equality among the senses. They have nothing to report. An occasional bleep, perhaps—the sway of an ass, a bottle breaking, a truck backfiring—but that's a rarity. Mostly, the people in Racine are never really *in* Racine. They are, instead, in 1985, 1932, or 2016. The present is a thing to be endured, a suspension bridge between the past and the future.

5. Oscillation: The Habit of Stupidity

How is it then that, after a year on Ibiza, I woke one morning to find myself consumed by a sad impatience, a melancholy that had no focus? And no matter how hard I tried to deny the feeling—to blame it on too much bad beer or the monotonous weather—the feeling gathered force until, by midafternoon, I was in an inconsolable fidget. I sat outside the Café Montesol chain-drinking espressos and telling myself that it was not as it seemed, it was not *homesickness,* not that, anything but that. And yet, there it was in all its symptoms: a disembodied remorse whose shapeless force kept my eyes spellbound with unwanted American images; an impatience with my surroundings; and the imbecilic repetition of the same pseudorecognition: "Gee, in twelve hours I could be home."

But how could that be? How could anyone be homesick for Racine, Wisconsin? As I thought about it, it occurred to me that I hadn't actually been there for more than ten years and that, in fact, it had never really been *home* in any meaningful sense—just a "permanent address" for income tax purposes, a kind of domestic Poste Restante from which my mother forwarded my mail. Like everyone else I knew, I'd been brought up in the nomadic style of the lower-upper-middle class. Living a kind of geographical roulette, my father had been "transferred" every two or three years, shifted from one malignant slurb to another until, as he neared retirement, a Universal Veep, he found himself at the Home Office in Racine. Like a silver ball that had finally come to rest on Double Zero.

It wasn't Racine, then, it was something else: a part of America that was common to *all* of America. Not the Blue Mountains, not the deserts, not the "amber waves of grain"—my homesickness had nothing to do with place. Or "home" either. It had instead to do with the common textures of the country—with nylon, air conditioning, and refrigerators humming through the night. With the baleful glow of television spreading its blue smear across carpets that run from wall to wall. With the eccentric convenience of electric can openers, blenders, toothbrushes, and drills. With the seductive labels in the supermarkets. My God! The supermarkets! Housewives wheeling the kiddies through fugues of Muzak, squeezin' the Charmin, writing "personal" checks, stuffing themselves with Twinkies, Devil Dogs, Oreos, and Ring Dings!

My nostalgia, then, went to the confectionery essence of the States, to the part that has no "roots" at all but, like moss and lichens, grows everywhere in undifferentiated profusion. It was the mass culture that I missed—the underwear of the Superpower.

And, while I felt some relief at the realization that it was not Racine per se that caused my sadness, but something subtler, I could take little pleasure in the knowledge that my expatriate malaise was only a kind of peanut-butter wistfulness. There was no element of romance in this nostalgia, and only the most neurotic affection. What had been lost by residence abroad was my connection to the banal meringue of daily life in the States. It was as if I'd been saddened by the loss of what I regarded as a disease, and remembered with affection the way my body sweated as its fever rose, the way my joints ached and head thrummed.

There was no way to slake this sadness on Ibiza: everything emphasized the lacunae.

In desperation I switched from coffee to bourbon—nothing

could be more American than its smooth cruelty to the throat—and bought a copy of *Playboy,* thinking that homesickness is the only illness that we feed. The advertisements drove me into a frenzy, of course. I kept imagining my arrival at the Playboy Club, tape deck blaring from the walnut dash of my E-Jag, some sequin'd honey at my side . . . after a few drinks, we'd walk out on the floor show, tool over to my suite in the Gonzo Towers, send down for a quart of Wesson Oil, and spend the night in an orgasmic froth. In the morning we'd slip into our tailored work shirts and overalls, and spend the day at community-action meetings. *That* was America. That was The Life.

And then, *sanctum sanctorum,* there was the Playmate herself—supine, relaxed, pudenda stapled into place upon the glossy centerfold. I read the details of her life with the same attention I'd have given to a poem by Wallace Stevens, and for the same reason: I was looking for clues that would tell me What It All Means, and I knew that there was some secret here, that the nudity disguised as much as it revealed.

Her name was Didi or Wanda or something and she'd given up a career in astrophysics or brain surgery in order to spend more time surfing. When not at the beach, she could be found beside the pool in the singles' apartment complex she called "home." In the magazine, she lay across the pages with her legs crossed and a look of lamial certitude on her face. Her pubic hair was trimmed to such equilateral perfection that, had he lived to see it, Pythagoras would have burst into applause. Her breasts, I noticed, were the same color as my mother's living room walls, and her eyes—coexistent with the carnal moue of her face—seemed to have been vacuum-cleaned of all expression. A Mona Lisa, albeit with big tits and two years of physics at UCLA.

Admittedly, the eyes gave me some reservations, but, like the Wesson Oil fantasy, the textures, and the Twinkies, they too were a part of my homesickness. (There's something about a callow girl.)

The perception that Playmates of the Month are empty-eyed is something of a cliché. The implication is that the woman's thrilling facade of sex is no more than a tent that covers dullness. A corollary to that implication, of course, is that the person who makes the observation is himself possessed of eyes that flash with intelligence and life. In fact, they hardly ever do, and that would be obvious if people scrutinized each other with the same prurient intensity that they reserve for their cyclic Didis.

There is, as the *I Ching* says, "no blame" in this. Living in the States requires a certain removal, an aloofness from the surrounding world. And that aloofness manifests itself in a habitually glazed demeanor, as if the eyes had been baked in kilns, lacquered, and set like pots on either side of the nose.

No one is exempt from this disconnected mien because it proceeds from the environment itself. It's a natural response to the technical apparat, a reaction to the culture's *fullness*. Even kids have that expression—as if they were listening to a high voice deep inside themselves. And no wonder: the average American kid witnesses more than 25,000 television commercials every year. Not to mention the billboards on the way to school, the radio at lunch, the packages on the food he eats, the ads in newspapers, magazines, and books. *Everything competes for our attention always.* There's no respite from our citizen's role as *customer,* and so we move as far inside ourselves as we can get, shutting out as much of the domestic world as possible simply because so little of it is compatible, or relevant, to our complicated needs. Since consciousness is the target of a conceptual barrage that never abates, since it's under continual siege, it's forced to contract in self-defense. Its "surface area" must be reduced or, if it remains open and receptive to all stimuli, the resultant excitation will devastate the psyche. After all, these stimuli aren't passive and neutral, but aggressive: they've been intelligently designed by people whose livelihoods depend on their ability to seize and, to some extent, control the consciousness of others. It seems certain that some forms of mental illness are, by nature or effect, nothing more than an excessive openness, a failure to generate the introversion which the technical plenum demands.

Advertisers (and, in fact, all communicators) respond to

the resulting dullness or distraction of their audience by intensifying, or renewing, the stimuli. Thus, Coca-Cola, whose logos had become so well accepted that they were virtually invisible, was forced to change its signs in order to reimpose its product on America's dwindling consciousness. Similarly, graphic violence becomes a staple of the art and entertainment industry, not because Americans are inherently violent or morbid, but because their attention is so elusive that it can be captured only by extremes. Violence, moreover, is like sex in that its climacteric fits conveniently into a commercial format characterized by frequent interruptions for advertisements. With our visual attention conditioned to the staccato, narrative rhythms of television, and our audial attention conditioned by the Top-40 format of AM radio, we've lost the capability of sustained concentration. "Concept" albums are financial suicide in the record industry because they receive little air play and because people simply can't listen to them all the way through: one of the best albums of the Sixties (Traffic's *John Barleycorn Is Dead*) went the way of *The Ring of the Nibelungs* because its complexity demanded too much (attention) from its listeners. In the same way, one of the most important novels in American letters—*Gravity's Rainbow*—is also one of the least read (as the Pulitzer judges noted when, in refusing its author an award, they described the mammoth book as "unreadable").

The physical characteristics of the National Gizmo are such that to live within it is to be engulfed—subsumed within a field of commercial stimuli, included within a program of consciousness modification that is no less coherent for the fact that it seems to be uncontrolled. Before we reach adulthood, we've exchanged our appreciation of the nuance for the jolts afforded by bold strokes and explosions.

Nothing illustrates this exchange better than the Arts, whether High- or Low-.

Pop and Op are successful styles because their crudities make them accessible to even the most withdrawn. In negating the viewer's conditioned introversion, they seize his attention in the same way that a foghorn or a suicide will do. By yanking us out of ourselves, however briefly, Pop and Op fulfill the first prerequisite for aesthetic experience: they provoke (which, for the most part, is more than Rembrandt's nuances are able to do). Unfortunately, the simplicity that grabs our attention does not allow the artist much room for conceptual maneuver: in the end, a goat with a tire around its midriff is, however interesting and curious, only a goat with a tire around its midriff. It says nothing but "LOOK!"

"Concrete poetry" says the same thing, and Pop music says "LISTEN!" but, finally, it is one phenomenon: since the advent of television, *all* the arts have been in retreat. And the first things to be cast to the wayside in that retreat are the ornamentation of subtleties and the heavy baggage of conception: ultimately, we return to the arresting "that-ness" of the hieroglyph, atrocity photo, and tom-tom's beat. When it's otherwise, as with *Gravity's Rainbow,* meaning sinks perception with a warning shot across the bows.

Survival within the National Gizmo, within what's rapidly becoming a technical plenum, requires a stunted consciousness in the same way that survival in the jungle demands an "expanded" consciousness—an absolute awareness of both dangers and opportunities. But the threat of the city, unlike that of the jungle, is not primarily to the body, but to the mind or spirit. And, therefore, to recognize the city's threat is to risk infatuation with it. Medusa comes to mind.

In a pinball demimonde such as New York's Forty-Second Street, the possibility of getting terminally hung up, transfixed with perception, is enormous. If we insist upon absolute receptivity, if we struggle against the imagery screens that our minds automatically erect, we'll certainly overload our senses and burn down consciousness to its wick. To function sanely in America we must acquire the habit of stupidity—just as the traveler in a poor land must learn to overlook, to ignore, the pus-running misery of the poor. Consciousness is made to oscillate and whole swatches of the world disappear routinely, and perhaps forever. In Mexico and Morocco we come to ignore the begging children because they're insatiable, threatening exhaustion and bankruptcy; in the States, we ignore *possibility* for the same reason.

We may on occasion tamper with this mechanism, spontaneously, or perhaps with the help of some good dope. But doing so is, however adventurous, folly of the most Icarian sort. Odysseus heard the Sirens in all their resonance, but his fate was restrained by his bondage to a mast. We have no restraint today; there is no mast to which the mind can be tied (not even ideology) and, if we open it to America's fullness, we'll drown. The asylums are full of awareness.

It's not a simple matter of "openness" in a "straight" society. The situation is not amenable to intentional change. What we are, and want, and do are functions of invisibilities, textures and processes that are so obvious as to be unnoticed. The *way* we think is not subject to any referendum of the brain, nor does the society around us evolve according to any cognitive plan: what happens, in the head as much as in the streets, takes place within an elemental framework that is at once intimate and unknowable. Even on a conscious, political level, it's safe to say that our collective thoughts are shaped less by Marx, de Tocqueville, and salutes to the flag than by Unca Scrooge, Orphan Annie, *Gunsmoke,* and "the gang at Riverdale High." The most popular American poem does *not* begin

> April is the cruelest month . . .

but

> You deserve a break today . . .

We may unlearn this acquired ignorance by an extraordinary act of will, intelligence, and luck. We may all become David Halberstams. But still, we'll not have gotten very far. We will have yet to deal with the invisible, with the textures, memories and things that are buried even deeper than what we take "for granted." The feel of an automobile accelerating, the high-school cheers, Coke commercials, half-time shows, billboards, stoplights, parking meters, hospital smells, televised assassinations, skies sliced by planes and traced by wires—consciousness doesn't have a chance. It gets slaughtered every time.

The emptiness in Didi's eyes proceeds not from some private dullness, not from her chauvinized surrender to the sufficiency of her body's beauty, but from the complex triviality of her world, and her reaction to it. Nothing could be more natural than, when forced to look away from the world, to look inward, become reflective, immerse oneself in a continuum of private narcissism.

It is *this* that one misses from abroad. The *tumult* of America, its subcutaneous groping and coping. The habit of stupidity which leads directly to an infatuation with the self and, therefore, to a special knowledge of the self as well. All this is gone. The pathos of the expatriate is that he no longer has any need of the special skills and defenses whose acquisition has taken a lifetime. Because he's abandoned his native culture, he looks back upon it, conscious of its lacunae. Because he lives in an alien environment—because he *is* an alien—he's turned outward and away from himself. Since his adopted universe is meaningless to his memory, its language unintelligible and customs impenetrable, it presents no threat to the mind. Unless he isolates himself within a "community" of expatriates, his consciousness begins to open. What he gains is a new appreciation of nuance, and a special knowledge of his native country. What he sacrifices is that unique self-knowledge that the narcissist acquires. He no longer narrates his own experience to himself; he ceases to be an actor studying an image—and lives *directly*.

Living outside the States, one feels like a prizefighter between bouts, a general between wars. It doesn't matter that the skills one possesses may be destructive—they've taken a lifetime to acquire, and leaving them fallow seems a tremendous waste. To place those skills in suspension therefore requires an almost transcendental lassitude of spirit, a willingness to rust from the very center of the self. A special kind of decadence.

They say—and I think they're right—it's worth it.

VII. America Flambé

1. Toynbee and the Metacrisis

Worth it, yes, but so rare as to be irrelevant. Expatriates are the aristocrats of decadent consciousness and, like any aristocracy, their import is confined to their own milieu. They speak to themselves only.

But what of those who remain? Their world inclines toward millenarian upheavals, bloody discontents which, because they proceed from the implications of Technique, are unavoidable. Social movements, both good and bad, are doomed by the nature of the media to premature, narcissistic decay. Awareness flounders as consciousness moves into a defensive sleep, a retreat from stimuli. What's to be done? What can be done?

Our technical interdependence is rapidly approaching a totality of completion such that the National Gizmo will soon be unable to afford *any* disruption. Each sector of the economy is linked to every other sector in such a way that a malfunction in one area generates a chain reaction throughout the infrastructure; it's fair to say that we live in the midst of an incipient economic avalanche that threatens to inter the culture. Mechanistic conceptions of man and society have led planners to create a precision machine of a nation whose high-powered performance is constructed upon an exquisite fragility. We near a time when America must run perfectly, or not run at all.

Arnold Toynbee, an historian of epic stature, has developed this view from a somewhat different perspective, one that emphasizes the inevitable depletion of strategic natural resources. In Toynbee's opinion, the developed nations will soon "find themselves in a permanent state of siege in which material conditions of life will be at least as austere as they were during the two world wars. The wartime austerity was temporary; the future austerity will be perennial, and it will become *progressively more severe*." The historian predicts that, faced with the prospect of disaster, governments will become ever more totalitarian, eventually resorting to draconian measures in a ruthless effort to preserve domestic order and conserve national resources. Free enterprise will be eliminated and daily life will approach a degree of regimentation heretofore known only in monastic communities.

The contemporary situation in the developed nations is clinically prefascist. If we acquiesce to the Orwellian controls that technogogues such as Daniel K. Bell, Herman Kahn, and B. F. Skinner would impose, we surrender whatever remnants of freedom we have. If we attempt to "muddle through" as we have in the past, trusting to Providence and confident that God and Science are on our side, we'll lose our ass. Those are the "alternatives."

So far in this book I've tended to concentrate on two things: a redefinition of recent history in millenarian terms, and the cultural characteristics that make our collapse seem to be inevitable. This has resulted in a somewhat rarified discussion, a reliance upon abstractions. The problem with analysis of this sort is that its force depends upon a recognition of threats that do not announce themselves with a flourish of trumpets— we cannot, after all, *see* the autonomous evolution of technique. And, like Pasteur, scholars such as Ellul find themselves in the position of one who warns the incredulous that they are threatened by organisms which they cannot see, touch, hear, or smell.

Toynbee reminds me that there are yet a few years before we arrive at the time of our unraveling and, before I proceed with the question of what, if anything, can be done, it might be useful to offer some sort of timetable. Cataclysm, after all, does not take place in the abstract: it is always quite specific, even visceral.

The problem is, of course, that the number of specific hazards is so large that a single timetable will not suffice; what's required is a finely printed *schedule* with all the natural resources listed down one side, and the dates scrawled across the top. Worked into this schedule would have to be a random factor representing the possibility of nuclear blunder, and floating footnotes would be needed to elaborate possible solutions (or substitutes) for each of the diminishing resources. And even then one would have covered only one aspect of the problem—the part in which we attempt to "muddle through"—and no consideration would have been given to such problems as overpopulation, pollution, ecocatastrophe, or man-devised Plague. Nevertheless, this is approximately what the Club of Rome has attempted to do, and readers who want to study models of future planet management, or the specifics of disaster-coping, are referred to *The Limits of Growth* (produced under the Club's auspices).

Without making reference to any monistic hazard, but referring to a panoply of threats deriving from a single cause (technical evolution), it's clear that Toynbee's metaphor of "siege" is accurate. We are entering upon a period of proliferating crises, a time in which one crisis succeeds another with so little interval between them that we may speak of a prevailing Metacrisis.

Indeed, it's happening already. E.g., an oil embargo leads to an increase in fertilizer costs that generates higher food prices which aggravate the difficulties of those who are unemployed by virtue of production cutbacks caused by the embargo, all of which combine to create economic uncertainties, depress consumption, stimulate retaliatory price rises, trade wars, layoffs in still other industries, and . . . the eventual result is a political crisis within the regime, a destabilization of the world order.

Because our culture is a plexus, rather than an amalgam of economic monads, crises tend to be synergistic and, therefore, to arrive in waves. The intervals between these "waves," these daisy chains of disaster, are getting shorter and it seems likely that perhaps within ten years we'll have arrived at a "normal" state of metacrisis. When that happens, the prevailing state of affairs will be one of instability and solutions will have to be provided instantaneously—which is to say, by administrative fiat rather than by democratic deliberation.

Totalitarianism will arrive in the United States, not by *coup d'état* or through some perverted manifestation of the "national will," but through the gradual surrender of popular authority to technical elites within the administrative, or military, branches of government. It will, in other words, be *delegated* into power, much in the same way that Congress has delegated, or abdicated from, so many of its responsibilities in favor of the Presidency. The change will appear "natural" and organic in that it will seem to be a *logical* response to extraordinary circumstances: it will represent a tacit recognition of the fact that the technical apparatus cannot survive the uncertainties of both diminishing resources and the facade of democratic deliberation. Americans will find themselves forced to choose between the comforts of technology, which advertising has transformed into "needs," and the *luxe* of freedom. There is little doubt which the people will choose; if they're called upon to decide, in effect, between the electric toothbrush and "representative" government, it is the voting booth and not the teeth that will suffer. And who could blame them (us?)? A democracy without a majority—such as the United States—is not much more than a tentative equilibrium among special interests with special influences. Indeed, all of this has already begun to happen: the acceptance of wage and price controls is partial evidence, and so is the fact that the people have themselves been transformed into a "special interest group" or nexus of groups.* They're "taken into consideration"

---

* Common Cause, John Gardiner's political organization, reifies this notion when it advertises itself for what it is: a "people's lobby."

when political decisions are made—which is to say that they're no longer the animus or *raison d'être* of democracy, but a mere constant within a complex political equation. The people are, like the Highway Lobby, the dairy industry, and the National Rifle Association, a *factor*.

2. Frankenstein: Seizing the Means of Reproduction

And yet, if America, or at least the Americans, are to be saved, their deliverance will have to be effected by the people, by themselves. A revolution, then? The Wad overturning the Gizmo? But the idea of Americans storming out of their "robot apartments" is ludicrous.

The cruel assessment of kindly Roel van Duyn, anarchist theoretician and a founder of the Dutch Provo rebellion, remains uncontradicted by events:

> We cannot convince the masses. We can scarcely even want to. How anyone can place any trust in that bunch of apathetic, unenterprising, witless cockroaches, beetles, and ladybirds is a mystery to me. . . . If only we could be revolutionaries. But we're more likely to see the sun rise in the west than a revolution. . . . We know our actions are useless. We also know that a demonstration is of no use in the long run; that is why it is so important to get as much as possible immediately out of demonstrating.[48]

That was written in the early Sixties and all that seems to have changed is that it's no longer possible to get *anything* out of demonstrating.

But, let us imagine for a moment that a revolution *is* possible. What would be gained? The national malaise goes deeper than politics and economics—it derives from the very nature of the culture, from the rational and mechanical underpinnings of the society. Revolution could accomplish nothing more than a change in the management of the disease. If that is vague, perhaps a metaphor from the Left will clarify the thought:

A book that's recently come to fascinate some Marxists is Mary Shelley's *Frankenstein*. The plight of the monster seems, in so many ways, to parallel the plight of the "masses." Consider the creature: he is a quilt of flesh, a collage of anatomical parts retrieved from paupers' graves and loonybins. A blacksmith's arm, the torso of a hod carrier, a farmer's stout legs . . . and so forth. It is easy to view the monster as the literal embodiment of Everyman (and perhaps Ms. Shelley intended us to do so).

The manipulator of the monster, his "bourgeois owner and exploiter," is the man who made him what he is—Dr. Frankenstein, the ingenuous genius whose laboratory is both the source of the creature's vitality and his only means of (re)production. When the monster undertakes an independent liberal education at the cottage of the unwitting De Lacey, he becomes self-conscious (and thereby prone to the fine, decadent sensibilities that inspire corrupt emotions and acts). As he comes to understand his own origins, to realize that he's the doctor's toy, a lab-dependent thing—he seeks out the good physician and makes *demands*. The monster wants an ugly woman, which is to say that he wants to exercise some control over what the laboratory produces. He wants to bend the laboratory to his own needs, to create a monster-lady and, in doing so, to obtain inhuman solace and affect the evolution of his own kind. (The doctor consents at first, but then reneges on the agreement, perhaps fearing the emergence of an abysmal union.)

A proper Leninist would urge the monster to take over the lab, evict the evil scientist, and thereby seize the means of production. But, even if he does this, what will he gain? The doctor is a mere appendix to the monster's real problem— which is that he's almost wholly a product of the laboratory and that, no matter who runs it, he's been flawed from conception. The monster's decay cannot be reversed by a purely *political* change in management: at most he'll only be able to prolong the duration of his own deterioration and perhaps repeat the doctor's original error, albeit in the feminine mode.

As it is with the monster, so it is with the people. Mere political solutions can have no substantial effect on problems that transcend politics. If there is no rain, there will be drought whether the nation is ruled by czar, parliament, or labor council. So it is that, in the United States, it is not a question of our relationship to the "means of production," but of the means themselves and, even more basically, of who and what we are. Herbert Marcuse states the problem exactly when, in looking forward to a great Refusal, he identifies the need for what he calls a "transvaluation of values."

"What is not at stake," he writes,[49] "are the needs themselves. At this stage, the question is no longer: how can the individual satisfy his own needs without hurting others, but rather: how can he satisfy his needs without hurting himself, with reproducing, through his aspirations and satisfactions, his dependence on an exploitative apparatus which, in satisfying his needs, perpetuates his servitude." (This is precisely the problem of Frankenstein's monster.) As Marcuse notes, "Technocracy, no matter how 'pure,' sustains and streamlines the continuum of domination. This fatal link can be cut only by a revolution which makes technology and technique subservient to the needs and goals of free men: in this sense, and in this sense only, it would be a revolution against technocracy." But, he adds (again correctly), "Such a revolution is not on the agenda." The "masses" are paralyzed by their dependence upon a system that exploits them, and revolutionary consciousness is generally confined to groups that have only a marginal social function—blacks and the middle-class young, each of whom is more or less expendable and relatively safe to repress. A "radical enlightenment," or Refusal, is possible only when the economy is critically weakened.

If Marcuse's analysis is accurate, the American revolutionary would seem to be charged with a task that is as awful as it is awesome. That is, he must abet and facilitate the immiseration of the people in order to accelerate the arrival of a "radical enlightenment." So long as the people's "needs" are met by the economic apparat, their exploitation and dehumanization will continue. In order to terminate the people's exploitation, the revolutionary must act as executioner to the economic apparat, weakening it whenever and wherever possible. He must, in other words, become an "enemy of the people" in order to become their savior.

What saves the American revolutionary from the necessity of this unsavory task is the fact that he's so powerless within the system that he can do virtually nothing to weaken it. Economically and politically, he is impotent, and therefore necessarily passive. Convinced that the system is afflicted with internal contradictions that will eventually destroy it, the American revolutionary has little choice but to wait for this to happen in its own time, or at least for the system to reach a stage of such critical fragility that even he may have some effect upon its demise. Until then, there's little he can actively do, except perhaps to establish a revolutionary party, or some other vehicle, for exploiting the anticipated social cataclysm.

Unfortunately, such "parties" seem to be inevitably prone to premature action, destroying the energies of their membership with quixotic and superfluous efforts at "consciousness raising," or reinforcing the established system by working for reforms that can only "streamline" and perpetuate "the continuum of domination." ("Consciousness raising" is quixotic because, so long as the people's needs are met by the system, they'll defend it to the last automaton; to raise their consciousness under such circumstances would require an hydraulic jack of metaphysics—mere leaflets will not suffice. Similarly, attempts to make the people more aware of their real condition are superfluous in that American consciousness will blast off *spontaneously* the moment that the Gizmo stops humming and begins to go clank-clank.)

The dilemma of the American revolutionary is existential: he has no meaningful task to perform in the present. Out of synch with history (through no fault of his own), he's condemned to the fate of theorist since all action must be either futile or (in the case of reform) counterrevolutionary. He is, in other words, Hamlet, when he's not Polonius.

3. Alpha and Omega Cultures

The fact that a political revolution is unlikely and even irrelevant (in so far as it would be purely political, redistributing the malaise of property) does not mean that there is no way for the Wad to transform the Gizmo. One can at least *conceive* of an Awakening, a spontaneous apostasy in which the great mass of people regurgitate the culture. But that is easier to conceive, as an idea, than it is to imagine as an occurrence. There is, so far as I know, no real precedent for cultural revolution. One thinks of the Luddite rebellion—but that was not a revolution. One thinks of the Chinese upheavals during the Sixties, but those were essentially reformist purges rather than stages in cultural revolution. In any case, I can't imagine millions of Americans running through the streets shaking copies of *Unsafe at Any Speed* and *Stalking the Blue-Eyed Scallop*.

And yet, this is precisely what the youth upheavals of the Sixties were about: they constituted rebellions against the culture itself and represented a "radical Enlightenment" that was no less bright for its short tenure and sometimes bizarre directions. Millenarian in nature, and confined for the most part to the middle-class young, the cultural revolts of the Sixties could, at least in our imaginations, be extended to include a larger segment of the population in the near future. A broad-based expression of such discontents and fears would certainly be different, in form and force, from that of the "counterculture," but it would reiterate many of the same basic rejections. The problem is: where would it come from? What would its animus be?

It seems obvious that, if such a Refusal were to take place, its origins would be buried deep within the culture; and if it were a mass Refusal, its animus would emerge from some part of the mass culture. Neither revolutionaries nor intellectuals will lead the people from their confectionery stupor —if the Wad is to be redeemed from the Gizmo's gears, it will redeem itself. Or it will not be redeemed at all.

"Mass culture," however, is a confusing term. Even if we think we know what it is that the term refers to, it's difficult to see how any part of *that* could constitute a fulcrum for Enlightenment or social action. One might even question whether there is such a thing as mass culture and, if there is, what would cause the "masses" to reject it.

The difficulty may be purely definitional. If we take the view that mass culture is simply the "culture of the masses," little will be learned. It is, instead, more profitable to distinguish between two kinds, or aspects, of "mass culture": that which derives from the people themselves (and over which they retain control), and that which is imposed upon them by the logic of technique (and over which they exercise no control).

As a kind of shorthand I'll refer to these aspects as the Alpha and Omega cultures, respectively.

Looked at from this dualistic vantage, several things become obvious. The first is that the popular, or Alpha, culture is infinitely smaller than the technical, or Omega, culture. This is, of course, no accident, but a function of the warlike relationship between the two. Omega culture expands at the expense of the Alpha culture, taking it over wherever possible, rationalizing and transforming it in the process. As an expression of technique, Omega culture is necessarily expansive, tending toward hegemony and completeness in all areas.

What this amounts to is cultural theft, and a history of mass culture as a whole could be written from that viewpoint. Examples of such thefts abound—in food, games, literature, music—throughout, in fact, the whole complex of popular cultural activity. The hamburger, for instance, has been rationalized by the McDonald's chain and others like it, transformed into a protein clone that amounts to the lowest common denominator in food, the nuts and bolts of digestion. Football has been similarly transformed, reduced from a Saturday-afternoon sandlot goof to an electronic spectacle of performing technicians. Rock and roll, once an expression of popular creative energies and romantic impulses, is now an industry whose product serves to pace radio advertisements and create subsidiary markets and spin-off industries (e.g., rock festivals). The formulas of successful fiction are by now well-known, but never before have they been applied so literally and self-consciously as *formulas*. In the case of action series such as *The Executioner* and *The Destroyer*—artifacts which make up an increasing part of the reading-entertainment market—the books are manufactured by a host of anonymous "authors" working with standard characters and plots that are, in effect, loaned to them by the publishing houses. The result is wok fiction, instant-fried entertainments.

Wherever the Omega culture has coopted activities whose origins were popular, the result has been loss. The people lose control over the activity they invented; the activity loses the vitality which the people gave to it; as the activity is taken over by technicians and organizers, food or fiction managers, its shape is standardized and its process made more predictable. Elements of creativity and surprise are eliminated as a corollary to the activity's rationalization, and what was formerly an entertainment degenerates into an addiction, or is abandoned as a fossil—a dull, dead thing.

The activity or artifact has been dehumanized—literally. And, in the process of that dehumanization, it becomes cheapened: experiencing it, our sensibilities are coarsened, our understanding blunted. Each contact with the Omega culture leaves us depleted, narcotized by the aftertaste of cheap thrills, and otherwise less than what we were before. Ultimately, we come to rely upon the confectionery blast conferred by the McDonald's tastepatty; the cardiac beat of mechanorock; the serial concussions of action literature; and the spectacle of statistoball. They are, in effect, the only games in town.

Thus it is that we eat without tasting, hear without listening, watch without playing, and read without learning. We live, in other words, as spectators within the complex vacuum of the Omega culture. What that culture has not co-opted has always been its own: the housing in which we live, and the work that we perform, is ours only in the sense that a disease might be. We have it, but don't choose it. It chose us, or revealed itself to us upon a rational consideration of what we can "afford" or what we're "trained to do." There is little to be learned about ourselves from a consideration of such "common bonds," except perhaps the extent of our symptoms, and the probable course of our illness.

There is, then, little or nothing in "mass culture" that would lead one to expect the radical Enlightenment which Marcuse anticipates. On the contrary, the Alpha culture has virtually dematerialized before the onslaught of the Omega. What remains (and passes for mass culture among many sociologists) is an irresistible and ubiquitous Anticulture, a black hole of custom that reduces all sensibilities and mores to a kind of primal brain meal. The fact that this Anticulture acts upon the people daily does not make it theirs. And there is consequently no reason to expect that anything positive will come from it.

4. Radical Nostalgia

It may be, however, that Marcuse's "Refusal" could be inspired by this very absence, or loss, of culture. It seems possible that, with their roots blasted, traditions crushed, and culture coopted, people may be moved to seize back what has been stolen from them.

If so, this would amount to nothing less than Revolutionary Nostalgia—an odd notion, if only because nostalgia has always been one of the most passive and polite sentiments in our emotional vocabulary. And yet, it needn't be so, and may not always have been so. Many of the countercultural outbursts seem to have been motivated by what amounted to a radical nostalgia, a nostalgia so deeply felt that it could only find an outlet in action (e.g., the battle at Wounded Knee).

And certainly the present is suffused with nostalgia, albeit of a false and wistful kind. A radical nostalgia, a Nostalgia worth capitalizing, would not merely mourn the loss of old values and ways, but would *take action* to have those values and ways reinstated. It would be the motive force behind what would amount to a reactionary renaissance. But for such a Nostalgia to emerge, Americans would first have to recognize the depth of their loss. They would have to realize that they are, as much as the Indians, resident upon a reservation devoted primarily to their cultural containment. It doesn't matter that the walls of the American reservation are built with coaxial cables, mortgages, organizational charts, magnetic tapes, and credit—the loss of control, culture, and independence is as thorough as barbed wire could make it.

But even with that realization in hand, the prospect for Refusal is dim. It took the Indians a hundred years of solitude and drunkenness for their desperation to climax in a Nostalgia sufficiently radical to bear the weight of a gun. And even then, at Wounded Knee, there were only a handful present. There is no reason to expect that the mass of Americans will experience a revolutionary Nostalgia any sooner than the Indians did, or in any greater numbers. Indeed, the idea is ludicrous. What would it be like? One imagines millions of Americans— beauty-salon blondes, hard hats, students, blacks, perfessers— marching down Pennsylvania Avenue chanting:

> BRING / BACK / THE GOOD OLD DAYS!
> BRING / BACK / THE GOOD OLD DAYS!
> BRING / BACK / THE GOOD OLD DAYS!

And, in their hands, posters reading *"We Want The Shadow!"*, *"Smash Progress!"*, and *"Revenge the 5¢ Cigar!"*

The scenario is deliberately absurd, but absurdity alone has never disqualified a possibility from becoming a happenstance. Indeed, revolutionary slogans, values, symbols, and actions often seem comic and surreal to those who anticipate them, precisely because they're revolutionary. What makes them surreal is that the means and ends of nascent radical contingents are necessarily "inappropriate." They have no "place" in the society (as it is) and, because they contradict the established order at the plenary level, they seem bizarre, unreal, and ridiculous. Anticipating the shape of future revolutionary modes is consequently about as difficult as estimating the cruising altitude of a "pig with wings."

Radical Nostalgia is therefore an absurdity, but not an impossibility. One can even find "evidence" for its emergence in the developing resistance to change as such, and in the increasingly militant (and sometimes "irrational") impedence of new public works. The message appears to be that, if we cannot recapture the past, we can at least preserve the present.

And yet, no matter how widespread the contemporary nostalgia is, it's unlikely to reach the proportions necessary to stimulate a "transvaluation of values." It is much more likely that the emotion will decay into a pervasive wistfulness that falsifies the past and serves, not as a lever in the present, but as an escape from it.

That process is already well under way. What began as an unselfconscious perception of loss has become an industry. A commodity like any other, nostalgia obsesses the supermarkets. And, just as we buy "the sizzle rather than the steak," we buy the wistfulness rather than (as in the case of Annie Greensprings) the wine.

Our nostalgia is no longer our own; it is served, rather than felt. Like so much else, it has been taken from us, remade, packaged and then sold back at a profit. No longer is it necessary to invent the emotion from within ourselves; it comes, along with the other Minimum Daily Requirements, in each package of Country Mornin' Cereal, in each rerun of *The Waltons* and *Happy Days*. The emotion is, of course, no more authentic than a hooker's love, but it tides us over. Unfortunately, that's all it does. Porn on the cob.

If continued "progress" is, as the Club of Rome and others

suggest, equivalent to disaster; if stagnation is made impossible by the autonomy of technique; then our only chance for survival would seem to rest with our ability to reinvent the past—to return. And yet, this too seems to be impossible. The people are used up, sapped and exhausted by the splendor and intricacy of America. A Refusal of the sort which Marcuse envisions demands an expenditure of energy that is, quite simply, beyond us. We're too civilized, too refined, to experience anything so intense as a Radical Nostalgia. Continued "progress" requires nothing more of us than a dead man's float toward the historical horizon. To retreat would involve an attack upon axioms, a long swim against the current of events. Why bother? It's far easier to accept America as our fate than it would be to remake it as our instrument. To be used, to be acted upon, requires only that we be. To act . . . that is a different matter.

5. Decadence

And so—incapable of resurrecting the past, and unable to affect the future—we're left in the present with the evidence of our decline. We become self-conscious and detached, morbid students of the national pathology. The certainty of our fate—the *inevitability* of America—renders us aloof and, in doing so, generates a clarity which, because it is impotent, finds its expression in irony. We give ourselves over to decay. We embrace decadence as the last heroism open to us.

And it *is* heroic. To give up all hope, to surrender to the future and decline *with gusto,* demands almost theatrical bravery and self-sacrifice. *Decadence is always radical: it eats at the roots.*

It is, of course, easier to be decadent in America than anywhere else. Our wealth and technical expertise—our *power*—provide us with extraordinary opportunities for decay. With the help of television, data processing, systems analysis, and a free press, it's entirely possible that we'll be able to accomplish within a decade what Rome required centuries to do.

Decadence is the jujitsu of history; we embrace our own destruction and, in doing so, endure—if not as a society and not as a people, then as people. It is the objectification of the self, the willingness to experience oneself as *an object in a setting*. As a process, decadence represents the *art of being in a place or time self-consciously*. Thus, for instance, we may be certain that a society is in a state of decay when its people begin to dwell upon their "role in history," their "national mission," and their "traditions." At that point, they're no longer being, but performing, *acting* the part of themselves.

This isn't to say that societies don't have traditions, but that, when the people become conscious of them *as such*, when they act *in behalf* of the traditions themselves (as with the impending Bicentennial), the people have lost their spontaneity and authenticity. They live at a remove from themselves. (Anyone who's been to the Grand Ole Opry in recent years, attended a contemporary rock "festival," or watched Senator-Sam Ervin quote Shakespeare will understand: each is an event trying to live up to its own significance and, thereby, failing to do so.)

Eventually, decadence becomes bloody. The nuance ceases to satisfy and, more or less rapidly, is phased out in favor of the blast. Only extremity serves to titillate, to stimulate. We come to demand the extravagant jolt, the beheading-pizza-and-Pisco-Sour of experience. Cruelty delights, excesses inform. Languor overtakes us and makes us "soft" even as our sensibilities contract and harden to an almost ceramic density. As our lives lose their content, their *affectiveness*, we learn how to live vicariously, depending upon others (in the news and in the arts) to manufacture experience. Or else we chase "the action," clambering through a matrix of superficial long shots, emerging with vertigo at the edge of probability: everything is transformed into a game and, having less and less to lose, we take dramatic chances; bet it all; on anything. Or else we contrive to energize our setting, immersing ourselves in the illusion of History, seeing what is ordinary as symptomatic, pursuing "records" (the hottest day, dryest month, most-Presbyterians-killed-on-county-roads-west-of-the-Mississippi-on-an-autumn-Wednesday). Or else we become crisis addicts, sensate only at the brink, demanding that the banal become sensational.

Because the civilization is no longer our own; because it is imposed upon us by the logic of unfolding methods no longer within our control; because we cannot participate with any effect . . . we become aliens and observers, tourists at home. We live at an existential apogee, an internal distance from ourselves and our surroundings. At this point there isn't much left but entertainment, unless we choose the rituals of some rude and secret heresy that promises to sensationalize existence through the auspices of an exquisite understanding (not available to the general public). We enlist in cults—breathing, screaming, chanting, dreaming, sitting, praying—placing our faith in E-meters, orgone blankets, broomsticks, mandalas, indoles, whatever spiritual nose cone holds promise. When everything's going, anything goes. And from this, at least, we may expect some singular validities to emerge: civilizations seldom reach their peaks until *after* their declensions have begun.

For most, however, there is only the possibility of passive entertainment; decadence may energize some, but it enervates millions. "Action" and amusement serve as a last refuge. And if our sensibilities are blunted—so what? We need only increase the stimulus. If ten volts cannot move us, a hundred may. And if we become accustomed to a hundred, then we may increase the voltage further—to a thousand or a billion! Any escalation of experience is possible, so long as it rescues the senses from oblivion.

The indolence characteristic of decadence undoes nothing so much as the imagination: its exercise becomes increasingly difficult. We seek, therefore, entertainments that are complete, that ask nothing of us but that we watch. We grow impatient with the abstract, the "difficult," the impressionistic: their hidden truths demand too much effort. What cultural hero has the patience left to read *Gravity's Rainbow,* or probe the occluded themes of Bergman? It's simpler to be Warholized, confronted with the unnerving facticity of a giant soup can, the serialized inertia of the Empire State Building, the lethal stillness of a Monroe photograph, the bloated ripeness of eternal flowers. Warhol manifests the consumptive bloom on our decay. Memorializing the mineral in images of exquisite tedium, he sensationalizes stasis itself. Mediocrity and the commonplace become, in his hands, spectacular and entertaining—not because he changes them, but because he does not. He regurgitates the culture, amusing us with the fact of its indigestibility, its resistance to the touch, its inhumanity. The effect, of course, is comical, a sort of gallows humor. And because Warhol makes no attempt at establishing the "significance" of his subjects, as an anthropologist or sociologist would be tempted to do, his realism is all the more rigorous: artful, rather than scientific, *because* it abstains from interpretation.

Too rigorous, in fact, for most of us. Closer to the center of our attention is the sensational realism of all contemporary popular entertainments from AIP * horror shows through *Superman Comics* and the *Six Million Dollar Man.* In these, the banal serves only as an anchor for our fantasies, a setting broad enough to support the weight of Jodorowsky's flaming bunnies, Peckinpagh's decapitations, and Polanski's good old knife in the nose. Warhol's nonaggression pact with the ordinary is unsigned by Peckinpagh, Stan Lee, and the others. Where the artist holds out the possibility of a reconciliation with the banal, the entertainer offers nothing more than a temporary escape from it. (Which is, after all, something. Which is, in fact, quite a bit.)

And yet, even entertainments are inadequate to the task of thwarting boredom, the scourge of decadence. Each *moment* must be inoculated with interest, and there is simply not

---

* American International Pictures.

enough to go around. (This, despite the fact that the average television viewer witnesses more than 13,000 simulated "killings" a year. Presumably, the number would be even higher but for the popularity of blood sports such as boxing and fist games such as hockey which, by virtue of their authenticity, have a qualitative edge over fictions.) It becomes necessary, therefore, to turn the world into a stage, to create an *existential* theater—a Forum, in fact. And because blood and pain are reliably à la mode, the Forum depends upon these for its subject matter. Death and injury offer the last opportunity for sustained sensation, recognition, and sympathy. And these, whether viewed as "news" or "drama," emerge as a steady diet. Fire, famine, hurricane, quake, assassination, riot, war, rape —we keep abreast of the country and the times.

Like pro football and the Indianapolis 500, politics becomes more popular as its practice becomes more brutal. The events of the Sixties—brought to us with the inevitable commercial interruptions—restored history to politics, a *de facto* de-Ike-ification. No effort was required to absorb the implications and impact of a man floating in space; a peasant village set afire with Zippos; young women heaved through the plateglass windows of the Loop; black kids chewed by dogs in Alabama; the spectacle of a million people massing; or an *espontáneo* execution on Dallas TV.

These proved to be the lowest common denominators of a decade so full that most remember it as an Age. Their force and flamboyance empurpled the times, compelling each of us to reenter history, *to live inside it,* play a role, follow the plot. The present bloated with a stipulated importance as the historic sensibility transformed the world into a gestalt of symbols, settings, and props. *Nothing* was exempt from the infestation of Meaning. Fucking, dishwashing, lettuce, trees, hair, grapes, soul food, hems, Volkswagens—each act and thing underwent a mythic inflation. Nothing was so insignificant that one could pass it by without a sort of knowing look, a wink in the mind's eye. All things belonged to some *class* of things, each act participated in a *trend;* and so both acts and things demanded to be taken seriously. They were Statements. They spoke to the dead. There was no such thing as a "private" life.

History moved through us like cocaine. It was impossible not to be "political." The Kennedys, those Evel Knievels of populism, always promised to self-destruct before our eyes —threatened, in effect, to make us a part of history, if only as witnesses. And, just as one anticipates the unlikely possibility of a no-hitter whenever one goes to the ballpark, so one could not attend a Kennedy rally, or watch a speech, without secretly wondering whether this. might. not. be. THE. NIGHT. That possibility informed the banal occasion with an immediacy, an expectation of shock that had theretofore existed only in Vincent Price films. And the Kennedys' misfortunes— the magnetic north of their charisma—proved transferable. Any politician worth his salt might explode. And several did, heating up the scene.

Even our metaphors bespoke our entry into a cerebral Astrodome, a Forum of gladiatorial expectations. Party hacks spoke glibly and at excruciating length of "the man in the Arena," comparing Vietnam with a "goal-line stand," and pointing to Agnew as "the man on deck." Nixon "called the signals" in Asia, delivering a yuletide "one-two punch" against Hanoi and Haiphong, while liberals "sat on the sidelines" awaiting their "turn at bat." And so on, *ad nauseam:* the world as spectator sport.

By the time the Seventies arrived, our excitement was tinged with the impatience of fans at an extra-inning ball game. Theoretically, the show could go on forever. More likely, however, it would end at any moment and, afterward, there would be fighting in the parking lots and traffic jams on the way home. The best place to be was next to an exit, bags packed, and ready to go.

VIII. Decadence: A Defense

> *. . . it is a biologic film.*
> William Burroughs

1. Existential Stardom

That was not, however, a practical option for most. To flee the Incurable, to expatriate and escape, has always been a minority enterprise, an alternative of the privileged. More common was a sense of cultural resignation, an acceptance of the inevitable. And this in turn produced a curious recognition: nothing is so relentlessly liberating as the realization that one's situation is Incurable.

To accept mortality as a *fait accompli*, a certainty both imminent and beyond remedy, is to experience a great release. Morbid prospects exempt us from the tyranny of ordinary cares, and deliver us to the very axis of possibility. Once we've lost hope, all experiences become equally probable. We decay, and sometimes magnificently.

A defense of decadence is nevertheless an ambitious undertaking, especially in a country that is at ease with parking meters and pay toilets. It is also somewhat futile since such a defense is unlikely to make converts of those who despise the decadent on grounds that are virtually a priori. Only a confrontation with mortality is likely to change all that.

Decadence and the Incurable are coefficients of each other. To acknowledge the imminent mortality of the self, or to recognize what is terminal within the society, is to accept the certainty of decay. It could hardly be otherwise. Few things are so pathetic, so embarrassing, as those who cling to a center which will not hold, who chirp their way into "that good night," insisting that the winter moon is actually a summer sun.

The vocabulary of apocalypse is increasingly familiar in the United States. It's apparent to many, perhaps most, that the next few years will inaugurate an age in upheaval. Crises will accumulate with a devastating synergy, and their natures will span the breadth of our categories: political, economic, cultural, ecological, and spiritual. The future impends, a Metacrisis.

Technogogues who perceive each problem monistically believe that each can be solved by the application of an appropriate technique. But what the technicians perceive to be a mere swirl of isolated motes, manageable in their disconnection, is actually a galaxy of dilemmas whose interaction renders them dynamic. The Metacrisis, incipient as a lump within the breast, is a gestalt, larger than the sum of our solutions.

That America is about to enter its final act, to reach its climax as a civilization, seems clear. Evidence in support of that view is widely available, and needn't be dwelt upon in this book. The skeptical optimist may attend to a vast body of literature on the subject—a sampler would include the works of Toynbee, Ophuls, Stent, Skinner, Heilbroner, Ellul, and the Club of Rome. He may ponder the *angst* which underlies artifacts such as *The Whole Earth Catalog,* trends such as nostalgia, and movements such as that which has returned so many of the urban young "to the land." If so inclined, the skeptic may listen to the rhetoric of the abounding millenarian sects (Children of God, Divine Light, United Family, et cetera) or to the analyses of the emergent conspiracy cults (e.g., the National Caucus of Labor Committees). Finally, he may do nothing at all—and merely wait for the evidence to *come to him* in the form of street fighting, trade wars, military conflicts, shortages, labor strikes, and an invasion of Orwellian social controls.

Our situation *seems* to be Incurable—whether it is or not—and, in view of that fact or apparition, it's only to be expected that decadent behavior will soon constitute a kind of trend. Some, of course, will insist upon punching the time clock even after the factory has disappeared, but those few may be dismissed as burned-out cases who never quite got over their first paper route. (Who, after all, is more contemptible: the one who fiddles while Brooklyn burns, or the stalwart who remains at his gas pump, waiting for his shift to end, while the station goes up in flames?)

A defense of decadence is therefore a timely undertaking, if only because its practice is about to be democratized. And it *needs* a defense, encumbered as it is with a panoply of popular misconceptions and malignant associations; for centuries, the subject has been mauled by the same people who delivered us into the hair-shirt, time-clock, neck-tie, and Work Ethic.

Decadence has a lousy image. It is, for instance, associated with the very rich (whom everyone hates), and with nasty acts that foreigners and eggheads are known to perform in the dark. In addition, the examples of decay which history has handed down have been uniformly negative: Roman winos giggling at the evisceration of God-fearing girls next door, French aristocrats lisping admonitions about the dietary practices of the poor, Nazi generals diddling each other in the trenches . . . most decadents seem to have been real slobs. Worse yet, decadence seems decidedly un-American, the prerogative of "winded civilizations" who no longer look at tomorrow and shout, "Can do!" And, because it is so often predicated upon a recognition of the Incurable, decadence appears to be without purpose, futile, and even cowardly.

But this is nonsense, a hatchet job the Puritans undertook in order to keep our collective nose to the grindstone (which the Puritans invented and own).

To defend decadence, one must first defuse the word itself, and scatter the misconceptions which attend it. Then, one may begin to redefine its practice in light of its real nature: the drive toward existential stardom.

2. An Ideology of Style?

Why has decadence always been within the behavioral province of the rich and the powerful, but never of the poor? Because decadence is inextricably bound up with, and inseparable from, *style*. And the poor, of course, have never had much style.

Why this should be so is easy to understand. Style entails the making of a choice—to do something in one way rather than in another. But to choose among alternatives, we must first have them. And the condition of the poor has always been such that their alternatives have been few or nonexistent. Preference is a luxury of the rich. (It is, for instance, meaningless to talk about the "life-style" of welfare recipients: lacking alternatives, they also lack style. Decadence is therefore beyond them.)

"Life-style" is itself a neologism of the industrial West, and has its genesis in the spiraling expectations of middle-class Americans. Formerly, only the aristocracy was called upon to make the kinds of choices that allow one to speak of a life-style. The economic boom that attended mechanization, however, extended those choices to a vast number of people who were, quite suddenly, called upon to develop *taste* (or, failing that, to acquire *tastes*). For what may have been the first time in history, the masses were expected to decide questions of an aesthetic nature: wing tips or sneakers? Viyella or lamb's wool? peas or lima beans? colonial or ranch? Mustang or Vega? Only a few decades earlier, they'd eaten what was set before them, worn what was available, slept where they'd always slept, and done what they'd been told. The affluence and variety which mechanization engendered, and upon which capitalism came to depend, made life-styles possible, and even mandatory. Decadence became accessible to the people for the first time—because style was.

In the United States, this seems to have happened relatively gradually. In some countries, however, it took place virtually overnight. In England, for instance, a postwar boom transformed the working classes and their young. Before the Second World War, young Britons had little or no opportunity for significant cultural expression (in terms of exercising style). After the war, that changed. For the first time, the working-class young had money in their jeans—and they spent it indulgently on the most garish clothes imaginable, on velvets, spangles, Edwardian suits, high heels, boots, and synthetic colors. They became peacocks. Unlike their parents, who were drab and thrifty with their new wealth, the British young developed a life-style. And, as if to prove it, they undertook a violent stylistic mitosis that ultimately boiled down to confrontations between the Rockers and the Mods.

Questions of hair length and tailoring, music and slang were sufficiently important to the British young that they beat and stabbed each other over them. It seems absurd that questions of taste should be made matters of life or death, but that they were (and are) is undeniable. The Rockers and Mods represented a dramatic cultural dialectic, a thesis and antithesis that were not resolved until the Beatles established their temporary harmonic synthesis.

Similar cultural clashes took place around the world—in Holland, Mexico, Japan, Italy, France, Germany, Spain—wherever the young were affluent enough to support a multiplicity of popular styles. And, in each case, particular styles came to be identified with special viewpoints. Indeed, the identification became so complete that one could speak of an emerging *ideology of style,* a politics of haberdashery and coiffure. Reason suggests that styles are adopted by individuals and groups in accordance with their intellectual or class biases; that is, one embraces a particular fashion *because* one is in sympathy with the view of those who have popularized it. In fact, however, the opposite is as often true. It frequently happens that the fashion one inherits, or adopts, causes one to accept virtually any set of beliefs which is associated with it. (Stick a kid in a Nazi uniform, and there's a good chance that he'll start clicking his heels.) Certainly this was true of the counterculture: thousands of young people, many of whom held no discernible political beliefs whatsoever, found themselves radicalized by the uniform they admired and adopted. Long hair—not because it had anything to do with the war, *per se,* but simply because it wasn't *short*—was for years a punchable offense in certain cultural zones, and only ceased to be so after it had achieved the political neutrality that chic confers.

Attempting to understand what decadence is, one quickly concludes that it's inseparable from style, and characteristic of certain styles. And yet style and decadence, while conjugally linked, are not synonymous. Decadence has characteristics of its own.

3. Playboys, Poets, and Cranks

The problem with defining decadence is that the word is itself sclerotic, referring to degeneration. That seems to be a result of Puritanical prejudices more than anything else, though, since "decadent" is most often invoked in a loose way. That is, the word is used as a kind of indiscriminate branding iron, and tends to be applied to any mode of behavior of which the speaker happens to disapprove (it's like "fascist" in this way).

And yet, however often the word is misapplied, it nevertheless refers to something real. There is an authentic decadence that exists independently of the observer and his values.

Real decadence is multidimensional, coherent, and complex. Its edges are defined by a preoccupation with the senses, an affection for the moment, and an insistence upon the supremacy or inconsequentiality of an individual's existence and acts. Decadence takes place at the extremity of self-indulgence, but it is seldom, if ever, marred by self-importance. (We do not think of the decadent as "serious" people, and neither do they.) Decadence is scandalous in its inclination toward excess, and often glamorous in its narcissism. It frequently seems nasty and luxurious, contemptible and enviable, all at once. (Think of Jackie O., or, better yet, think of the way that most people think of Jackie O.*)

But most of these characteristics are secondary, and proceed from a common source: that is, the decadent have somehow been released from the consequences of their acts and live in wholesale disregard of the future. They are, in other words, "irresponsible."

The origins of that inconsequentiality can be several. A drastic sense of one's mortality is enough. Extraordinary wealth serves the same end, and so does the radical naïveté that children share with the senile.

According to the origins of their release from future cares, the decadent can be divided into three groups: poets, playboys, and cranks, each of which differs from the other in strategic ways. Only by making these distinctions about origins can we explain the fact that the annals of decadence include an equal number of saints, savages, and yo-yo's. Byron, de Sade, Henry Miller, Blake, Farouk, Gille de Rais, Rimbaud, Proust, Huysmans, the Borgias, Rubirosa, Verlaine, Baudelaire, Ludwig of Bavaria, Dick Haymes, Coleridge, Dick Diver —each pursued a decadent course, but with different results. The origins of their decadence go a long way toward explaining the outcome of each.

The poets seem to have suffered the same catastrophic recognition, to have understood their mortality at an almost molecular level. This morbid understanding effectively severs them from the future, or renders it distressingly finite, thereby turning their attentions to the present with a vengeance. We obscure their excesses and reckless self-indulgence only because their decay is redeemed by literature (or, in Ludwig's case, public monuments and tourist attractions).

While poets achieve fame, playboys seldom acquire more

---

* Or—best of all—think of the way that Jacqueline de Bouvier de Kennedy d'Onassis thinks of "Jackie O."

than a notorious celebrity that is precisely as fleeting as their lives or potency. Their decadence is an especially happy variety in that it is not particularly plagued by intimations of mortality. Inheriting a fortune, as much as a facility with pentameter and a familiarity with death, immunizes one from the society's customs and consequences.

The crank is a third case altogether. His position is the most extreme because his disregard of consequences proceeds from a thoroughly barbaric naïveté. Cranky decadence, as distinguished from other kinds, tends to be brutal. The very young and the very old frequently share an identical lacuna: where their empathy should be, there is a hole. Each has an excuse, of course. The young are frankly ignorant, savages setting winos and turtles on fire out of curiosity. And the old are tired, damaged by a lifetime of usefulness and consequences that they have, inexplicably, outlived; like the very young, the very old have a treasury of pardons, prerogatives, and exemptions.

But we don't think of kids and geezers as decadent, even though their behavior would otherwise qualify. Their naïveté is mostly unintentional and out of control; it's not so much stylistic as hormonal. And, because the consequences of their acts are invisible to them, rather than disregarded by them, society forgives. (In addition, the old have earned the right to their decay.)

Cranky decadence would, therefore, be an unviable category if it were not for the fact that the naïveté which motivates it is cultivated by some (Gilles de Rais, de Sade, and Rimbaud are notorious examples).

Having made those distinctions, acknowledging that there are often bridges between one category and another, the point can be made: decadence is a particularized behavioral style whose causes are specific and limited. That is, it has certain preconditions without which it cannot exist: a mortal insight, the liberation that affluence affords, a deluded naïveté, or a combination of those.

The mortality of a society (perceived by the many as imminent) can lead to a *collective* decadence, a mass disregard for social consequences. And this will always be a radical and revolutionary course because, in acting upon the premise that the society is nearly defunct, the perception turns out to be self-fulfilling. Rightly or wrongly, prematurely or not, the future is given up. It is abandoned as the lost cause it quickly becomes.

Historians tend to see decadence as a malaise, a virus which civilizations catch at their apex: traditions are ignored, institutions corrupted, and morals overthrown. The grindstone spins unattended, and the society comes unzipped: the people grow sexy and solipsistic; they ask not what they can do for their country, but what their country can do for them. They lack the inclination to defend the society with their time or energies, which are instead wholly committed to the immediate gratifications of the present. Eventually, history's bozos— barbarians and ruder peoples who *just know* that God gave man hands in order that he might strangle—arrive upon the scene, and make short work of it.

The decadents are assassinated in their tubs.

And this is seen as a kind of tragedy, *de causibus*. We regret the collapse of great civilizations, the fall of nations and kings, for the same reason that we regret an incompleted forward pass: a remarkable possibility (*a record!*) seems to have been cheated of actuality.

Usually, our regret is tempered by the cluckings of moral superiority: "My God, if only they hadn't grown so *decadent* —think what they might have achieved! Why, they could have subjugated the entire world!" But it's an unconvincing reproach since societies decay only when their own limits, and the possibilities they contain, have been reached and exhausted. At that point they become international pushovers, or get their limits redefined through revolution. Or else they simply fall apart from within. (It's a safe bet that if the pharaohs had endured an extra thousand years, the wisdom of Egypt and man would not have been appreciably increased

—only the size of subsequent pyramids would have grown.)

But the plaint against decadence is particularly unconvincing in the United States, where decadence is institutionalized; where, indeed, decadence is the promise which the state has made to the people. America long ago passed the stage where the majority aspired to be released from "need." And, in passing that stage, it entered into the reach of its destiny: to release the people from their *cares*.

Immigrants may have been content to reach a land so apparently rich that circumstances seemed to guarantee a chicken in every pot. But that wasn't the promise America made to her *native* sons. To them, it whispered and cooed: "Stick with me, and I'll do the cooking too!"

It was not entirely credible that "any kid might grow up to be president"—but that any kid might grow up to be Lance Reventlow, racing and balling his way across the landscape, seemed feasible and, in fact, more desirable. If we excuse decadence from its negative connotations, it's found to be the American Dream: a Corvette in every garage, a stereo in every bath, servants from the Land of Somewhere Else.

A defense of decadence is therefore a defense of the American Dream. What made the Dream possible was the happenstance of historical serendipity: the birth of a nation coinciding with the onset of mechanization. In putting new distance between labor and productivity, formerly coefficients of each other, mechanization shifted the economic base from work to consumption. An abundance of natural resources, coupled with the sheer *horsepower* of our machinery and the efficiency of our organizational techniques, allowed us to take productivity almost for granted, and to concentrate our attentions upon escalating demand, realizing the Dream.

In making mass consumption a cornerstone of the society, America took the "decay" out of decadence. The health of the economy was directly tied to the rising expectations of the folk, and to the material realization of those expectations. In so far as we "decayed," or came to be released from *basic* needs and cares, we came into our own: the country boomed because it was predicated upon the possibility that "decadence" might be strength.

All that stood in the way of the Dream's realization, its endurance, was the finitude of raw materials and the possibility that the people themselves would become bored with their compulsive consumption. If the materials ran out, or became too expensive, expansion would stop, wants would begin to go unmet, and the economy would unravel because growth itself was the economy's fuel. Similarly, if the people became reluctant consumers, the primary need of expanding production—expanding demand—would not be met, and the same disintegration would occur.

The American Dream was therefore threatened on two different flanks. Access to sufficient raw materials, and to foreign markets, was a military and diplomatic problem that could be dealt with in the conventional way. The military/intelligence apparatus might be relied upon to guarantee the access we required. Guaranteeing the continued expansion of demand, however, was a separate and subtler problem. To guard the Dream's internal flank, a unique entity evolved: Madison Avenue.

4. The Avenue

Madison Avenue is both the machinery of our decadence and its first line of defense. To keep the country running, it must transform the imaginations of the citizenry almost daily, cultivating an enduring discontent, an obsession with new wants.

It's been said that the purpose of the counterculture was to make everyone a superstar. Whether that's true or not, it's certainly the purpose of Madison Avenue. The Avenue's basic function is to create settings in which each of us may star: by acquiring the setting (e.g., a Cadillac) we acquire stardom as well. The whole thrust of advertising, its *modus operandi*, is to incorporate the customer or mark within the ad itself. To place him *there*, on the Marlboro range or in the Arpège café, to reinterpret his identity in the light of some new product or service.

People's access to such delights was formerly confined to priestly sermons about the hereafter, and to the vicarious luxuries of dime novels. Madison Avenue requires the same suspension of disbelief that religious faith and the novel do, but has the advantage that the commodity is available at a price. Advertising asks that we not be skeptical of *ourselves,* that we believe in the mystique which the Avenue creates for us. It promises to make a wonderland of our lives if only we'll believe in the magic of the image it deliberately creates.

What this amounts to is narcissistic magic. That is, products are transformed into environments—the vehicles of concocted identities—and into talismans, conferring upon the owner whatever condition the advertiser happens to associate with his product.

As an environment, the product (e.g., a perfume or cigarette) establishes a setting or frame of reference in which we may perform. Our identity becomes a function of what we buy or use, since the product makes its idiosyncracies our own. We live within *its* context, and *its* content becomes ours.

As a talisman, the product is found to possess a quality more important, albeit less tangible, than its supposed function. The business of a Cadillac, for instance, is transportation, but that isn't the basis on which it's sold. Instead, Cadillac advertisements sell success first, and the vehicle hardly at all; it just happens, the ads imply, that Cadillacs are the mechanisms required to confer success upon the citizen. They suggest, in other words, that the Cadillac is not the result of having wealth—but its cause. Own one, and you'll be rich too.

It used to be the case that changing one's identity required the intervention of a judge, or at least the issuance of a false passport. Today, changes in identity can be accomplished simply by changing brands. Consider, for instance, a guy—

call him "Woody"—who, let us say, smokes the "new," proletarianized Benson & Hedges cigarettes. Those are the ones whose length is so enormous that they're forever getting caught in closing elevator doors and jammed into any device within unexpected reach of their lighted ends (*"America's Favorite Cigarette Break"*). Chances are, Woody is a pretty goofy guy (and knows it) or he wouldn't smoke Benson & Hedges.

What does Woody drive? Well, certainly not a Ford Mustang II (which is advertised as *"The Right Car at the Right Time"*). Nor does he drive a Cadillac, which is, in fact, almost unthinkable in view of his brand of cigarettes. (Cadillac owners are dead serious; after all, they can afford to be.) No, Woody drives a "bug," a beige Volkswagen that probably has a dent in its right front fender.

Now, this isn't to suggest that Woody's a dope. On the contrary, he thinks for himself, disregards appearances, and has a lot of fun with his thrift. His cigarettes last longer (packing more cancer to the pack), and so does his gas. What does he care if people laugh at him?

There are some other things that we might guess about Woody. He wears, in all likelihood, H.I.S. pants (*"For a Truly Touching Experience"*), and thinks of himself as a sensible member of the counterculture's left wing. If he drinks, Woody's a beer man, opting for "Gusto" over the other brands; he might, on occasion, order a Harvey Wallbanger just for the fun of saying it, but that's about it.

One day, however, Woody's girl ("Sandy" or "Wendy" or "Barb") leaves him. Woody is absolutely shattered. Deep in despair, he visits the neighborhood bar and, abandoning his quest for Gusto, starts drinking Jack Daniels. Doubles. Naturally, he smashes up his car later in the evening.

The next day, released from the hospital with only minor cuts and bruises, Woody goes out to buy a new car. Does he get another Volkswagen? He does not. He buys a "muscle car," a Dodge Charger, perhaps. (Or, better yet, a Corvette.) Woody is ready to *charge*. (Or *'vette,* as the case may be.)

Waiting impatiently in his new car for the street light to change, Woody lights up a cigarette. But the Benson & Hedges are somehow unsatisfactory. They've ceased to amuse. Now that Sandy's left him, he couldn't care less about "economy." *He's ready for a shorter smoke.* Buying a pack of Camels, he lights up, and lets the smoke slide through his teeth. (Castrating bitch!) People begin to call him Steve (which is, after all, his given name). He doesn't drink beer anymore (fuck Gusto!)—he's into Scotch (Johnnie Walker Black) and has, moreover, phased out his chinos in behalf of double knits. Sandy's dying to get him back now, but does he care? HAH! He's having a goddamn ball. . . .*

Enough of Woody.

If the business of Madison Avenue was confined to selling commodities—rather than marketing images and styles as well—it wouldn't be much more than the instrument of a manic materialism (which isn't, in itself, decadent). But because the nation's industrial health depends upon the constant turnover of commodities, rather than upon their mere collection, the Avenue goes further. It fulfills a psychiatric function. The mental pathologies of the citizenry (their phobias, fetishes, and insecurities) are carefully monitored and exploited via "market research." Personalities are reordered through the prescription of commodities whose images are often stronger than the consumer's own identity, and new behavioral norms are established through the calculated invasion of new styles. Traditions are discarded as inhibitions, or rooted out as fixations, and consciousness itself is subject to stylization. (*"You've Come a Long Way, Baby."*)

The Avenue's psychiatric intervention in the marketplace has made Americans more involved in the things they own, while paradoxically diminishing their attachment to them.

---

* Woody-Steve's story goes on and on. When he meets Lissa he switches to Marlboros, and trades in his old car for a new Mustang II. He then switches to Courvoisier. After Lissa and Steve tie the knot, he moves over to a pipe and Borkum Riff Tobacco, acquires a Ford LTD and starts hitting the martinis pretty hard. The divorce shakes him up, though, and . . . so forth.

Materialism gives way to something else, a newer philosophy, or world view—Stylism, perhaps. Wallace Stevens tells us that reality is "not ideas about the thing, but the thing itself." While this may be the operative premise on Parnassus, it isn't so on the Avenue. There, ideas about the thing *are* the thing itself.

It's possible, of course, that the poet and the huckster are both right—Stevens' materialism is *surpassed* by the Avenue's stylism, rather than contradicted by it. The ad men never promised realism, only ideas about the thing.

The Avenue's psychiatric function, however, isn't restricted to changing commodities into ideas. The Avenue is also responsible for carrying out that function *in reverse*. That is, *it changes ideas into commodities*. In this second role, Madison Avenue acts as the great co-opter of movements and concepts. It arbitrates the country's internal dialogue, synthesizing opposing views, reaching compromises in the public's behalf—deciding, in other words, which ideas *sell*.

Counterculture and women's liberation are classic examples of movements "processed" by the Avenue. The spectacular energies of the young during the 1960s and the insurgence of feminism reorganized the intellectual landscape, questioning, provoking, and polarizing the country. In their naïveté, the young and the women believed that the issues they raised would be resolved "democratically": that is, in Congress, in dialogue, and in the streets. What happened, however, was entirely different. The most strategic ideological battles took place in none of those forums, but in the suites of Avenue account execs, in the minds of copywriters, on television, and on the advertising pages of the nation's magazines.

It was there that America accommodated itself to the new ideas or rejected them. What made those ideas virtually impossible to ignore was the economic strength which the young possessed and, just as important, the attention they commanded from their envious elders. In co-opting the young and the women's movement, the Avenue exercised its usual care for the stability of the social boat, going to extraordinary lengths in its efforts to separate the movements' styles, slogans, symbols, heroes, and catchwords from their essences and contents.

Sometimes the Avenue's efforts were amusing, especially when the advertisers adopted the symbols and rhetoric of causes that were, in themselves, absolutely at odds with the commodity being sold.

"*Vogue* says: to be pretty, you must be natural. *Angel Face* [makeup] is for girls who agree—girls like Sian Houston." *Vogue* and Angel Face then tell us that "natural" means the application of Angel Face Makeup Mousse (Pretty Creamy shade) topped off with a swath of Pretty Pansy Cream Blusher, some Wineshine Lipstick, and a few hits of Silver Pearl Eye Shadow modified with a touch of something called Blue Haze. The result is about as "natural" (undertones of ecological awareness, health foods, spontaneity, and unspoiled nature) as a waxwork at Madame Tussaud's.

Indeed, "naturalness" was something that the Avenue could really sink its prose into.

"My world is evergreens and old blue jeans. Fresh, clean air. And *Dep* for my hair."

"Right Guard's newest anti-perspirant—*Natural Scent*. A light clean scent. Not perfumey or chemical. A scent that comes from real, natural ingredients. Not a lot of artificial ones. And it's Right Guard. You know it has the best wetness fighter in any anti-perspirant spray."

Reading Right Guard's ad, one is ready to believe that, after years of underarm gassing, the company has managed to develop a scent which will return the smell of sweat to the consumer. For a price, of course. (First we pay to get rid of it because it's "body odor," then we pay to get it back because it's a male "scent"; it is, in a sense, free enterprise's way of recycling attitudes.)

In each of these ads, the ecology and natural-environment enthusiasts are solicited by corporate allusion to their catchwords (e.g., "natural"), seeking to identify the product with the movement—or else to affiliate the uninvolved with the values of the movement by making it accessible to them through the agency of the product. The same contradictions were apparent in the Avenue's relationship to the women's movement.

The Powers modeling school, for instance, urged womankind to "Liberate Yourself" by paying to enroll in a course designed to turn out professional models. The pitch was that the (financial) rewards of modeling would enable a woman to free herself. The advertisement neglected to mention that the price of freedom might be the soul since models are, above all, pro sex objects. Nor did the advertisement mention that most women who enroll in such schools never become successful models, but must content themselves with having learned the techniques of modeling: makeup application, "poise," "walking," posture, smile tactics, and so forth—all of which may be desirable from a man's point of view, but none of which have any obvious relationship to women's liberation. Indeed, they seem antithetical to it in so far as they reinforce sexist stereotypes.

If a prize for the most grotesque example of bad faith had to be given, however, Ma Griffe perfume would probably take it. As one of their ads reported (urged?):

> You're liberated.
> You don't believe in marriage.
> You tell him so.
> You wear Ma Griffe.
> He slips on the ring.
> (It's five carats.)

The ad's message seemed to be: "Okay, girls, insist on all this claptrap about women's lib. But, if you do, you're going to need Ma Griffe, and need it bad." It suggested that women might have their ideological cake and eat it too. Ma Griffe pronounces the reader "liberated," and offers evidence: she doesn't "believe in marriage." Proof of her liberation is then advanced: she "tells him so."

"Him," on the other hand, is some poor shmuck who *does* believe in marriage. We know this because—despite her unconvincing ideological brief (or perhaps because of it)—he nevertheless "slips on the ring." Who is this guy? Who knows? Who cares? *It's five carats!* (Ordinarily, this behavior might seem rather boorish—even whorish. One can imagine the scene.

"I don't believe in marriage," she whispers huskily.

"Of course you don't, sweetlips, but try this baby on for size. It's five, count 'em, *five* carats!"

"In that case," she purrs, extending her hand.)

It goes on and on. The word "revolutionary" supplants the phrase "brand new." (*Cosmopolitan's Love Book* "revolutionises any girl's sex life.") Hush Puppies comes up with a pair of "New Generation" shoes. Ultressa markets "Female Chauvinist, an authoritative shirt . . . soft, silky ($14)." Customers in Hertz Rent-A-Car advertisements come to look disturbingly like Peter Fonda, with long hair and cosmic neckties. (You *still* couldn't rent one without a credit card, though.) The "generation gap" was bridged by booze, as filmmaker Dennis Hopper proved when he posed for a Jim Beam ad—*avec* pageboy, mustache, beads, and denim jacket—with old-timer John Huston. Levi's funded a set of assy commercials so erotic and "liberating" that, in one London theater where it was shown, the fans rioted. H.I.S. pants went even "more countercultural than thou," doing everything but call for the legalization of marijuana.

The young's reaction was predictable. They complained about "cultural exploitation" and co-optation, but saw little that they could do about it. What they didn't seem to understand, however, was that co-optation works both ways. The Avenue co-opted the symbols and rhetoric of the young in order to sell their clients' products but, in doing so, it also sold the thing which it'd co-opted. Advertisements for Angel Face, Dep, Jim Beam, Levi's, Ma Griffe, H.I.S., Hertz, and Right Guard hawked the values of the counterculture and women's lib even as they touted makeup, hair conditioner, bourbon, pants, deodorants, and perfume. Women's liberation became exactly as acceptable as Ma Griffe, and equally chic. It doesn't matter that industry's endorsement of the movement was mercenary and ripe with hypocrisy. What counted was the effect of that endorsement: women who were ambivalent or skeptical about the movement understood, at least subliminally, that its values were literally "in *Vogue*." Not to accept those values, or to neglect the rhetoric, was tantamount to being "lame," unattractive, and cloddish. Ma Griffe spoke to the fashionable women of America, and pronounced them "liberated"; in doing so, the perfume makers struck a greater blow for the women's movement than all the books about *Vaginal Politics* and all the "consciousness-raising sessions" held to date.

In selecting and packaging the symbols of social movements, Madison Avenue exerts a profound and unyielding influence on all Americans. That this psychiatric influence is virtually unnoticed makes it all the more potent since its messages are absorbed without reflection or questioning: we may reject the product being sold, but the imagery is beneath or beyond our notice. We grow accustomed to the symbols and slogans which the Avenue employs, and our acceptance of them "softens us up" for their content. We aren't *converted* to a cause by exposure to its emblems, but our receptivity to its message is heightened.

In the case of the women's movement, and other progressive groups, this is fine. But the Avenue is a commercial highway, progressive from expedience rather than from necessity. Concerned with the turnover of commodities, it will use any style or symbolism which is eye-catching. Imagine, for instance, opening a women's magazine to the following words, illustrated by a moony photograph depicting a beautiful woman, a diamond ring, and a Yeshiva student (the woman should be in the foreground):

> You're a Nazi.
> You don't believe in Jews.
> You tell him so.

You wear *Totenkopfverbande* perfume.
He slips on the ring.
(It's five carats.)

Turning the page, one comes across an ad for:

STORMTROOPERS: THE BOOTS
WITH THE BUILT-IN KICK ($59)

The illustration shows a foot protruding through a shattered door. On the facing page, an article describes the latest rage in women's fashions: "The Gestapo Look . . . slim . . . severe . . . practical . . . no-nonsense . . . a classic and a must! For the authoritative woman who says 'You *vill*' more often than 'I do.'" Elsewhere in the same fantasy mag, an advertisement for a data retrieval system shows a puzzled executive listening to his boss demand, "Vere are your papers?" And, perhaps, on the last page, a montage of locomotives and timepieces advertising a popular wristwatch:

WE MADE THE TRAINS RUN ON TIME.
NOW IT'S UP TO YOU.

One of the greatest fears liberals and libertarians share in the United States is that the government will intervene in the affairs of the press, "managing" the news. "Big Brother" scenarios imagine a populace made wildly nationalistic by propaganda disguised as information. Certainly this is a legitimate concern, particularly in view of the Nixon Administration's efforts to bludgeon the media into docility. But I don't think it constitutes a danger. The First Amendment offers some protection against such attempts, of course, but what makes the Big Brother scenario even more improbable is the integrity of most journalists and the public's almost visceral skepticism toward the "news." A greater danger of the scenario's realization exists on Madison Avenue. For all practical purposes, advertising is unprotected by constitutional guarantees: federal and state governments routinely, and sometimes drastically, intervene in the Avenue's affairs, and the public takes it for granted since it's assumed that the government is acting in the people's best interests. That assumption seems naïve, and it would unquestionably meet with public rejection if it were applied to news and editorial content. Where advertising is concerned, however, the state is free to meddle almost at will, banning certain advertisements from particular kinds of media, dictating wording, and generally overseeing content in order to monitor "claims." The umbilical relationship between advertising and government, particularly with regard to the latter's regulatory functions vis-à-vis *both* advertising and the electronic media, is inherently Orwellian. What makes it even more dangerous is the fact that advertising is designed to seduce, whereas journalism is written to inform or convince by rational means. The advertiser's integrity is not the journalist's and, moreover, the industry is conditioned to comply with all governmental demands. Finally, the public's skepticism toward reportage is not transferred to advertising, and is therefore no protection. We may doubt the excellence of a particular product, and its value, but the imagery by which it's sold is usually overlooked, subverting consciousness rather than convincing it.

If the State embarked upon a campaign for the management of minds, a Brotherly blitz directed at behavioral control, the news media would be at the very periphery of its strategy. At the center would be Madison Avenue—skilled at the techniques of manipulation, subject to an apparatus of already existing controls, venal, and more seductive in its influence than any editorial medium. In order to exercise power over the nation's half-dozen most influential news publications, the State would be compelled to establish new mechanisms of control, to act forcefully and blatantly in disregard of existing laws. The risks would be enormous and, even if the project succeeded, the results mediocre. While a few people read *The New York Times,* most doubt it. On the other hand, everyone would agree that Hush Puppies aren't a fancy shoe; they're just *dumb* (and that's good). Behavioral controls could be far more effectively implemented through the capture of the country's largest advertising firms, businesses responsible for the content and design of perhaps half the national advertising in the United States. That's a lot of newspaper space, particularly in view of the fact that it's almost entirely devoted to persuasion, rather than to information. It is, in other words, "editorial space" that's paid for and over which the newspaper exercises little or no control.

How likely is it that such a scenario could come to pass? I have no idea. But perhaps that's the wrong question. How certain are we that it hasn't already and, if it had, how certain would we be that it hadn't? How would we know? Admittedly, the notion of CIA agents poring over the Right Guard and Ivory Snow accounts is bizarre. To suggest that this might actually be the case is to commend oneself to the ambiance of a rubber room and canvas coat. But then again—keeping the activities of the Messrs. Hunt & Liddy & McCord in mind, and the CIA's subsidization of *Fodor's Guide*—the notion is not entirely implausible. That is, there are some among us who could conceivably believe it.

5. Tea at the Palaz of Hoon (Bye-bye, Canada Dry)

This may seem to be a few furlongs from the subject of decadence. Having begun with a defense of that condition, we've trudged up Madison Avenue to arrive at speculation concerning the Central Intelligence Agency's relationship to deodorant and detergent ads. The connection may seem obscure, but it's real. Decadence seeks to make the banal sensational, rooting out all that's exquisite in the commonplace; the paranoia which leads "conspiracy theorists" to elaborate extraordinary scenarios accomplishes the same thing. In each case, the banal is elevated to some special status through a trick of perspective. It's seen to have special import by virtue of a concealed meaning, sinister connection, or secret quality that is, to all but the initiated (the decadent and the paranoid), invisible.

Whether decadence takes sensory or intellectual indulgence as its context, the result is an identical megalomania; the present is inflated, blown up with a significance that borders upon the absolute. The gorgeous meal, divine recognition, compulsive fuck, and millenarian conspiracy are one. To the gourmet, each meal is his last; to the mystic and nympho, each moment is final; and to the conspiracy theorist, history is at its climax. Our proximity to what we believe is "the edge of history," the social terminus, makes each of us a superstar in a theater of ejaculation. The uniqueness and finality of the situation ("It's just a shot away") releases the decadent from ordinary cares and responsibilities: old rules no longer apply because, when the future disappears, so must prudence.

Millenarian sects of the past were built upon divinely apocalyptic foundations. Religious elites announced that secular history was at an end, and prepared the masses for their detention in Eternity. Conventional laws and customs were discarded as inherently corrupt or irrelevant, while each millenarian threw out his chest at the realization of his special role, his Election. The cosmic dispensation, a Christian *fatum,* accounted for everything.

Like their religious counterparts, the emergent conspiracy cults are inspired by a radical pessimism, a vatic glimpse of the culture's ruin. Differences between the two types are superficial, technical rather than substantial—despite the fact that each is literally "a world apart" from the other.

Consider, for instance, Moses David Berg and Lyn Marcus. Berg's Children of God sect is, like Marcus's National Caucus of Labor Committees (NCLC), a highly disciplined, hierarchically organized doom cult. Both groups anticipate the world's impending transformation, and the establishment of a new society following an Armageddon-like struggle.* Each would agree that we're at the American climax. For Berg, the struggle is between the forces of God and Evil, categories to which Marcus never refers. Instead, the head of the NCLC sees the

---

* A vision, not incidentally, which Hitler shared.

battle as a struggle between the People and a cabal of fascist intelligence agencies which would enslave them. Berg's Devil, in other words, is Marcus's CIA. Each man is equally a prophet to his followers; and, if both are autocratic, it's only because both are accorded a "special vision," a unique authority or cosmic pipeline. They *know*.

What does it matter that Moses David Berg sees the sinner as a soul seduced by the Devil, while Lyn Marcus views the average citizen as the victim of CIA conditioning and brainwashing? In either case, the sinner and the victim have lost their souls. And, of course, both can regain what they've lost by committing themselves totally (that is to say, by surrendering their time *and* assets) to the organizations of their choice.

If Marcus and Berg were unique, they could be dismissed as aberrations, curdled extremists and nothing more. But they aren't unique. On the contrary, as the country's pessimism swells, so do their congregations and their counterparts. It's tempting to regard such groups as oddball wampeters, isolated religious fanatics and political crank cases whose persuasion is limited and whose influence is nil. But that view fails to take into account the vast number of unorganized, dissatisfied individuals who—without knowing one another—constitute a commune of the depressed.

It is a very large commune, mostly passive and resigned to the collective *fatum*. The religious millenarian groups may be fully subscribed, but the commune isn't. Its numbers are increased by a rising tide of "conspiracy fans" who believe in common that the society is jammed and dominated by the manipulation of sinister (usually venal) forces. Their pantheon of demons is varied and suitably mythic in their supposed influence: a random sample includes the CIA, the Mafia, the Oil Barons, Howard Hughes, the Rockefellers, the Council on Foreign Relations, the Kennedys, Mormons, LEAA—almost anything and anyone will serve. One man's antichrist is another man's savior.

The "commune of the depressed" represents what may be America's last majority. While the nation undergoes its nu-

clear splits, atomizing into particles of opposing granfalloons *
based upon religion, region, gender, politics, and "ethnic heritage"—an unpleasant consensus emerges. It is the consensus of persecution, a collective agreement which proposes that malevolent forces are conspiring to destroy whatever it is that one holds to be precious. Moses David Berg, Lyn Marcus, and their colleagues have merely formalized, and particularized, a paranoia that is general. In a way, that paranoia is a result of the Faustian belief in the efficacy of our techniques. Convinced that there is nothing this nation of experts can't accomplish, it becomes almost reasonable to think that whatever transpires is the result of someone's intention. The oil crisis is therefore seen to be a manufactured disaster visited upon the public by boardroom plotters. Inflation is believed to be the work of gold bugs, ruthless financiers, corrupt politicians, and agrarian cabals. Who killed Marilyn Monroe? Why are we in Vietnam? What's the *real* story behind the JFK assassination, Chappaquiddick, Martin Luther King, and Altamont?

Somewhere along the line, Americans stopped believing in their own mistakes, in coincidence, and the Lone Assassin. Instead, they came to believe, as Faust did, that the world "is governed by demons." (The "them.") It suddenly seemed incredible that history could be deflected by the whim of an individual, or that the priests of science and economics (with their computers and formulae) could blunder unintentionally. For decades we'd been taught that America was "fail-safe," a Superpower whose destiny was bedded down with Progress. If the Superpower was in crisis—if the public suffered—it must be so *by design*. And once that belief became commonplace, so did the search for scapegoats: commies, chauvinists, honkies, hoods, militants, cops, multinationals, welfare mothers, the liberals, the press, the Japs, the Jews, the CIA, the "gnomes of Zurich". . . the country came to boil with

---

* "Granfalloon" is a neologism of Kurt Vonnegut, Jr. It refers to associations which are built upon the *deluded* belief that their members have something important in common. Mensa and the D. A. R. are classic examples of the granfalloon.

exasperation and self-loathing. With the possible exception of the Seabees, nothing and no one was spared the identification of one or another role: victim or oppressor, demon or exorcist. Since fallibility didn't exist, Evil must. Or so it seemed to many.

The 1960s were exceedingly affluent years and, as the Dow-Jones Average climbed to new highs, so did social consciousness. But what began (with the civil rights movement) as an Awakening decayed, by the decade's end, into an epidemic of cultural hypochondria. Americans undertook a self-examination so morbid and narcissistic that it bordered on paranoia, a solipsistic search for the symptoms of a national malignancy. The Them. Everyone knew they were there.

Part of this was nostalgia for Vietnam, a wistful search for new scabs. Because it divided us so passionately, the war reminded us that we held something important in common—otherwise, how could we have been so deeply divided, so caring? With "Vietnamization," the country seemed to lose its internal focus, to sink back into the amorphous wad of its discontents. The anger which the war brought to the surface (but didn't create) became untethered with the conflict's "end," and floated across the landscape in search of a place to land.

And yet the war's disappearance from the news did nothing to release us from the conviction that the civilization was nearing its climax, that dramatic changes were gathering on the horizon. History had become an iron lung, an engulfing context that was awful, but vital and impossible to forget. The fade-out of the war, like the diaspora of the counterculture, cut the nation loose from its fetishistic preoccupations with Asia and youth—thereby demolishing *the matrix* of our discontents, but having little effect upon the discontents themselves.

Deprived of that matrix, the age became newly incoherent. If nothing else, the 1960s had been a decade of great certainty. At least, everyone knew what the question was—*Why are we in Vietnam?*—and understood that the answer was to be found at home, in the culture and institutions of America. By 1971, however, we were not in Vietnam, not publicly, and the "question" was therefore meaningless. We found ourselves reduced to the deathbed retort of Gertrude Stein. Asked "What is the answer?" she replied, quite sensibly, "What is the question?" Our situation was no longer the relatively simple one of finding a solution to a discrete problem-mantra, but was, instead, the much more serious one of identifying the question itself.

The unhappiness with which the Seventies began was rootless and detached from external events. It had neither point nor cutting edge, and therefore no chance of release. Watergate arrived in time to confirm the obvious—that the country had been captured by a cabal of infinitely corrupt nitwits—but, just as the war had been "Vietnamized," the political corruption of Watergate was "Nixonized." The President's withdrawal from the White House was, like the withdrawal of troops from Vietnam, a palliative that served only to obscure an institutional crisis that went much deeper. Once again, the symptoms were treated in such a way as to frustrate the possibility of cure.

The importance of Watergate had little to do with the change in Administrations, the revolving personalities of Nixon, Agnew, Ford, and Rockefeller. Rather, its importance lay in the fact that it bolstered the rootless cynicism of the times, and ratified the widespread belief in the manipulative authority of conspiratorial cliques. The early defense of the Watergate principals, the assertion that "everyone's doing it," did nothing to relieve their culpability before the law, but was widely believed nonetheless. Purging Nixon and the others from the White House smacked of a coup, rather than a housecleaning, and it seemed to many that the country had been given an enema when it needed surgery. The "integrity" of America's institutions, the eighteenth-century *demos* supposed to inhabit them, was invoked throughout the Watergate dramaturgy, but was never called upon to play an active role. Instead, it sat with the people, eating sandwiches and watching the televised parade of amnesiacs, apparatchiks, image hustlers, and party hacks as they checked, balanced, and spun the controls of state. After two years of rehearsed testimony, bowdlerized tapes, closed-door meetings, and eristic argument, nothing was clear but that justice had been masticated in the gears of "due process." The "system worked" (everyone could see that), but, like a pardon without a crime, it accomplished invisible purposes or none at all. Inconsequential or diabolical—take your pick.

The journey from Woodstock to Watergate was baptismal, a ritual initiation that submerged the country in the proof of its decay. In the course of that baptism, the counterculture drowned . . . but that was to be expected. It had sought salvation through solutions, intending to repair, renovate, and make well. Nothing could have been more responsible than the dream of the young. Or more pathetic in the end. Like a terminal cancer patient searching Tijuana for Krebiozen, Laetrile, or psychic surgery, the counterculture refused to recognize the fact that the condition they sought to remedy was Incurable. Instead, they rushed through a metaphysical Tijuana of their own, desperate for panacea and willing to pay any price: yoga, mushrooms, acid, magic, venal gurus, music, megavitamins, T-groups, chanting, screaming, Zen, bombs, trepanation, pilgrimages to Kathmandu, Goa, and Mu—anything seemed worth a try.

When the young stopped believing in themselves as culture bearers, when they became refugees from their own visions, our decadence became complete: the Incurable went unchallenged. Speculations about "a new chapter" in history, a "new stage" in man's cultural evolution (rallying cries of the Sixties), gave way to meditations on the cultural *dénouement*. Pessimism engendered by the failures of the past and by the deterioration of the present * sufficed to keep us on the edge of our seats, waiting for the age to reach its climax—but reminded us also that we were *spectators,* voyeurs whose intervention would be useless if not impossible. The counterculture, having begun with a cultural war dance, ended in a swoon of relaxed futility. The same generation which jammed daisies down the barrels of M-16s, capitalizing on their perfected innocence, watched Watergate with the passive detachment of a

---

* A deterioration in the "quality of life" *and* in the "standard of living," environment, political institutions, and . . . so on.

boozy peasantry: nodding, clucking, taking sides, and disdaining action. That would seem to be the operational style of the Seventies and, indeed, of the foreseeable future.

The "commune of the depressed" is a large one, united only in the abstract characteristics of their decadence. It includes the religious millenarians, with their visions of Armageddon and utopia; the "conspiracy fans," with their secular, Faustian paranoias; the "expatriates" who've left Gomorrah for the Maine woods or Ibiza, never looking back; the psychic fetishists who would immunize themselves against the future through some mental leap or esoteric knowledge; and, of course, it includes the commune's fodder, the poets, playboys, and Warholized naïfs.

What holds the commune together is the fact that, in one way or another, *all* its members have been released from the cares and responsibilities usually associated with the, ummm, "democratic enterprise." In that *social* sense, their decadence is communal. The millenarians have completely written off the society, regarding it as Evil beyond corruption, and expecting some cosmic intervention to redefine its course—their only task is one of self-purification, which is, after all, nothing more than a survival chore. The conspiracy fans are equally liberated from responsibility: convinced that the United States is a colony of the CIA, Howard Hughes, the male gender, or some other "special interest" or apparat, their victimization is complete, their preoccupations solipsistic and survival-oriented. The expatriates, whether they've gone abroad or "back to the land," are so convinced of the nation's impending disintegration that they no longer live in it; a visit to Esalen, Lindesfarne, or to any of the backwoods communes is like taking a trip into another world or century, into the Middle Ages or deep future. Which is as it's supposed to be. Each such group or family is organized as a social monad; each expects to be the inheritor of a society in shambles; none feel they owe anything to a society that is moribund. The psychic fetishists, immersed in the marvels of biofeedback, Arica, and other esoterica, are simply "expatriates" of a different order.

As to the commune's fodder, they remain at Ground Zero, reconciled to their pleasures, to the finality of the present and to whatever sensations can be wrung from it.

Describing this mélange as a commune of the depressed is somewhat misleading, at least in so far as it suggests a prevailing unhappiness. In fact, its depression is more theoretical than actual—like that to be found in a singles bar, it hovers in the background, occluded by desperate enterprises. It is a *stipulated* depression, a depression that *ought* to be there but which, in fact, is more often drowned out in the buzz of conversation, the slosh of beer, the migrations between tables.

If a "generation" is defined in its own terms, if it is "Lost" or "Beat" because it believes itself to be so, then the present generation ought properly to be called the Last. Resigned to the Incurable, the Last Generation is beyond social interventions of any sort, content to let the cultural machine wind down around them. It is, as it seems to be, out of their hands —a Gizmo stoked by phantom elites, technicians of the endless means. Nothing could be more human or humane than to step aside and let the inevitable take its course without delay.

The Seventies have so far proven to be an elusive decade, if not a sloppy one. No rock group has succeeded in capturing the spirit of the time (as the Beatles and Stones once did), nor has anyone emerged with an insight or style capable of inspiring a movement large enough to define the age. Indeed, we're beyond movements, however committed we may be to factions. If the character of a decade becomes identifiable in its fourth year (and it usually does), then the Seventies would seem to be a conglomerate of Watergate, unemployment lines, and waiting. Which is to say: conspiracy, dissatisfaction, and apprehension.

And yet, if nothing's happening, if there are no movements, well, that too is remarkable. Decadence—whether it proceeds from the ministrations of Madison Avenue, or from a brush with the Incurable—is no less significant for the fact that it seems purposeless and ineffectual. Nor is it necessarily permanent, in any case. On the contrary, the lassitudes of the present may be nothing more than an interregnum between upheavals. The Left, in particular, is convinced that this is so, and it may well be correct.

If economic conditions, at home and abroad, continue to deteriorate at their present pace (as seems likely), then the number of plausible scenarios are few. Either the American economy will be provided with the cocaine of a new Vietnam (perhaps in the Middle East), or the federal bureaucracy will implement an ameliorative economic strategy that seems bound to require the imposition of stringent social controls.

With an all-volunteer army, and a good press, such a war could be profitably fought and protracted for as long as need be. Unfortunately, it would do nothing to solve the long-range problems of diminishing resources, ecological disruptions, and the depredations of technical evolution. On the contrary, such a conflict seems certain to accelerate all of these incipient catastrophes, even while it improves the "standard of living" in the short run.

An ameliorative economic strategy seems equally futile. The success of such a strategy depends upon the tractability, patience, and goodwill of the populace—qualities which are presently conspicuous by their absence. Moreover, it's unreasonable to expect contemporary Americans to accept economic disability with the perplexed, almost good-natured despair ("Happy Days Are Here Again!") that kept the Thirties politically stable. Mass education has made latent populists of us all and the living standards of the middle class have come to be viewed as an American birthright. If it should become impossible for the majority to achieve or maintain such standards, they will react not with the resignation of the disappointed, but with the fury of the disinherited.

Carl Oglesby, one of the most imaginative and coherent theoreticians on the New Left, muses on this scenario, and confesses to the expectation that the Left and Right will coalesce in the coming adversity. Oglesby looks forward to a spontaneous mass movement based upon the patriotic concerns which people on the Left and Right share equally. He predicts that the movement will be catalyzed by revelations apropos to political conspiracy (probably involving the Kennedy assassinations). If Oglesby is right, this would not be a movement in the conventional sense, but a sort of democratic spasm, an explosive repossession of power by the public.

Bridges between the Left and Right have already been built and, while differences between the two groups remain substantial, they share many things: a deep mistrust of the present regime, a belief that existing institutions have been corrupted, suspicions of ruthless conspiracies, details of those conspiracies, and a profound hatred of the liberal power bloc. "People are just going to get fed up with being manipulated," Oglesby says, and he may be right. But the problem with such a coalition is that, in transcending political differences by ignoring them, it becomes hopelessly nonideological, capable of negative therapies ("Throw the bastards out!") but not much else. Should a coalition of this sort emerge, its character would be more demagogic than democratic, a mob rather than a movement. This isn't what Oglesby (or anybody else) wants, but it may be what the country will get. And, if this happens, the federal apparat will either acquiesce to the popular will, or repress it. If it does the former, then there is an excellent chance that fascism will come to power "from below." If, on the other hand, it chooses to repress such a movement, then we may expect a police state mandated from above.

It may be, however, that the "interregnum" of the early Seventies is characteristic of the decade as a whole—that we are, as we seem to be, "beyond movements" of any kind. If so, then our situation is indeed "Incurable" and, in that at least, we may take a perverse hope.

History recycles cultures more completely and often than revolutions do. When a culture has exhausted the possibilities inherent in it, when the people have nothing more to look forward to than smaller cars and bigger picture tubes, when a country comes up against those limits which proceed from within (e.g., the need for continued growth in the face of shrinking resources and markets)—then implosion is certain. The country or culture will undergo an upheaval of historic dimensions, a sundering at the seams. The United States is nearing that point today and, in so far as American culture is contagious, so is the rest of what *Time* magazine calls "the Free World." We're about to get recycled.

But before the end and the new beginnings that must follow is a period of simple decadence that's strategic to each.

Decadence is the interval between decline and . . . fall, the pause between recognition and impact. Reconciling oneself to the mortality of the times, *moving beyond movements,* is an act of private liberation that withdraws obstacles from the path of history. Letting the society strangle on its own dilemmas, rather than nagging it with attempts at its preservation in modified form, is a revolutionary path in that the society is severed from its roots, its sources of renewal. Keeping "abreast of the Incurable" is an inspirational activity in that—by giving up the past and future alike—we're immersed in the here and now of the self: *the present,* **no** longer diluted by promises and nostalgia, is rediscovered **and** made sensational. Narcissism, that state of transcendental self-attention, divides the self from within and, in doing so, guarantees our decadence. Each of us becomes an audience to his or her own private performance, simultaneously both narrator and observer of whatever playlet we choose. What does it matter that, in reducing ourselves to *objets d'art,* spontaneity is forbidden unless it's undertaken in its own behalf? Irony has more charm. Like the nymph on the ginger ale bottle, we stare at our own reflections, waiting for the image to move, waiting for history while we haunt ourselves from the water's edge. Like Wallace Stevens, we take "Tea at the Palaz of Hoon":

> What was the sea whose tide swept through me there?
> Out of my mind the golden ointment rained,
> And my ears made the blowing hymns they heard.
> I was myself the compass of that sea:

> I was the world in which I walked, and what I saw
> Or heard or felt came not but from myself;
> And there I found myself more truly and more strange.[50]

In the confines of the moment, we become conscious for perhaps the first time, innovative with our heads and hands and hearts. Because *this is it*. There is nothing else. No hope. No fear. No desire. No lack. No . . . nothing. Fraud is impossible. We are, because we've stopped becoming.

Decadence is its own defense.

Acknowledgments

The investigations and meditations which led to this book could not have been undertaken without the generous support of the Alicia Patterson Foundation, assisted by funds from the Rockefeller Foundation. Despite my analysis, both institutions continue to operate on the assumption that the world is *not* about to end; it must be obvious, therefore, that they bear no responsibility for the contents of *Decadence*.

I'd also like to acknowledge my debts to Eric, the Dobkins, Scott and Devorah Spencer, Sam and Libby Johnson, and Jim Landis. They came through.

Dave Wagner, the poet, crank, and Hegelologist, deserves thanks for his (rather vehement, I thought) criticism, and for his insights concerning *Frankenstein*.

Other debts, of an intellectual sort, may be obvious to the reader. Jacques Ellul's *The Technological Society* is easily one of the most important books of the twentieth century; to read it is to fall under its influence forever. Much of what I have to say about technique is a direct result of this philosopher's earlier analysis.

A similar debt is owed to Norman Cohn, whose book *The Pursuit of the Millennium* is quoted throughout my first chapter.

Recommendations

A few words of introduction, explanation, or warning ought to preface the following list which is, by any standard, almost supernaturally idiosyncratic. Besides works of obvious relevance to my own, there are a substantial number of novels, poetry chapbooks, broadsides, and even movies—whose inclusion must seem curious.

And yet, if the purpose of a bibliography is to show the reader where the writer's "coming from," and to provide references to materials which supplement or expand upon the writer's concerns, then it would be foolish to exclude such intuitive works and entertainments. Often the most difficult notions and most firmly held views derive, not from the products of intellectual investigators and academicians, but from accidental encounters and almost casual insights. Clearly, the best introduction to the plenum of decadence is three months spent in Tangiers. Similarly, a rather clear notion of narcissism (as I've defined the term) could conceivably be obtained from a weekend at the movies: *Pierrot le Fou, The Revolutionary, Performance, The Man from Rio,* and *Castle Keep* all deal with the subject, in some cases quite explicitly.

Moreover, many of our best poets and novelists (such as d. a. levy and William Gaddis) have dealt with many of the themes discussed in *Decadence,* and readers inclined to explore those themes further would be as well advised to read levy's freewheeling "Suburban Death Monastery Poem" as, for example, Giedion's excruciating *Mechanization Takes Command.*

Finally, some of the references below (*Alternative London, VRIL, The Cosmic Forces of Mu,* and others) are cited more as "exhibits" than anything else. Those remarks aside, the following have been helpful:

Allen, Diogenes, "Deliberation and Regularity of Behavior." *American Philosophical Quarterly,* Volume 9, Number 3.

Allen, Donald M., ed., *The New American Poetry 1945–1960.* New York, Grove Press, 1960.

Andrzeyevski, George, *Ashes and Diamonds.* Middlesex, Penguin Books, 1965.

Auerbach, Erich, *Mimesis: The Representation of Reality in Western Literature.* Princeton, Princeton University Press, 1953.

Bateson, Gregory, *Steps to an Ecology of Mind: Collected Essays in Anthropology, Psychiatry, Evolution, and Epistemology.* St. Albans, Paladin, 1973.

Bebel, August, *Society of the Future.* Moscow, Progress Publishers, 1971.

Bell, Daniel K., *The Coming of Post-Industrial Society: A Venture in Social Forecasting.* New York, Basic Books, 1973.

Bergier, Jacques, *Extraterrestrial Visitations from Prehistoric Times to the Present.* New York, The New American Library, 1974.

Bleibtreu, John, *The Parable of the Beast.* London, Paladin, 1971.

Bookchin, Murray, *Post Scarcity Anarchism.* Berkeley, Ramparts Press, 1971. (See, especially, the section entitled "Listen, Marxist!")

Boorstin, Daniel J., *The Image: A Guide to Pseudo-Events In America.* New York, Harper & Row, 1964.

Bukowski, Charles, *A Bukowski Sampler.* Madison, Quixote Press, 1969.

———, *The Days Run Away Like Wild Horses Over the Hills.* Los Angeles, Black Sparrow Press, 1969.

———, *Mockingbird Wish Me Luck.* Los Angeles, Black Sparrow Press, 1972.

———, *Notes of a Dirty Old Man.* North Hollywood, Essex House, 1969.

———, *Post Office.* Los Angeles, Black Sparrow Press, 1971.

Burroughs, William S., *Dead Fingers Talk.* London, Tandem, 1966.

———, "Interview with William Burroughs: The Art of Fiction XXXVI." *Paris Review,* #35.

---, *Naked Lunch*. New York, Grove Press, 1966.
---, *Nova Express*. New York, Grove Press, 1965.
---, *The Ticket That Exploded*. New York, Grove Press, 1967.
---, *The Wild Boys: A Book of the Dead*. New York, Grove Press, 1971.
Camus, Albert, *The Plague*. New York, Random House.
---, *The Stranger*. New York, Vintage Books, 1962.
Carroll, Paul, ed., *Big Table*. Chicago, Big Table, Inc., 1960.
Céline, Louis-Ferdinand, *Death on the Installment Plan*. New York, New Directions, 1966.
Charroux, Robert, *One Hundred Thousand Years of Man's Unknown History*. New York, Berkley Medallion Books, 1971.
Churchward, James, *The Cosmic Forces of Mu*. New York, Paperback Library, 1968.
Cioran, E. M., *The Temptation to Exist*. Chicago, Quadrangle Books, 1968.
Cohn, Norman, *The Pursuit of the Millennium: Revolutionary Millenarians and Mystical Anarchists of the Middle Ages*. London, Paladin, 1970.
Cortázar, Julio, *Hopscotch*. New York, Random House, 1967.
von Däniken, Erich, *Chariots of the Gods?*. Great Britain, Souvenir Press, 1969.
Daraul, Arkon, *A History of Secret Societies*. New York, The Citadel Press, 1968.
Daumal, René, *Mount Analogue: An Authentic Narrative*. London, Vincent Stuart Ltd., 1959.
Delta: A Review of Arts, Life, and Thought in the Netherlands, Provo 13 issue. Amsterdam, Delta International Publication Foundation, 1967.
Dickson, Paul, *Think Tanks*. New York, Ballantine Books, 1972.
Disch, Thomas M., "The Asian Shore," in James Sallis, ed., *The Shores Beneath*. New York, Avon Books, 1971.
Ellul, Jacques, *The Political Illusion*. New York, Random House, 1973.
---, *Propaganda: The Formation of Men's Attitudes*. New York, Alfred A. Knopf, 1968.
---, *The Technological Society*. New York, Random House, 1954.

Fitzgerald, F. Scott, *Tender Is the Night.* New York, Charles Scribner's Sons, 1934.

Fuller, Buckminster, *Nine Chains to the Moon.* Carbondale, Southern Illinois University Press, 1963.

———, *The Buckminster Fuller Reader,* James Meller, ed. Middlesex, Penguin Books, 1972.

Ford Foundation Energy Policy Project, *Exploring Energy Choices.* Washington, D.C., Ford Foundation, 1974.

Gaddis, William, *The Recognitions.* Cleveland, Meridian Books, 1962.

Gardner, Martin, *Fads and Fallacies in the Name of Science.* New York, Ballantine Books, 1956.

Giedion, Sigfried, *Mechanization Takes Command.* New York, W. W. Norton & Co., 1969.

Ginsberg, Allen, *The Fall of America, Poems 1966–1971.* San Francisco, City Lights Books, 1972.

———, *Howl and Other Poems.* San Francisco, City Lights Books, 1956.

———, *Indian Journals.* San Francisco, City Lights Books, 1968.

Guenon, René, *The Reign of Quantity and The Signs of the Times.* Middlesex, Penguin Books, 1972.

Hayden, Tom, *Rebellion and Repression.* Cleveland, The World Publishing Co., 1969.

Heinlein, Robert A., *Stranger In a Strange Land.* New York, Berkley Medallion Books, 1968.

Herbert, Frank, *Dune.* New York, Chilton Books, 1965.

Herlihy, James Leo, *All Fall Down.* New York, E. P. Dutton & Co., Inc., 1960.

Huizinga, Johan, *Homo Ludens: A Study of the Play Element In Culture.* London, Paladin, 1971.

The Humanist, Volume XXXIV, No. 5, an issue devoted to "The New Cults." Buffalo, The American Humanist Association and the American Ethical Union, 1974.

Huysmans, J. K., *Against the Grain.* New York, Dover, 1969.

Illich, Ivan D., *Celebration of Awareness: A Call for Institutional Revolution.* Garden City, New York, Doubleday & Co., 1971.

———, *Deschooling Society.* New York, Harper & Row, 1971.

Jung, C. G., *Synchronicity: An Acausal Connecting Principle.* London, Routledge and Kegan Paul Ltd., 1972.

Kaplan, Bert, ed., *The Inner World of Mental Illness: A Series of*

First-Person Accounts of What It Was Like. New York, Harper & Row, 1964.

Katz, Steve, *The Exaggerations of Peter Prince*. New York, Holt, Rinehart and Winston, 1968.

Koestler, Arthur, *The Act of Creation*. New York, Dell Publishing Co., Inc., 1967.

Kropotkin's Revolutionary Pamphlets, Roger N. Baldwin, ed. New York, Dover, 1970.

Lanternari, Vittorio, *The Religions of the Oppressed: A Study of Modern Messianic Cults*. New York, Alfred A. Knopf, 1963.

Layne, McAvoy, *How Audie Murphy Died In Vietnam*. Garden City, New York, Anchor Books, 1973.

Leary, Timothy, and Ralph Metzner, *The Psychedelic Experience: a Manual Based on the Tibetan Book of the Dead*. New York, Universe Books, 1964.

levy, d. a., *The Madison Poems and the Suburban Death Monastery Poem*. Madison, Quixote Press, 1968.

———, *Red Lady*. Cleveland, Para-Shakti Press, 1969.

The Italian State Massacre. London, Libertaria Books, 1972.

Lilly, John C., *The Centre of the Cyclone: An Autobiography of Inner Space*. London, Paladin, 1973.

Luttwak, Edward, *Coup d'État: A Practical Handbook*. Middlesex, Penguin Books, 1969.

Lytton, Sir Bulwer, *VRIL: The Power of the Coming Race*. New York, Rudolf Steiner Publication, 1972.

Mailer, Norman, Interview conducted by Richard Stratton in *Rolling Stone*, January 16, 1975.

———, "The White Negro," in *Advertisements for Myself*. New York, G. P. Putnam's Sons, 1959.

———, *Why Are We In Vietnam?* New York, G. P. Putnam's Sons, 1968.

Marcuse, Herbert, *An Essay on Liberation*. Boston, Beacon Press, 1968.

Marine, Gene, *America the Raped: The Engineering Mentality and the Devastation of a Continent*. New York, Avon Books, 1970.

McCay, Winsor, *Little Nemo in Slumberland*. New York, McCay Features Syndicate, 1945.

McLuhan, Marshall, *Understanding Media: The Extensions of Man*. New York, McGraw-Hill Book Company, 1965.

———, *The Medium is the Massage: An Inventory of Effects,* with Quentin Fiore. London, Bantam Books, 1967.

———, *Through the Vanishing Point: Space in Poetry and Painting,* with Harley Parker. New York, Harper & Row, 1968.

Meadows, Donella H. and Dennis L., with Jorgen Randers and William W. Behrens III, *The Limits to Growth.* New York, New American Library, 1972.

Miller, David L., *Gods and Games: Toward a Theology of Play.* New York, Harper & Row, 1973.

Miller, Henry, *The Air-Conditioned Nightmare.* New York, Avon Books.

Mishan, E. J., *Technology and Growth.* New York, Praeger, 1971.

Mitchell, Juliet, *Woman's Estate.* Middlesex, Penguin Books, 1971.

Muller, Herbert J., *The Children of Frankenstein: A Primer on Modern Technology and Human Values.* Bloomington, Indiana University Press, 1971.

Mumford, Lewis, *Technics and Civilization.* New York, Harcourt, Brace, and Co., 1934.

Musil, Robert, *The Man Without Qualities.* New York, Capricorn Books, 1965.

Neville, Richard, *Play Power.* New York, Random House, 1970.

Nizan, Paul, *Aden, Arabie.* Boston, Beacon Press, 1968.

Nuttall, Jeff, *Bomb Culture.* London, Paladin, 1971.

Olson, Charles, *Mayan Letters.* London, Jonathan Cape Ltd., 1968.

Percy, Walker, *The Last Gentleman.* New York, Farrar, Straus, & Giroux, 1967.

———, *Love In the Ruins.* New York, Farrar, Straus & Giroux, 1971.

———, *The Moviegoer.* New York, Alfred A. Knopf, 1961.

Poniatowska, Elena, *Massacre In Mexico.* New York, The Viking Press, 1975.

Portola Institute, *Whole Earth Catalog* (and Supplements). Menlo Park, Calif., Portola Institute, 1968.

Purdy, James, *Malcolm.* New York, Farrar, Straus & Cudahy, 1960.

Pynchon, Thomas, *Gravity's Rainbow.* New York, The Viking Press, 1973.

Reich, Wilhelm, *The Mass Psychology of Fascism.* New York, Farrar, Straus & Giroux, 1970.

Revel, Jean-François, *Without Marx or Jesus*. London, Paladin, 1972.
Ridgeway, James, *The Last Play: The Struggle to Monopolize the World's Energy Resource*. New York, E. P. Dutton & Co., Inc. 1974.
Rienow, Robert, and Leona Train Rienow, *Moment in the Sun*. New York, Ballantine Books, 1969.
Rosemont, Franklin, ed., *Arsenal/Surrealist Subversion*. Chicago, Franklin Rosemont, Publisher, 1974.
Rosenberg, Bernard, and David Manning White, eds., *Mass Culture: the Popular Arts in America*. New York, The Free Press, 1964.
Rosenberg, Samuel, *The Confessions of a Trivialist*. Baltimore, Penguin Books, 1972.
Roszak, Theodore, *The Making of a Counter-Culture*. Garden City, New York, Doubleday & Co., 1969.
————, *Where the Wasteland Ends: Politics and Transcendence in Postindustrial Society*. Garden City, New York, Doubleday & Co. 1972.
Sartre, Jean-Paul, *Nausea*. New York, New Directions, 1964.
Saunders, Nicholas, *Alternative London: Survival Guide for Strangers*. London, Nicholas Saunders, 1972.
Schickel, Richard, *The Disney Version*. New York, Avon Books, 1969.
Schmielewski, Yogi Alfred, ed., *The Gospel of the Twentieth Century*. Toronto, Yoga Forum of Canada.
Selye, Hans, *The Stress of Life*. New York, McGraw-Hill Book Company, 1956.
Shelley, Mary, *Frankenstein*. London, J. M. Dent & Sons, 1970.
Sidran, Ben, *Black Talk*. New York, Holt, Rinehart, and Winston, 1971.
Skinner, B. F., *Beyond Freedom & Dignity*. New York, Alfred A. Knopf, 1972.
Slater, Philip, *The Pursuit of Loneliness*. Boston, Beacon Press, 1971.
Snyder, Gary, ed., *Riprap & Cold Mountain Poems*. San Francisco, Four Seasons Foundation, 1966.
Sontag, Susan, *Against Interpretation and Other Essays*. New York, Dell Publishing Co., Inc., 1966.

Spencer, Scott, *Last Night at the Brain Thieves Ball.* Boston, Houghton Mifflin, 1973.
Stansill, Peter, and David Zane Mairowitz, eds., *BAMN (By Any Means Necessary): Outlaw Manifestos and Ephemera 1965–1970.* Middlesex, Penguin Books, 1971.
Stent, Gunther S., *The Coming of the Golden Age: A View of the End of Progress.* Garden City, New York, The Natural History Press, 1969.
Stevens, Wallace, *The Collected Poems.* London, Faber & Faber, 1971.
Strawson, P. F., *Individuals: An Essay in Descriptive Metaphysics.* Garden City, New York, Doubleday & Co., 1963.
Strayer, Joseph R. *Western Europe in the Middle Ages: A Short History.* New York, Appleton-Century-Crofts, 1955.
Thompson, William Irwin, *At the Edge of History: Speculations on the Transformation of Culture.* New York, Harper & Row, 1972.
de Tocqueville, Alexis, *Democracy in America,* 2 volumes, New York, Harper & Row, 1966.
Toffler, Alvin, *Future Shock.* London, Pan Books Ltd., 1973.
Tolkien, J. R. R., *Lord of the Rings.* Boston, Houghton Mifflin Company, 1966.
Tompkins, Peter, *Secrets of the Great Pyramid,* New York, Harper & Row, 1971.
Turner, Nigel G., *Community Radio in Britain: A Practical Introduction.* Bottisham, Cambs., Whole Earth Tools, 1973.
TZARAD, Issue #1, edited by Lee Harwood. London, Lee Harwood, 1965.
Urban, G. R., ed., *Can We Survive Our Future?* New York, St. Martin's Press, 1971.
Van Duyn, Roel, *Message of a Wise Kabouter.* London, Gerald Duckworth & Co., 1972.
Velikovsky, Immanuel, *Worlds In Collision.* New York, Dell Publishing Co., Inc., 1967.
Vonnegut, Kurt, Jr., *Breakfast of Champions: Goodbye Blue Monday!* New York, Delacorte Press, 1973.
——— *Cat's Cradle.* New York, Holt, Rinehart, and Winston, 1964.
——— *Player Piano.* New York, Avon Books, 1967.

Waddington, C. H., ed., *Biology and the History of the Future.* Edinburgh, Edinburgh University Press, 1972.
Wagner, Dave, "Interview with Donald Duck." *Radical America,* Vol. 7, No. 1, Boston.
Wain, John, *Hurry On Down.* New York, The Viking Press, 1953.
Wakefield, Dan, *Going All the Way.* New York, Delacorte Press, 1970.
Walter, W. Grey, *Observations on Man, His Frame, His Duty and His Expectations.* Cambridge, Cambridge University Press, 1969.
Watt, Bob, *Watt's Happening.* Madison, Quixote Press.
Wilhelm, Richard, translator, *The I Ching or Book of Changes.* New York, Random House, 1964.
Wolfe, Tom, *The Electric Kool-Aid Acid Test.* New York, Farrar, Straus & Giroux, 1968.
———, *The Kandy-Kolored Tangerine-Flake Streamline Baby.* New York, Farrar, Straus, & Giroux, 1965.
Woodcock, George, *Anarchism: A History of Libertarian Ideas and Movements.* Middlesex, Penguin Books, 1962.
Wooldridge, Dean E., *The Machinery of the Brain.* New York, McGraw-Hill Book Company, 1963.
Worsley, Peter, *The Trumpet Shall Sound: A Study of 'Cargo' Cults in Melanesia.* London, Paladin, 1970.
Wurlitzer, Rudolph, *Quake.* New York, E. P. Dutton & Co., Inc., 1972.

AND

Badlands, directed by Terrence Malick, 1974.
Castle Keep, directed by Sydney Pollack, 1969.
End of the Road, directed by Aram Avakian, 1970.
The Harder They Come, directed by Perry Henzell, 1973.
The Lickerish Quartet, directed by Radley Metzger, 1970.
Performance, directed by Donald Cammell and Nicholas Roeg, 1970.
The Revolutionary, directed by Paul Williams, 1970.
The Damned, directed by Luchino Visconti, 1969.
THX 1138, directed by George Lucas, 1971.
Two-Lane Blacktop, directed by Monty Hellman, 1971.

Footnotes

1. Susan Sontag, "The Imagination of Disaster," in *Against Interpretation* (New York, 1966), pages 212–228.
2. Jacques Ellul, *The Technological Society* (New York, 1964).
3. Gunther Stent, *The Coming of the Golden Age* (Garden City, New York, 1969).
4. Buckminster Fuller, *Nine Chains to the Moon* (Philadelphia, 1938).
5. B. F. Skinner, *Beyond Freedom & Dignity* (New York, 1971).
6. Lawrence E. Rocks and Richard Runyon, *The Energy Crisis* (New York, 1972). See also *The Futurist,* February, 1974.
7. Daniel K. Bell, *The Coming of Post-Industrial Society* (New York, 1973).
8. William Ophuls, "The Scarcity Society," *Harper's Magazine* (April, 1974), pages 47–48.
9. William Irwin Thompson, *At the Edge of History* (New York, 1972).
10. Norman Cohn, *The Pursuit of the Millennium* (London, 1970), page 53.
11. *Ibid.,* page 87.
12. *Ibid.,* page 150.
13. *Ibid.,* pages 157–158.
14. *Ibid.,* page 350.
15. *Ibid.,* page 286.
16. C. H. Waddington, *Biology and the History of the Future* (Edinburgh, 1972), pages 8–11.
17. *Ibid.,* page 9.

18. *Ibid.*, page 9.
19. *Ibid.*, page 5.
20. Stanley Milgram, *Obedience to Authority, An Experimental View* (New York, 1973).
21. Ebiezer Coppe, "A Fiery Flying Roll: A Word from the Lord to all the Great Ones of the Earth, whom this may concerne: Being the last WARNING PIECE at the dreadful day of JUDGEMENT. For now the Lord is come to 1) Informe 2) Advise and warne 3) Charge 4) Judge and sentence the Great Ones. As also most compassionately informing, and most lovingly and pathetically advising and warning London. With a terrible Word, and fatall Blow from the Lord, upon the Gathered CHURCHES. And all by his Most Excellent MAJESTY, dwelling in, and shining through AUXILIUM PATRIS, alias, Coppe. With another FLYING ROLL ensuing (to all the Inhabitants of the Earth)." "Imprinted at London, in the beginning of that notable day, wherein the secrets of all hearts are laid open; and wherein the worst and foulest of villanies, are discovered, under the best and fairest outsides" (London, 1649), quoted in Cohn, pages 318-330.
22. Alvin Toffler, *Future Shock* (New York, 1970).
23. William Burroughs, *Nova Express* (New York, 1964).
24. *The Paris Review,* No. 35 (Fall, 1965) (Paris).
25. *Ibid.*
26. *Ibid.*
27. William Burroughs, *Naked Lunch* (New York, 1966), pages 32-33.
28. Siegfried Giedion, *Mechanization Takes Command* (New York, 1969).
29. Waddington, *op. cit.*, page 67.
30. E. M. Cioran, *The Temptation to Exist* (Chicago, 1970), page 55.
31. Philip Slater, *Earthwalk* (New York, 1974).
32. Marshall McLuhan, *Understanding Media: The Extensions of Man* (New York, 1964).
33. Rousseau, from *Emile,* quoted in Skinner, *op. cit.*, pages 37-38.
34. E. M. Cioran, *op. cit.*, pages 61-62.
35. Siegfried Giedion, *op. cit.*, page 714.

36. *Ibid.,* page 715.
37. E. L. Doctorow, "The Bomb Lives," *Playboy* (March, 1974).
38. "Talk of the Town" column, the *New Yorker* (March 17, 1973).
39. *The New Scientist* (24 May, 1973) (London publication); see pages 466–495.
40. *Ibid.,* page 492.
41. Paul Dickson, *Think Tanks* (New York, 1972), pages 171–177.
42. Peter Stansill and David Zane Mairowitz, editors, *BAMN: Outlaw Manifestos and Ephemera 1965–70* (Middlesex, 1971), pages 266–267.
43. *The Whole Earth Catalog* (Menlo Park, Calif., 1969).
44. Richard Neville, *Play Power* (New York, 1970), page 278.
45. Herman Kahn and Anthony J. Weiner, *The Year 2000* (New York, 1967), page 277.
46. Murray Bookchin, "Listen, Marxist!," *Post Scarcity Anarchism* (Berkeley, 1971).
47. Edward Luttwak, *Coup d'Etat* (New York, 1969).
48. *Delta: A Review of Arts, Life and Thought in the Netherlands* (Autumn, 1967), page 21.
49. Herbert Marcuse, *An Essay On Liberation* (London, 1972); pages 14, 16, and 61 contain the relevant quotes.
50. Wallace Stevens, "Tea at the Palaz of Hoon," in *The Collected Poems* (London, 1971), page 65. Reprinted by permission of Alfred A. Knopf, Inc. Copyright 1923, renewed 1951 by Wallace Stevens.